New Home Plans for 2001

Visit Our Website

www.familyhomeplans.com

AUTHENTIC
VeriSign
SITE
CLICK TO VERIFY

All Website
Credit Card
Transactions
Are Secure With
VeriSign Encryption

Cover Design By
Andy Russell

We Welcome Your Feedback!
Email us at: editor@garlinghouse.com

Library of Congress No.: 99-76701
ISBN: 0-938708-93-7
Submit all Canadian Plan orders to:
The Garlinghouse Company
102 Ellis Street,
Penticton, BC V2A 4L5
Canadian Orders Only: 1-800-361-7526
Fax No. 1-250-493-7526

the Garlinghouse company

Design by Greg Marquis & Associates

Plan # 93447

BL

See order pa
& index for in

Optional Master Bath

Garage
20/8 x 22

Walk

Units	Single
Price Code	A
Total Finished	1,474 sq. ft.
Main Finished	1,474 sq. ft.
Garage Unfinished	454 sq. ft.
Deck Unfinished	72 sq. ft.
Porch Unfinished	142 sq. ft.
Dimensions	43'x42'6"
Foundation	Crawl space
	Slab
Bedrooms	3
Full Baths	2
Main Ceiling	9'
Primary Roof Pitch	8:12
Secondary Roof Pitch	4:12
Max Ridge Height	22'
Roof Framing	Stick
Exterior Walls	2x4

Master
16 x 13
9' Ceiling

Dining
10 x 10/6
9' Ceiling

Kitchen
14 x 10

Pantry

Br. #3
10 x 11

Family Room
21/4 x 15
12' Ceiling Vaulted

Br. # 2
12/5 x 11/2
9' Ceiling

Porch
23/6 x 6

MAIN FLOOR

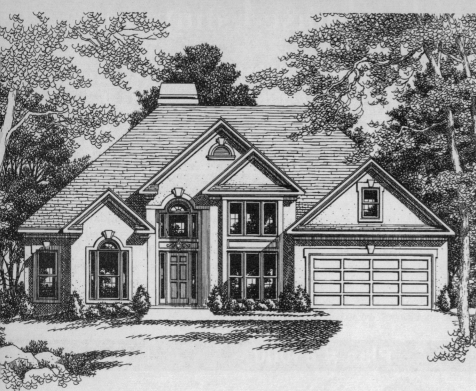

Units	Single
Price Code	B
Total Finished	1,715 sq. ft.
Main Finished	1,715 sq. ft.
Basement Unfinished	1,715 sq. ft.
Garage Unfinished	450 sq. ft.
Dimensions	55'x51'6''
Foundation	Basement
	Crawl space
	Slab
Bedrooms	3
Full Baths	2
Main Ceiling	9'1''
Primary Roof Pitch	12:12
Max Ridge Height	25'
Roof Framing	Stick
Exterior Walls	2x4

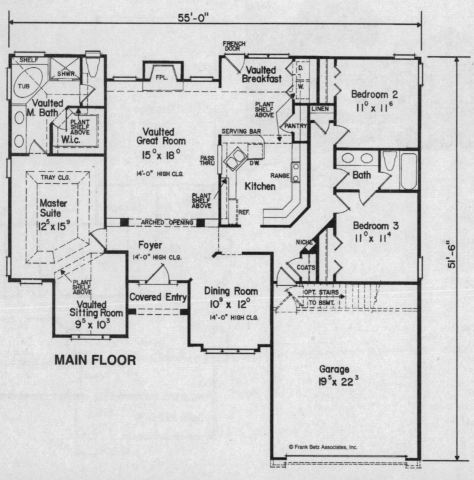

MAIN FLOOR

© Frank Betz Associates, Inc.

3

The Garlinghouse Company
is pleased to present
Home Design Services, Inc.

New to the Garlinghouse Company, but not new to the home design field, Home Design Services, Inc. has over 8,000 plans that have been built across the United States and in 57 countries worldwide. The company's president and founder, James E. Zirkel has been in the architectural and residential design business for over 33 years. He has won over 150 Parade of Homes awards including six Grand Awards. In addition, some of his designs have been awarded the coveted Aurora Award. He has been published in Better Homes and Gardens Special Interest Publications, Home Magazine Home Plans, Good Housekeeping Home Plans just to name a few. Welcome to our esteemed Design Network, Home Design Services, Inc.!

Design by Home Design Services, Inc. **Plan # 63000** BL See order pa & index for i

Units	Single
Price Code	A
Total Finished	1,442 sq. ft.
First Finished	1,442 sq. ft.
Garage Unfinished	437 sq. ft.
Dimensions	51'x70'8''
Foundation	Slab
Bedrooms	3
Full Baths	2
Primary Roof Pitch	6:12
Max Ridge Height	15'5''
Roof Framing	Stick
Exterior Walls	2x4

MAIN FLOOR

2 Car Port

Utility

Storage

Nook

Kitchen

Bedroom 2
12⁰ · 11⁴

Bath

Bedroom 3
10⁰ · 11⁴

Master
Bath

Family
22⁰ · 15⁸

Master
Bedroom
17⁴ · 12⁰

W.I.C.

Foyer

Covered Porch

Entry

4

Units	Single
Price Code	E
Total Finished	2,307 sq. ft.
First Finished	1,530 sq. ft.
Second Finished	777 sq. ft.
Bonus Unfinished	361 sq. ft.
Garage Unfinished	576 sq. ft.
Dimensions	61'4"x78'
Foundation	Slab
Bedrooms	4
Full Baths	3
Half Baths	I
First Ceiling	9'
Second Ceiling	8'
Primary Roof Pitch	8:12
Secondary Roof Pitch	4:12
Max Ridge Height	24'9"
Roof Framing	Truss
Exterior Walls	2x4

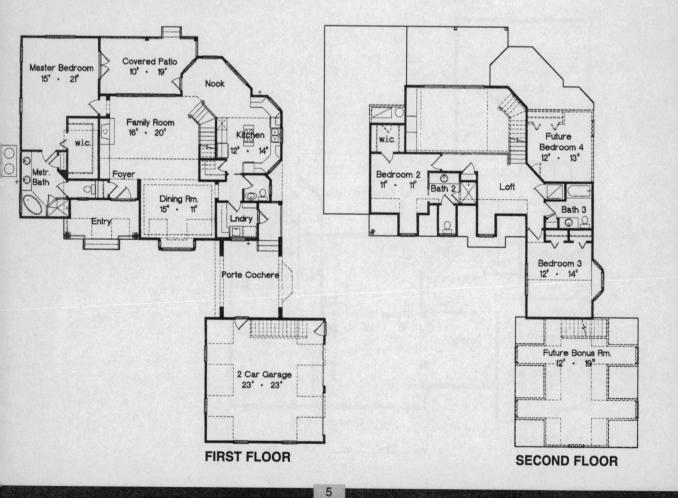

FIRST FLOOR

SECOND FLOOR

Units	Single
Price Code	C
Total Finished	1,963 sq. ft.
Main Finished	1,963 sq. ft.
Garage Unfinished	501 sq. ft.
Porch Unfinished	216 sq. ft.
Dimensions	58'x66'8"
Foundation	Basement
	Slab
Bedrooms	3
Full Baths	2
Primary Roof Pitch	7:12
Secondary Roof Pitch	12:12
Max Ridge Height	20'2"
Roof Framing	Truss
Exterior Walls	2x4

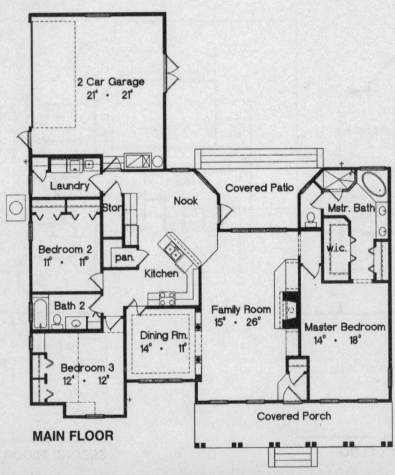

2 Car Garage 21' • 21'

Laundry

Stor

pan.

Bedroom 2 11⁰ • 11⁰

Nook

Covered Patio

Kitchen

Mstr. Bath

w.i.c.

Bath 2

Family Room 15⁸ • 26⁰

Master Bedroom 14⁰ • 18⁰

Dining Rm. 14⁰ • 11⁰

Bedroom 3 12⁴ • 12⁰

Covered Porch

MAIN FLOOR

Units	Single
Price Code	F
Total Finished	2,660 sq. ft.
Main Finished	2,660 sq. ft.
Garage Unfinished	527 sq. ft.
Porch Unfinished	465 sq. ft.
Dimensions	66'4"x74'4"
Foundation	Slab
Bedrooms	3
Full Baths	3
Main Ceiling	10'
Primary Roof Pitch	6:12
Max Ridge Height	23'
Roof Framing	Truss
Exterior Walls	2x4

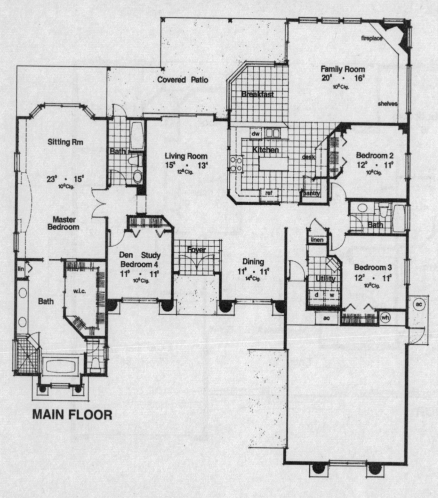

MAIN FLOOR

Units	Single
Price Code	E
Total Finished	2,308 sq. ft.
Main Finished	2,308 sq. ft.
Garage Unfinished	505 sq. ft.
Dimensions	67'x56'8''
Foundation	Slab
Bedrooms	4
Full Baths	2
Primary Roof Pitch	7:12
Max Ridge Height	25'
Roof Framing	Truss

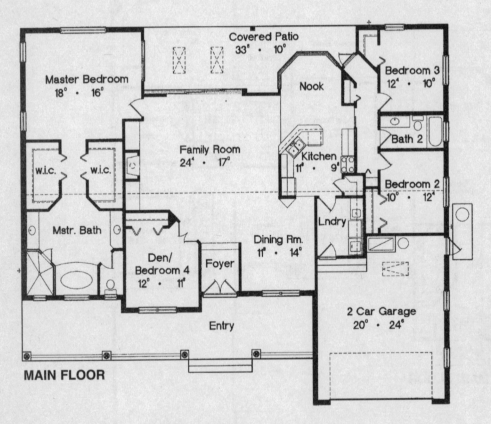

Covered Patio 33⁸ • 10⁰

Master Bedroom 18⁰ • 16⁰

Nook

Bedroom 3 12⁴ • 10⁰

Family Room 24⁴ • 17⁰

Kitchen 11⁰ • 9⁰

Bath 2

w.i.c.   w.i.c.

Bedroom 2 10⁴ • 12⁴

Mstr. Bath

Lndry

Den/ Bedroom 4 12⁰ • 11⁰

Foyer

Dining Rm. 11⁰ • 14⁰

Entry

2 Car Garage 20⁰ • 24⁶

MAIN FLOOR

8

Units	Single
Price Code	F
Total Finished	2,666 sq. ft.
First Finished	1,908 sq. ft.
Second Finished	758 sq. ft.
Garage Unfinished	640 sq. ft.
Deck Unfinished	426 sq. ft.
Porch Unfinished	426 sq. ft.
Dimensions	50'x86'
Foundation	Slab
Bedrooms	3
Full Baths	2
Half Baths	1
First Ceiling	9'
Second Ceiling	9'
Primary Roof Pitch	9:12
Max Ridge Height	29'2''
Roof Framing	Truss
Exterior Walls	2x4

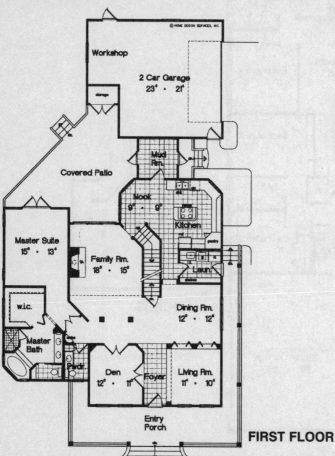

FIRST FLOOR

Workshop

2 Car Garage
23⁴ · 21

Covered Patio

Mud Rm.

Nook
9⁰ · 9⁰

Kitchen

pantry

Master Suite
15⁰ · 13⁴

Family Rm.
18⁰ · 15²

Laun

w.i.c.

Master Bath

Pwdr.

Den
12⁰ · 11

Foyer

Living Rm.
11⁰ · 10⁴

Dining Rm.
12⁰ · 12⁰

Entry Porch

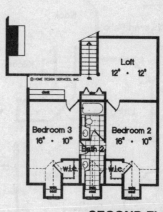

SECOND FLOOR

Loft
12⁰ · 12⁰

Bedroom 3
16⁰ · 10¹⁰

Bath 2

Bedroom 2
16⁰ · 10¹⁰

w.i.c.

w.i.c.

Units	Single
Price Code	D
Total Finished	2,224 sq. ft.
Main Finished	2,224 sq. ft.
Bonus Unfinished	262 sq. ft.
Garage Unfinished	554 sq. ft.
Dimensions	58'6''x72'
Foundation	Slab
Bedrooms	4
Full Baths	3
Main Ceiling	10'
Primary Roof Pitch	9:12
Max Ridge Height	26'
Roof Framing	Truss

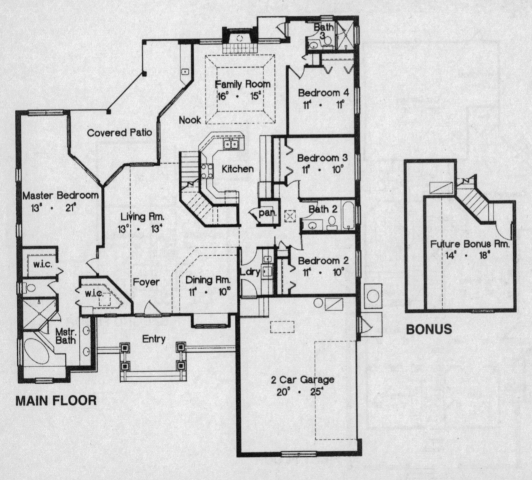

MAIN FLOOR

BONUS

Units	Single
Price Code	F
Total Finished	2,731 sq. ft.
First Finished	2,270 sq. ft.
Second Finished	461 sq. ft.
Garage Unfinished	468 sq. ft.
Porch Unfinished	280 sq. ft.
Dimensions	70'x73'8''
Foundation	Slab
Bedrooms	3
Full Baths	3
First Ceiling	10'
Primary Roof Pitch	7:12
Max Ridge Height	25'4''
Roof Framing	Truss

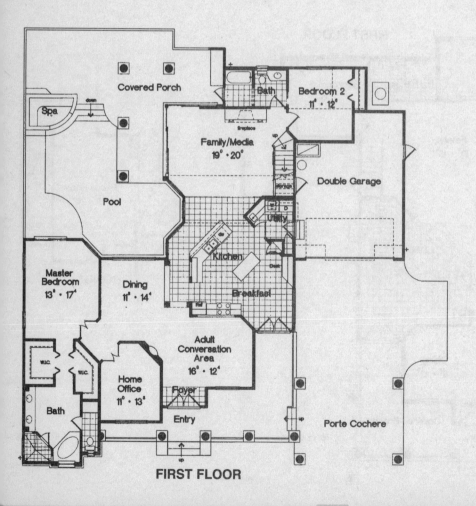

FIRST FLOOR

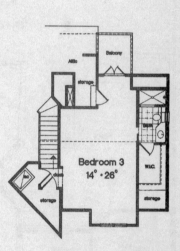

SECOND FLOOR

Units	Single
Price Code	E
Total Finished	2,270 sq. ft.
First Finished	2,270 sq. ft.
Bonus Finished	461 sq. ft.
Garage Unfinished	468 sq. ft.
Porch Unfinished	280 sq. ft.
Dimensions	70'x70'
Foundation	Slab
Bedrooms	3
Full Baths	3
Primary Roof Pitch	7:12
Max Ridge Height	25'4''
Roof Framing	Truss

FIRST FLOOR

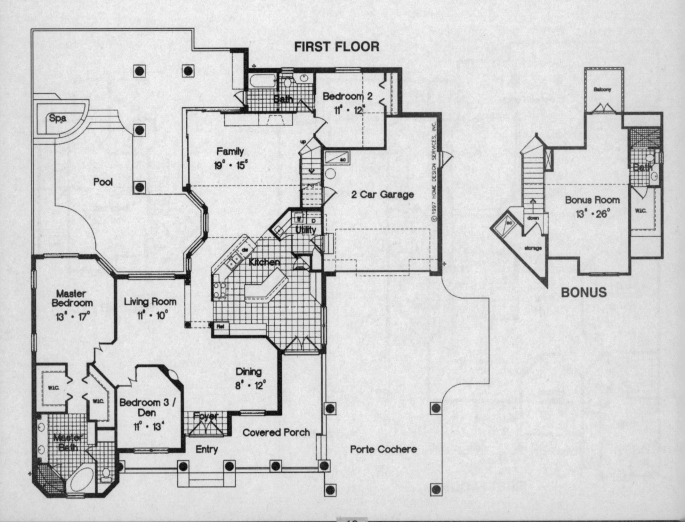

12

Units	Single
Price Code	H
Total Finished	3,119 sq. ft.
Main Finished	3,119 sq. ft.
Garage Unfinished	142 sq. ft.
Dimensions	60'x90'
Foundation	Slab
Bedrooms	4
Full Baths	4
Main Ceiling	10'
Primary Roof Pitch	6:12
Max Ridge Height	23'8"
Roof Framing	Truss

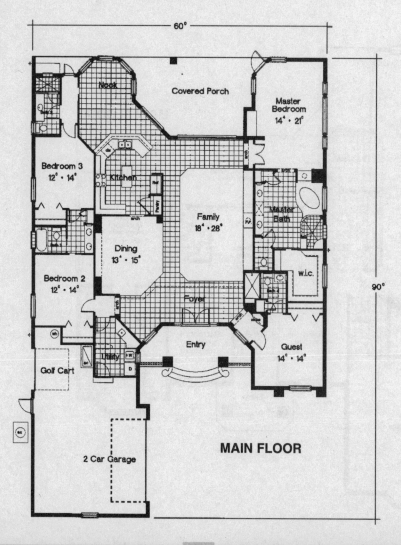

MAIN FLOOR

Units	Single
Price Code	E
Total Finished	2,362 sq. ft.
Main Finished	2,362 sq. ft.
Garage Unfinished	522 sq. ft.
Dimensions	65'8''x73'4''
Foundation	Slab
Bedrooms	4
Full Baths	3
Main Ceiling	10'
Primary Roof Pitch	6:12
Max Ridge Height	20'
Roof Framing	Truss

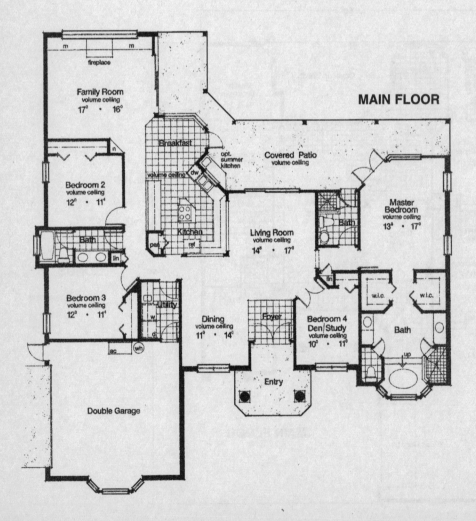

MAIN FLOOR

Family Room
volume ceiling
17⁰ · 16⁰

fireplace

Breakfast
volume ceiling

opt. summer kitchen

Covered Patio
volume ceiling

Bedroom 2
volume ceiling
12⁰ · 11⁴

Kitchen

Bath

Master Bedroom
volume ceiling
13⁸ · 17⁰

Living Room
volume ceiling
14⁴ · 17⁰

Bath

Bedroom 3
volume ceiling
12⁸ · 11¹

Utility

w.i.c.   w.i.c.

Dining
volume ceiling
11⁰ · 14⁰

Foyer

Bedroom 4
Den/Study
volume ceiling
10⁰ · 11⁰

Bath

Entry

up

Double Garage

Units	Single
Price Code	G
Total Finished	2,755 sq. ft.
Main Finished	2,755 sq. ft.
Bonus Unfinished	440 sq. ft.
Garage Unfinished	724 sq. ft.
Porch Unfinished	419 sq. ft.
Dimensions	73'x82'8''
Foundation	Slab
Bedrooms	4
Full Baths	3
Primary Roof Pitch	8:12
Max Ridge Height	22'
Roof Framing	Truss

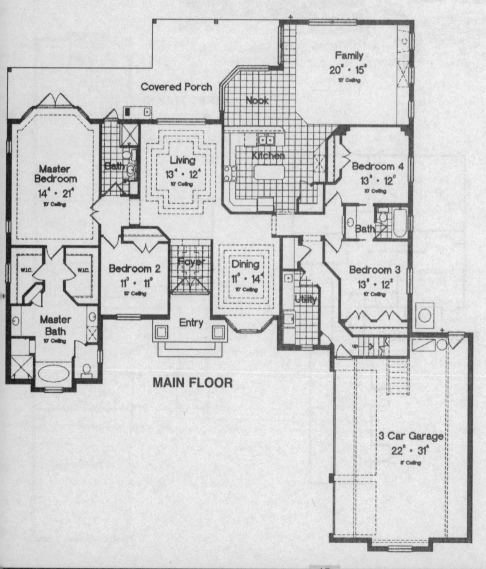

MAIN FLOOR

Covered Porch

Master Bedroom 14⁴ · 21⁴ 10' Ceiling

Bath

Living 13⁴ · 12⁴ 10' Ceiling

Nook

Kitchen

Family 20⁶ · 15⁶ 10' Ceiling

Bedroom 4 13⁸ · 12⁰ 10' Ceiling

Bath

W.I.C.   W.I.C.

Bedroom 2 11⁰ · 11⁰ 10' Ceiling

Foyer

Dining 11⁰ · 14⁴ 10' Ceiling

Utility

Bedroom 3 13⁸ · 12² 10' Ceiling

Master Bath 10' Ceiling

Entry

3 Car Garage 22⁰ · 31⁴ 8' Ceiling

BONUS

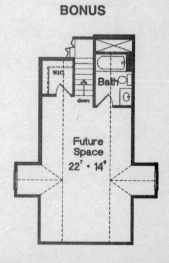

W.I.C.

Bath

down

Future Space 22⁷ · 14⁰

Units	Single
Price Code	F
Total Finished	2,600 sq. ft
First Finished	1,878 sq. ft
Second Finished	722 sq. ft.
Bonus Unfinished	356 sq. ft.
Garage Unfinished	489 sq. ft.
Dimensions	38'8''x95'
Foundation	Slab
Bedrooms	3
Full Baths	2
Half Baths	1
First Ceiling	10'
Primary Roof Pitch	12:12
Max Ridge Height	31'8''
Roof Framing	Truss

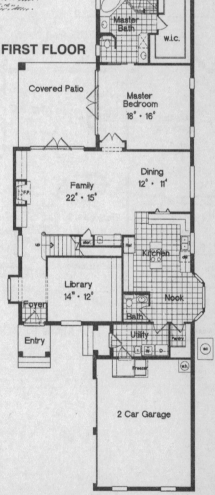

FIRST FLOOR

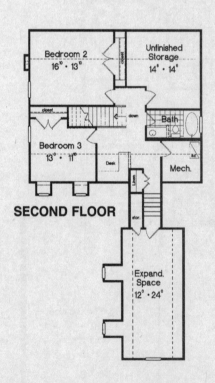

SECOND FLOOR

16

Units	Single
Price Code	I
Total Finished	3,338 sq. ft.
First Finished	2,854 sq. ft.
Second Finished	484 sq. ft.
Garage Unfinished	688 sq. ft.
Dimensions	77'4''x94'
Foundation	Slab
Bedrooms	4
Full Baths	3
Half Baths	I
First Ceiling	10'
Primary Roof Pitch	9:12
Max Ridge Height	28'
Roof Framing	Truss

Rear Elevation

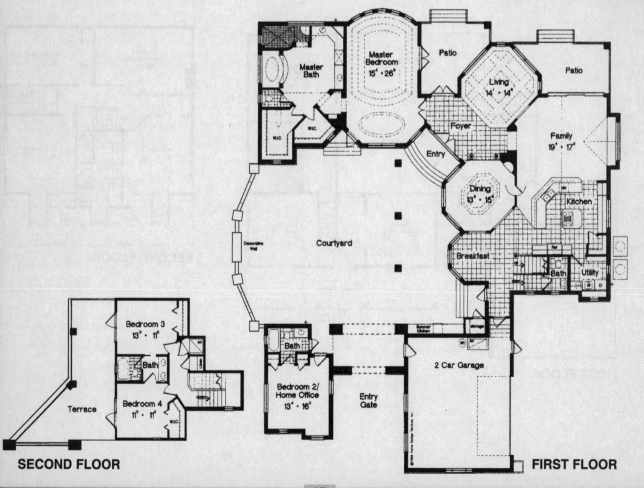

SECOND FLOOR

FIRST FLOOR

Master Bath

Master Bedroom 15'⁴·26'⁶

Patio

Living 14'·14'

Patio

Foyer

Family 19'·17'

Entry

Dining 13'·15'

Kitchen

Courtyard

Breakfast

Bath   Utility

Decorative Wall

Bedroom 3 13'·11'

Bath

Bedroom 4 11'·11'

Terrace

Bath

Bedroom 2/ Home Office 13'⁴·16'⁶

Entry Gate

2 Car Garage

17

Units	Single
Price Code	F
Total Finished	2,711 sq. ft.
First Finished	1,808 sq. ft.
Second Finished	903 sq. ft.
Garage Unfinished	609 sq. ft.
Dimensions	70'4"x59'4"
Foundation	Slab
Bedrooms	4
Full Baths	3
Half Baths	1
First Ceiling	10'
Second Ceiling	8'
Primary Roof Pitch	8:12
Max Ridge Height	28'6"
Roof Framing	Truss
Exterior Walls	2x4

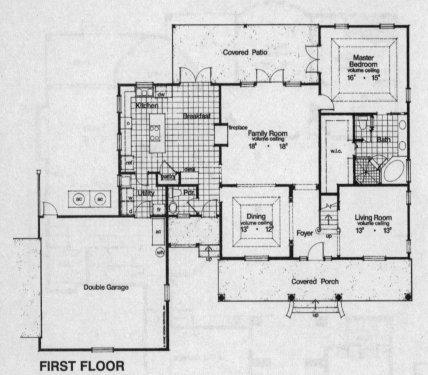

FIRST FLOOR

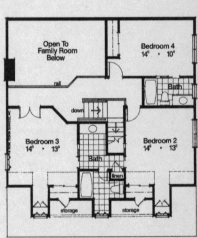

SECOND FLOOR

Order Today! 1-800-235-5700 or order online at www.familyhomeplans.com

Units	Single
Price Code	J
Total Finished	3,680 sq. ft.
First Finished	2,285 sq. ft.
Second Finished	1,395 sq. ft.
Garage Unfinished	766 sq. ft.
Dimensions	73'8"x76'2"
Foundation	Slab
Bedrooms	3
Full Baths	3
Half Baths	1
First Ceiling	10'
Primary Roof Pitch	8:12
Max Ridge Height	32'8"
Roof Framing	Truss
Exterior Walls	2x6

Rear Elevation

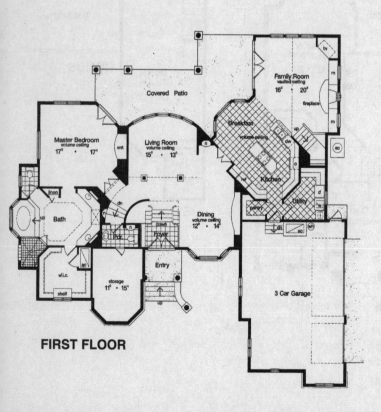

FIRST FLOOR

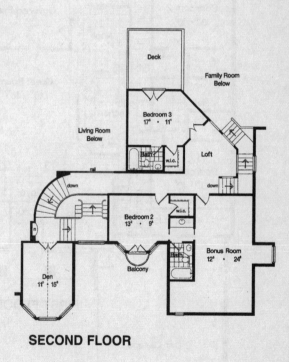

SECOND FLOOR

Order Today! 1-800-235-5700 or order online at
www.familyhomeplans.com

Units	Single
Price Code	D
Total Finished	2,237 sq. ft.
First Finished	2,237 sq. ft.
Bonus Finished	397 sq. ft.
Garage Unfinished	679 sq. ft.
Dimensions	60'x70'
Foundation	Slab
Bedrooms	3
Full Baths	2
First Ceiling	9'
Primary Roof Pitch	7:12
Max Ridge Height	22'4"
Roof Framing	Truss
Exterior Walls	?

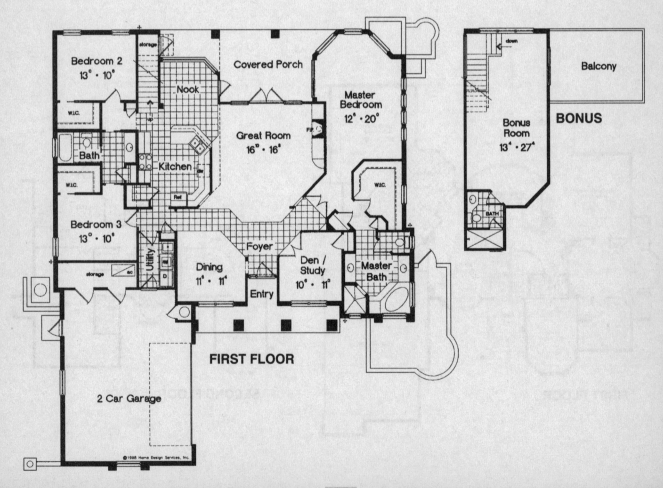

FIRST FLOOR

Bedroom 2
13⁰ · 10⁰

Nook

Covered Porch

Master Bedroom
12⁸ · 20⁰

Great Room
16⁰ · 16⁰

Kitchen

Bath

Bedroom 3
13⁰ · 10⁰

Utility

Dining
11⁰ · 11⁴

Foyer

Entry

Den / Study
10⁰ · 11⁰

Master Bath

2 Car Garage

Balcony

Bonus Room
13⁴ · 27⁴

BONUS

BATH

Units	Single
Price Code	I
Total Finished	3,434 sq. ft.
First Finished	3,434 sq. ft.
Garage Unfinished	814 sq. ft.
Dimensions	82'4"x83'8"
Foundation	Slab
Bedrooms	3
Full Baths	4
First Ceiling	10'-12'
Primary Roof Pitch	6:12
Max Ridge Height	23'5"
Roof Framing	Truss

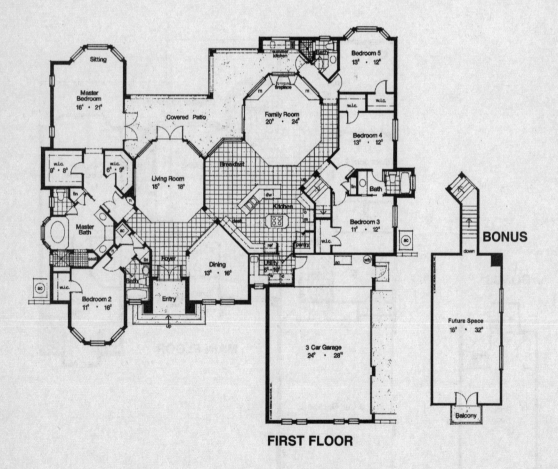

FIRST FLOOR

Units	Single
Price Code	F
Total Finished	2,713 sq. ft.
Main Finished	2,713 sq. ft.
Bonus Unfinished	440 sq. ft.
Dimensions	66'4''x80'8''
Foundation	Slab
Bedrooms	3
Full Baths	3
Main Ceiling	10'
Primary Roof Pitch	8:12
Max Ridge Height	25'4''
Roof Framing	Truss

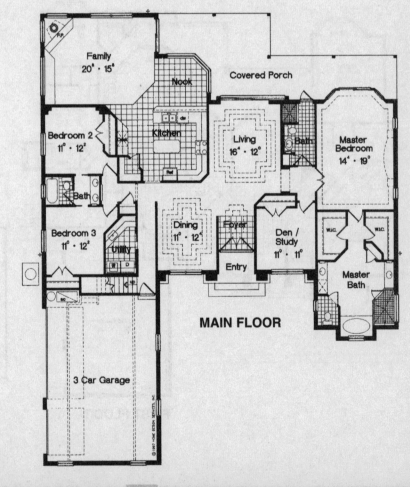

BONUS

Bonus Room
14⁰ · 21⁸

MAIN FLOOR

Family 20⁰ · 15⁸

Nook

Covered Porch

Bedroom 2 11⁰ · 12²

Kitchen

Living 16⁴ · 12⁰

Bath

Master Bedroom 14⁴ · 19⁰

Bath

Bedroom 3 11⁰ · 12²

Utility

Dining 11⁰ · 12⁸

Foyer

Den / Study 11⁰ · 11⁰

W.I.C.

W.I.C.

Entry

Master Bath

3 Car Garage

Units	Single
Price Code	J
Total Finished	3,723 sq. ft.
First Finished	3,723 sq. ft.
Bonus Unfinished	390 sq. ft.
Garage Unfinished	850 sq. ft.
Dimensions	82'4''x89'
Foundation	Slab
Bedrooms	5
Full Baths	5
First Ceiling	12'
Primary Roof Pitch	10:12
Max Ridge Height	29'6''
Roof Framing	Truss

BONUS ROOM

Bonus Room
16° · 22°

FIRST FLOOR

- sitting
- Master Suite 17⁴ · 17⁰
- Covered Patio
- Family 20⁴ · 16⁸
- Bedroom 4 14⁰ · 13⁰
- w.i.c.
- w.i.c.
- Living 14⁰ · 16⁰
- Breakfast
- Bedroom 3 14⁰ · 12⁰
- Bath
- Master Bath
- Kitchen
- Bath
- Bedroom 2 15⁴ · 12⁴
- Bath
- Foyer
- Dining 12⁴ · 16⁴
- L'ndry
- Guest/Den 11⁴ · 15⁴
- Entry
- 3 Car Garage 22' · 36'
- Covered Patio
- summer kitchen
- Bath

Units	Single
Price Code	F
Total Finished	2,636 sq. ft.
Main Finished	2,636 sq. ft.
Bonus Unfinished	337 sq. ft.
Garage Unfinished	789 sq. ft.
Dimensions	96'6"x52'4"
Foundation	Slab
Bedrooms	4
Full Baths	3
Main Ceiling	10'
Primary Roof Pitch	8:12
Max Ridge Height	29'9'

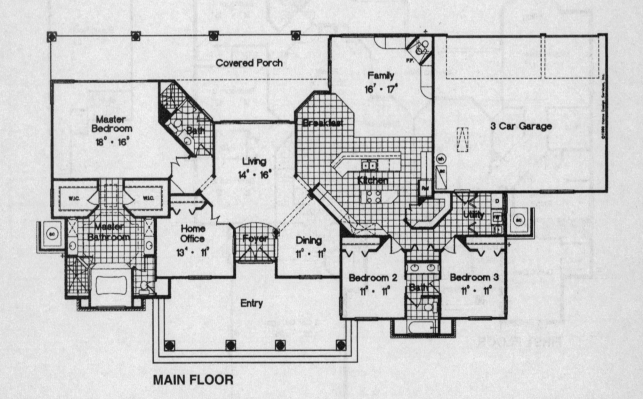

Covered Porch

Family
16'⁷ · 17'⁸

3 Car Garage

Master Bedroom
18° · 16°

Bath

Breakfast

Living
14° · 16°

Kitchen

W.I.C.   W.I.C.

Utility

Master Bathroom

Home Office
13⁴ · 11°

Foyer

Dining
11° · 11°

Bedroom 2
11° · 11°

Bath

Bedroom 3
11° · 11°

Entry

MAIN FLOOR

Units	Single
Price Code	1
Total Finished	3,432 sq. ft.
First Finished	2,390 sq. ft.
Second Finished	1,042 sq. ft.
Garage Unfinished	503 sq. ft.
Deck Unfinished	115 sq. ft.
Dimensions	70'x76'4"
Foundation	Slab
Bedrooms	5
Full Baths	3
Half Baths	1
First Ceiling	10'
Second Ceiling	9'4"
Primary Roof Pitch	6:12
Max Ridge Height	28'
Roof Framing	Truss

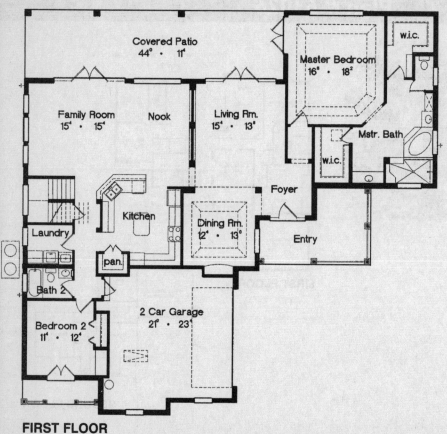

FIRST FLOOR

Covered Patio 44⁰ · 11⁰

Family Room 15⁴ · 15⁴

Nook

Living Rm. 15⁴ · 13⁰

Master Bedroom 16⁰ · 18²

w.i.c.

Mstr. Bath

w.i.c.

Foyer

Kitchen

Laundry

Dining Rm. 12⁴ · 13⁰

Entry

pan.

Bath 2

Bedroom 2 11⁴ · 12⁴

2 Car Garage 21⁰ · 23⁰

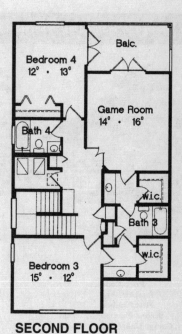

SECOND FLOOR

Bedroom 4 12⁰ · 13⁰

Balc.

Game Room 14⁰ · 16⁰

Bath 4

w.i.c.

Bath 3

w.i.c.

Bedroom 3 15⁰ · 12⁰

Plan # 63023

Units	Single
Price Code	J
Total Finished	3,557 sq. ft.
First Finished	2,761 sq. ft.
Second Finished	796 sq. ft.
Bonus Unfinished	284 sq. ft.
Garage Unfinished	863 sq. ft.
Dimensions	74'x85'
Foundation	Slab
Bedrooms	4
Full Baths	4
Half Baths	1
First Ceiling	10'
Second Ceiling	8'
Primary Roof Pitch	8:12
Max Ridge Height	29'4''
Roof Framing	Truss

FIRST FLOOR

SECOND FLOOR

Plan # 63026

Units	Single
Price Code	K
Total Finished	3,910 sq. ft.
First Finished	3,097 sq. ft.
Second Finished	813 sq. ft.
Garage Unfinished	481 sq. ft.
Dimensions	75'4"x80'8"
Foundation	Slab
Bedrooms	4
Full Baths	3
Half Baths	1
First Ceiling	10'
Primary Roof Pitch	6:12
Secondary Roof Pitch	8:12
Max Ridge Height	28'
Roof Framing	Truss

FIRST FLOOR

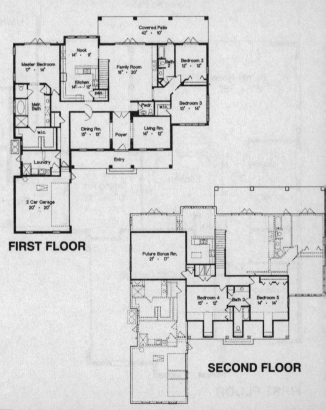

SECOND FLOOR

Units	Single
Price Code	F
Total Finished	2,660 sq. ft.
Main Finished	2,660 sq. ft.
Garage Unfinished	543 sq. ft.
Dimensions	66'4''x73'4''
Foundation	Slab
Bedrooms	4
Full Baths	3
Main Ceiling	10'
Primary Roof Pitch	8:12
Max Ridge Height	27'6''
Roof Framing	Truss
Exterior Walls	2x4

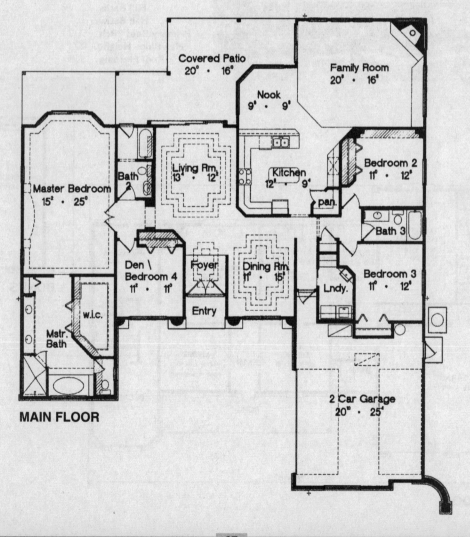

MAIN FLOOR

Covered Patio 20⁰ · 16⁰

Family Room 20⁰ · 16⁸

Nook 9⁸ · 9⁸

Bedroom 2 11⁰ · 12⁸

Living Rm. 13⁴ · 12²

Kitchen 12⁴ · 9⁴

pan.

Bath 3

Master Bedroom 15² · 25⁰

Bath 2

Den \ Bedroom 4 11² · 11⁰

Foyer

Dining Rm. 11⁴ · 15⁸

Lndy.

Bedroom 3 11⁰ · 12⁸

w.i.c.

Entry

Mstr. Bath

2 Car Garage 20⁸ · 25⁴

HOT OFF THE DRAWING BOARD

We are pleased to bring you this exciting feature. A special section that presents to you the newest home designs from our talented network of designers. We have entitled this section "HOT OFF THE DRAWING BOARD." These designs use innovative floor plans and are on the cutting edge of today's market. These plans have the ultimate in convenience and style, not to mention luxurious detailing. The varying styles represented are the result of the different personalities of the talented designers responsible for each plan. By grouping these designs together, we present to you many style variations. Time is of the essence. Your dream home is waiting to be chosen. Take a moment to thumb through pages 28-43. You may have just found the "key" that opens the first door to your very special home.

Units	Single
Price Code	C
Total Finished	1,988 sq. ft.
Main Finished	1,988 sq. ft.
Bonus Unfinished	366 sq. ft.
Garage Unfinished	650 sq. ft.
Porch Unfinished	480 sq. ft.
Dimensions	76'10"x44'10"
Foundation	Basement
	Crawl space
	Slab
Bedrooms	3
Full Baths	2
Half Baths	I
Primary Roof Pitch	7:12
Max Ridge Height	22'4"
Roof Framing	Stick
Exterior Walls	2x4

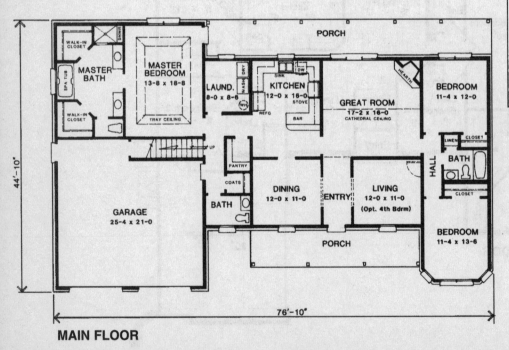

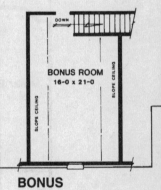

MAIN FLOOR

Units	Single
Price Code	E
Total Finished	2,384 sq. ft.
Main Finished	2,384 sq. ft.
Bonus Unfinished	364 sq. ft.
Basement Unfinished	2,384 sq. ft.
Garage Unfinished	636 sq. ft.
Porch Unfinished	678 sq. ft.
Dimensions	82'4"x59'
Foundation	Basement
	Crawl space
Bedrooms	3
Full Baths	3
Primary Roof Pitch	8:12
Secondary Roof Pitch	12:12
Max Ridge Height	24'6"
Roof Framing	Stick
Exterior Walls	2x4

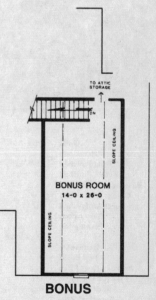

New Design

HOT OFF THE DRAWING BOARD

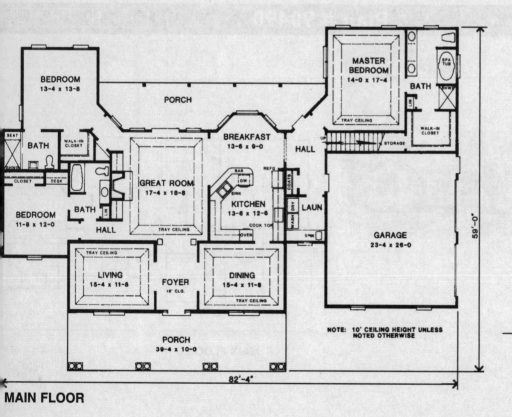

MAIN FLOOR

BONUS

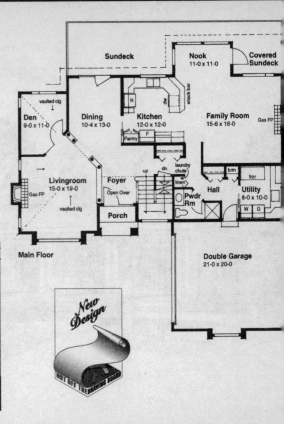

Main Floor

Sundeck | Nook 11-0 x 11-0 | Covered Sundeck

vaulted clg

Den 9-0 x 11-0 | Dining 10-4 x 13-0 | Kitchen 12-0 x 12-0 | Family Room 15-6 x 16-0 | Gas FP

snack bar

R, dw

Pantry, F

Livingroom 15-0 x 19-0 | Foyer Open Over | up | dn | laundry chute | linen | Hall | Utility 8-0 x 10-0

Gas FP | vaulted clg | Porch | Pwdr Rm | bm | frzr | W D

Double Garage 21-0 x 20-0

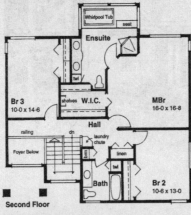

Whirlpool Tub | seat

Ensuite

twl

Br 3 10-0 x 14-6 | shelves | W.I.C. | MBr 16-0 x 16-8

Hall

railing | dn | laundry chute | linen

Foyer Below | bm

Bath | twl | Br 2 10-6 x 13-0

Second Floor

New Design

HOT OFF THE DRAWING BOARD

Units	Single
Price Code	E
Total Finished	2,497 sq. ft.
Main Finished	1,470 sq. ft.
Second Finished	1,027 sq. ft.
Basement Unfinished	1,470 sq. ft.
Garage Unfinished	440 sq. ft.
Deck Unfinished	353 sq. ft.
Porch Unfinished	35 sq. ft.
Dimensions	52'x58'6"
Foundation	Basement
Bedrooms	3
Full Baths	2
3/4 Baths	1
Main Ceiling	8'
Second Ceiling	8'
Primary Roof Pitch	6:12
Secondary Roof Pitch	7:12
Max Ridge Height	25'9"
Roof Framing	Truss
Exterior Walls	2x6

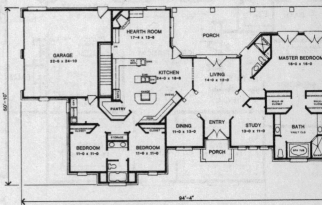

HEARTH ROOM 17-4 x 13-6 | PORCH

GARAGE 32-6 x 24-10 | KITCHEN 24-0 x 18-6 | LIVING 14-0 x 12-0 | MASTER BEDROOM 18-0 x 16-0

50'-10" | PANTRY | RANGE | OVENS | WALK-IN CLOSET | WALK-IN CLOSET

CLOSET | STORAGE | DINING 11-0 x 13-0 | ENTRY | STUDY 13-0 x 11-0 | BATH

BEDROOM 11-0 x 11-0 | BEDROOM 11-0 x 11-0 | PORCH | SPA TUB

94'-4"

MAIN FLOOR

New Design

HOT OFF THE DRAWING BO

Units	Single
Price Code	F
Total Finished	2,575 sq. ft.
Main Finished	2,575 sq. ft.
Basement Unfinished	2,575 sq. ft.
Garage Unfinished	624 sq. ft.
Porch Unfinished	572 sq. ft.
Dimensions	94'4"x50'10"
Foundation	Basement, Crawl space
Bedrooms	3
Full Baths	3
Primary Roof Pitch	8:12
Max Ridge Height	24'6"
Roof Framing	Stick
Exterior Walls	2x4

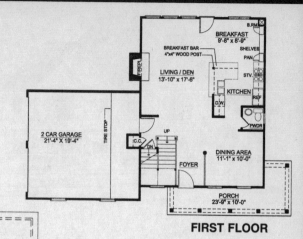

BREAKFAST
9'-8" x 8'-9"

BREAKFAST BAR
4"x4" WOOD POST

B.RM

SHELVES

PAN.

LIVING / DEN
13'-10" x 17'-6"

KITCHEN

STV.

D.W.

REF.

FIREPL

PWDR

2 CAR GARAGE
21'-4" X 19'-4"

TIRE STOP

UP

DINING AREA
11'-1" x 10'-0"

C.C.

DN

FOYER

PORCH
23'-9" x 10'-0"

FIRST FLOOR

Units	Single
Price Code	B
Total Finished	1,668 sq. ft.
First Finished	771 sq. ft.
Second Finished	897 sq. ft.
Garage Unfinished	400 sq. ft.
Porch Unfinished	330 sq. ft.
Dimensions	46'x31'
Foundation	Basement
Bedrooms	3
Full Baths	2
1/2 Baths	1
First Ceiling	9'
Second Ceiling	8'
Primary Roof Pitch	12:12
Max Ridge Height	29'9"
Roof Framing	Stick
Exterior Walls	2x4

GARDEN TUB

BEDROOM #2
11'-4" X 10'-7"

CLOSET

MASTER BATH

LC

BATH.

MASTER BEDRM.
15'-6" X 13'-0"

NICHE

ATTIC ACCESS

DN OPEN RAIL

BEDROOM #3
12'-8" X 10'-5"

LINEN

CLO.

LDRY

CLOSET

SECOND FLOOR

New Design
HOT OFF THE DRAWING BOARD

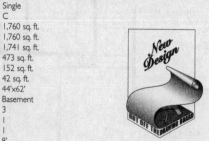

New Design
HOT OFF THE DRAWING BOARD

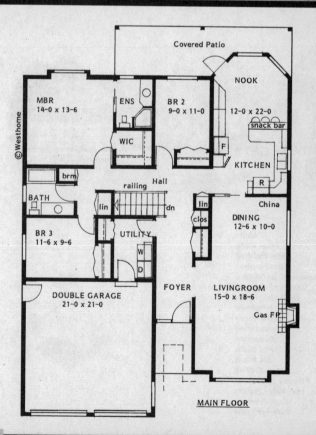

Covered Patio

NOOK
12-0 x 22-0

MBR
14-0 x 13-6

ENS

BR 2
9-0 x 11-0

snack bar

WIC

F

KITCHEN

R

brm

railing

Hall

China

BATH

lin

lin

clos

DINING
12-6 x 10-0

BR 3
11-6 x 9-6

dn

UTILITY

W
D

FOYER

LIVINGROOM
15-0 x 18-6

DOUBLE GARAGE
21-0 x 21-0

Gas FP

©Westhome

MAIN FLOOR

Units	Single
Price Code	C
Total Finished	1,760 sq. ft.
Main Finished	1,760 sq. ft.
Basement Unfinished	1,741 sq. ft.
Garage Unfinished	473 sq. ft.
Deck Unfinished	152 sq. ft.
Porch Unfinished	42 sq. ft.
Dimensions	44'x62'
Foundation	Basement
Bedrooms	3
Full Baths	1
3/4 Baths	1
Main Ceiling	8'
Primary Roof Pitch	5:12
Max Ridge Height	18'6"
Roof Framing	Truss
Exterior Walls	2x4

Plan # 98243

FIRST FLOOR

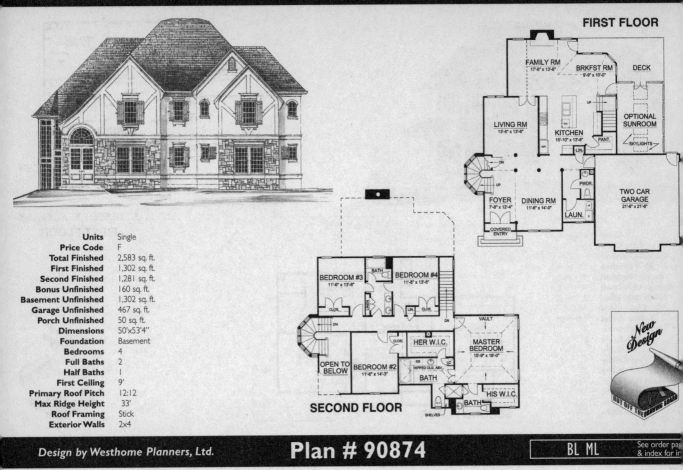

Units	Single
Price Code	F
Total Finished	2,583 sq. ft.
First Finished	1,302 sq. ft.
Second Finished	1,281 sq. ft.
Bonus Unfinished	160 sq. ft.
Basement Unfinished	1,302 sq. ft.
Garage Unfinished	467 sq. ft.
Porch Unfinished	50 sq. ft.
Dimensions	50'x53'4"
Foundation	Basement
Bedrooms	4
Full Baths	2
Half Baths	1
First Ceiling	9'
Primary Roof Pitch	12:12
Max Ridge Height	33'
Roof Framing	Stick
Exterior Walls	2x4

SECOND FLOOR

New Design

Plan # 90874

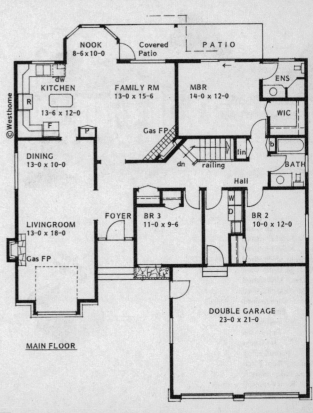

Units	Single
Price Code	C
Total Finished	1,770 sq. ft.
Main Finished	1,770 sq. ft.
Basement Unfinished	1,770 sq. ft.
Garage Unfinished	516 sq. ft.
Deck Unfinished	143 sq. ft.
Porch Unfinished	24 sq. ft.
Dimensions	50'x61'
Foundation	Basement
Bedrooms	3
Full Baths	1
3/4 Baths	1
Main Ceiling	8'
Primary Roof Pitch	5:12
Max Ridge Height	17'6"
Roof Framing	Truss
Exterior Walls	2x6

New Design

MAIN FLOOR

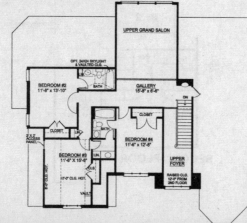

FIRST FLOOR

DECK

MORNING/KEEPING ROOM 20'-0" x 11'-6"

GRAND SALON 15'-0" x 19'-0"

MASTER STATEROOM 17'-0" x 14'-0"

KITCHEN 15'-0" x 11'-6"

M.BATH

UTILITY

DINING ROOM 11'-2" x 17'-0"

2 CAR GARAGE 21'-0" x 22'-8"

TWO STORY FOYER

COVERED PORCH

LIBRARY 11'-4" x 11'-0"

SECOND FLOOR

UPPER GRAND SALON

BEDROOM #2 11'-8" x 13'-10"

GALLERY 15'-8" x 6'-8"

BEDROOM #3 11'-6" X 15'-8"

BEDROOM #4 11'-8" x 12'-8"

UPPER FOYER

Units	Single
Price Code	G
Total Finished	2,870 sq. ft.
First Finished	1,963 sq. ft.
Second Finished	907 sq. ft.
Basement Unfinished	1,963 sq. ft.
Garage Unfinished	483 sq. ft.
Deck Unfinished	308 sq. ft.
Dimensions	58'x51.6'
Foundation	Basement
Bedrooms	4
Full Baths	3
Half Baths	1
Primary Roof Pitch	12:12
Max Ridge Height	35'
Roof Framing	Stick
Exterior Walls	2x4

Units	Single
Price Code	G
Total Finished	2,900 sq. ft.
Main Finished	2,900 sq. ft.
Basement Unfinished	2,900 sq. ft.
Dimensions	79'8"x86'
Foundation	Basement
Bedrooms	2
Full Baths	2
Half Baths	1
Primary Roof Pitch	8:12
Max Ridge Height	26'4"
Roof Framing	Stick
Exterior Walls	2x4

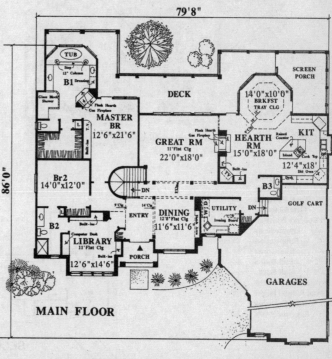

79'8"

86'0"

TUB
B1

DECK

SCREEN PORCH

BRKFST 14'0"x10'0" TRAY CLG

MASTER BR 12'6"x21'6"

GREAT RM 11'Flat Clg 22'0"x18'0"

HEARTH RM 15'0"x18'0"

KIT 12'4"x18'

Br2 14'0"x12'0"

B3

B2

DINING 12'8"Flat Clg 11'6"x11'6"

UTILITY

GOLF CART

ENTRY

LIBRARY 11'Flat Clg 12'6"x14'6"

PORCH

GARAGES

MAIN FLOOR

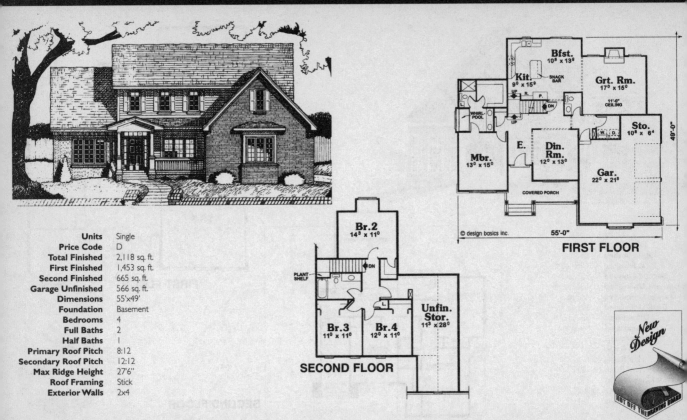

FIRST FLOOR

© design basics inc. 55'-0"

Units	Single
Price Code	D
Total Finished	2,118 sq. ft.
First Finished	1,453 sq. ft.
Second Finished	665 sq. ft.
Garage Unfinished	566 sq. ft.
Dimensions	55'x49'
Foundation	Basement
Bedrooms	4
Full Baths	2
Half Baths	1
Primary Roof Pitch	8:12
Secondary Roof Pitch	12:12
Max Ridge Height	27'6"
Roof Framing	Stick
Exterior Walls	2x4

SECOND FLOOR

FIRST FLOOR

61'8"

65'0"

Units	Single
Price Code	G
Total Finished	2,906 sq. ft.
First Finished	2,060 sq. ft.
Second Finished	846 sq. ft.
Dimensions	61'8"x65'
Foundation	Basement
Bedrooms	4
Full Baths	3
Half Baths	1
Primary Roof Pitch	12:12
Max Ridge Height	28'6"
Roof Framing	Truss
Exterior Walls	2x4

SECOND FLOOR

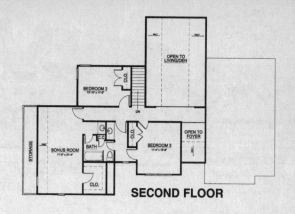

SECOND FLOOR

Units	Single
Price Code	D
Total Finished	2,206 sq. ft.
First Finished	1,616 sq. ft.
Second Finished	590 sq. ft.
Garage Unfinished	430 sq. ft.
Dimensions	65x46'
Foundation	Crawl space
Bedrooms	4
Full Baths	2
Half Baths	1
First Ceiling	9'
Primary Roof Pitch	12:12
Max Ridge Height	33'
Roof Framing	Stick
Exterior Walls	2x4

FIRST FLOOR

New Design — HOT OFF THE DRAWING BOARD

FIRST FLOOR

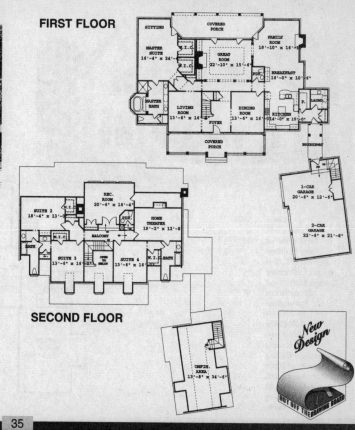

SECOND FLOOR

Units	Single
Price Code	L
Total Finished	5,106 sq. ft.
First Finished	2,920 sq. ft.
Second Finished	2,186 sq. ft.
Bonus Unfinished	564 sq. ft.
Garage Unfinished	890 sq. ft.
Dimensions	86'7"x103'6"
Foundation	Crawl space
Bedrooms	4
Full Baths	3
Half Baths	2
First Ceiling	10'
Second Ceiling	9'
Primary Roof Pitch	12:12
Max Ridge Height	35'6"
Roof Framing	Stick
Exterior Walls	2x4

New Design — HOT OFF THE DRAWING BOARD

© design basics inc. 1986

FIRST FLOOR

Kit. 9'x13'   Bfst. 10'x13'   Fam. rm. 17'x19'

Gar. 20'8"x24'   Dn. 12'x11'   Liv. 11'8"x11'

WRAP AROUND PORCH

58'-0"

40'-0"

SECOND FLOOR

SKYLIGHT

Br. 12'x11'   Mbr. 13'x17'4"

Br. 8'0"x11'x11'   Br. 11'x13'

Units	Single
Price Code	E
Total Finished	2,360 sq. ft.
First Finished	1,188 sq. ft.
Second Finished	1,172 sq. ft.
Garage Unfinished	504 sq. ft.
Dimensions	58'x40'
Foundation	Basement
	Slab
Bedrooms	4
Full Baths	2
Half Baths	1
First Ceiling	8'
Primary Roof Pitch	6:12
Secondary Roof Pitch	8:12
Max Ridge Height	25'6"
Roof Framing	Stick
Exterior Walls	2x4

New Design

HOT OFF THE DRAWING BOARD

FIRST FLOOR

DECK / TERRACE

MASTER SUITE 15'-10" x 16'-6"

FAMILY ROOM 14'-10" x 15'-8"

BREAKFAST 12'-10" x 9'-6"

MASTER BATH   W.I.C.   KITCHEN 14'-0" x 13'-2"

LAUND.   UP   OPEN TO ABOVE

GARAGE 20'-0" x 20'-0"   FOYER

PDR.   PORTICO   DINING ROOM 11'-10" x 13'-8"

SECOND FLOOR

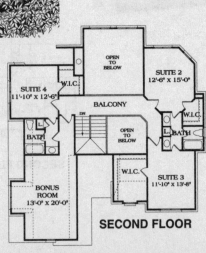

SUITE 4 11'-10" x 12'-6"   W.I.C.   OPEN TO BELOW   SUITE 2 12'-6" x 15'-0"

BALCONY   W.I.C.

BATH   DN   OPEN TO BELOW   BATH

W.I.C.   SUITE 3 11'-10" x 13'-8"

BONUS ROOM 13'-0" x 20'-0"

Units	Single
Price Code	G
Total Finished	2,807 sq. ft.
First Finished	1,805 sq. ft.
Second Finished	1,002 sq. ft.
Bonus Unfinished	340 sq. ft.
Garage Unfinished	434 sq. ft.
Dimensions	49'10"x60'8"
Foundation	Crawl space
Bedrooms	4
Full Baths	3
Half Baths	1
First Ceiling	8'
Second Ceiling	9'
Primary Roof Pitch	12:8
Secondary Roof Pitch	12:12
Max Ridge Height	34'6"
Roof Framing	Stick
Exterior Walls	2x4

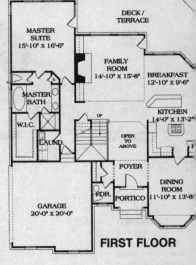

New Design

HOT OFF THE DRAWING BOARD

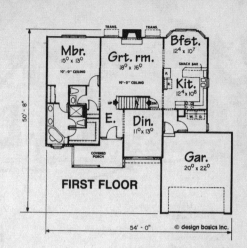

FIRST FLOOR

Mbr. 15⁰ x 13⁰ — 10'-0" CEILING
Grt. rm. 18⁰ x 16⁰ — 10'-0" CEILING
Bfst. 12⁴ x 10⁷
Kit. 12⁴ x 10⁸
E.
Din. 11⁰ x 13⁰
Gar. 20⁰ x 22⁰
COVERED PORCH
TRANS. TRANS.
UP
DN
50' - 8"
54' - 0"
© design basics inc.

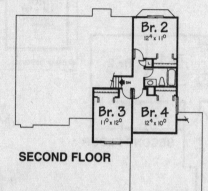

SECOND FLOOR

Br. 2 12⁴ x 11⁰
Br. 3 11⁰ x 12⁰
Br. 4 12⁴ x 10⁰
DN

Units	Single
Price Code	C
Total Finished	1,996 sq. ft.
First Finished	1,398 sq. ft.
Second Finished	598 sq. ft.
Garage Unfinished	460 sq. ft.
Dimensions	54'x50'8"
Foundation	Basement
Bedrooms	4
Full Baths	2
Half Baths	1
First Ceiling	8'
Primary Roof Pitch	8:12
Secondary Roof Pitch	8:12
Max Ridge Height	24'10"
Roof Framing	Stick
Exterior Walls	2x4

New Design
HOT OFF THE DRAWING BOARD

SECOND FLOOR

FIRST FLOOR

GARAGE 24'-6" X 22'-0"
LAUN.
BREAKFAST 12'-2" X 11'-0"
COVERED TERRACE
MASTER SUITE 14'-0" X 15'-10"
KITCHEN 12'-2" X 13'-0"
GATHERING ROOM 14'-6" X 18'-0"
MASTER BATH
W.I.C.
P.
PDR.
DINING ROOM 14'-0" X 13'-0"
FOYER
STUDY 14'-0" X 13'-0"
PORCH
UP

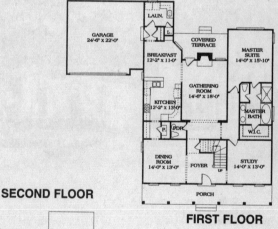

RECREATION ROOM 14'-6" X 13'-0"
BATH
W.I.C.
W.I.C.
BATH
SUITE 3 14'-0" X 13'-0"
OPEN TO BELOW
SUITE 2 14'-0" X 13'-0"
DN

Units	Single
Price Code	G
Total Finished	2,932 sq. ft.
First Finished	1,905 sq. ft.
Second Finished	1,027 sq. ft.
Deck Unfinished	124 sq. ft.
Porch Unfinished	252 sq. ft.
Dimensions	66'10"x61'2"
Foundation	Crawl space
Bedrooms	3
Full Baths	3
Half Baths	1
First Ceiling	9'
Second Ceiling	9'
Primary Roof Pitch	10:12
Secondary Roof Pitch	12:12
Max Ridge Height	31'
Roof Framing	Stick
Exterior Walls	2x4

New Design
HOT OFF THE DRAWING BOARD

Order Today! 1-800-235-5700 or order online at
www.familyhomeplans.com

Plan # 97438

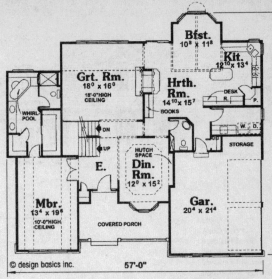

© design basics inc.   57'-0"

FIRST FLOOR

Grt. Rm.
18⁰ x 16⁰
18'-0" HIGH
CEILING

Bfst.
10⁸ x 11⁸

Kit.
12¹⁰ x 13⁴

Hrth. Rm.
14¹⁰ x 15⁷

DESK

WHIRL POOL

BOOKS

DN

UP

E.

HUTCH SPACE

Din. Rm.
12⁰ x 15²

W. D.

STORAGE

Mbr.
13⁴ x 19⁶
10'-0" HIGH CEILING

COVERED PORCH

Gar.
20⁴ x 21⁴

Units	Single
Price Code	F
Total Finished	2,512 sq. ft.
First Finished	1,795 sq. ft.
Second Finished	717 sq. ft.
Garage Unfinished	472 sq. ft.
Dimensions	57'x51'
Foundation	Basement
Bedrooms	4
Full Baths	2
Half Baths	1
Primary Roof Pitch	10:12
Secondary Roof Pitch	12:12
Max Ridge Height	30'
Roof Framing	Stick
Exterior Walls	2x4

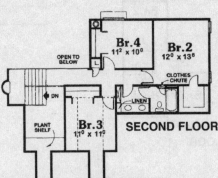

Br.4
11² x 10⁰

Br.2
12⁰ x 13⁶

OPEN TO BELOW

DN

CLOTHES CHUTE

LINEN

PLANT SHELF

Br.3
11⁰ x 11⁰

SECOND FLOOR

New Design
HOT OFF THE DRAWING BOARD

Plan # 96950

MASTER SUITE
14'-6" x 16'-6"

TERRACE

W.I.C.   W.I.C.

FAMILY ROOM
16'-0" x 14'-6"

BRKFST

MASTER BATH

PDR

KITCHEN
12'-10" x 13'-0"

LAUN.

P.

FOYER

DINING ROOM
12'-0" x 14'-0"

ENTRY

PORTICO

GARAGE
21'-2" x 21'-0"

FIRST FLOOR

SUITE 2
14'-6" x 12'-0"

BATH

OPEN TO BELOW

SUITE 3
10'-6" x 12'-0"

DN

SUITE 4
12'-0" x 14'-0"

OPEN TO BELOW

BATH

BONUS ROOM
13'-0" x 17'-2"

SECOND FLOOR

Units	Single
Price Code	F
Total Finished	2,674 sq. ft.
First Finished	1,688 sq. ft.
Second Finished	986 sq. ft.
Bonus Unfinished	341 sq. ft.
Garage Unfinished	444 sq. ft.
Dimensions	63'11"x68'11"
Foundation	Crawl space
Bedrooms	4
Full Baths	3
Half Baths	1
Primary Roof Pitch	12:8
Secondary Roof Pitch	12:4
Max Ridge Height	35'6"
Roof Framing	Stick
Exterior Walls	2x4

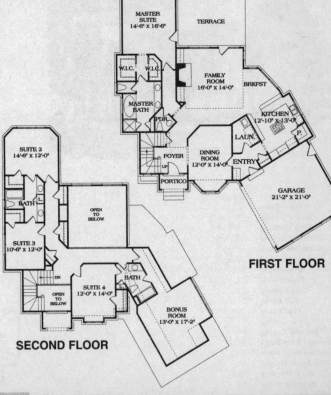

New Design
HOT OFF THE DRAWING BOARD

Plan # 97448

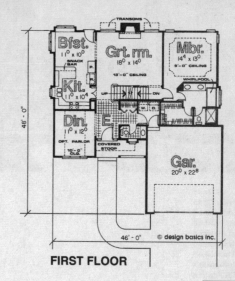

FIRST FLOOR

© design basics inc.

Units	Single
Price Code	B
Total Finished	1,660 sq. ft.
First Finished	1,265 sq. ft.
Second Finished	395 sq. ft.
Garage Unfinished	475 sq. ft.
Dimensions	46'x48'
Foundation	Basement
	Slab
Bedrooms	3
Full Baths	2
Half Baths	1
First Ceiling	8'
Primary Roof Pitch	8:12
Secondary Roof Pitch	10:12
Max Ridge Height	25'
Exterior Walls	2x4

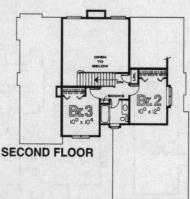

SECOND FLOOR

Plan # 97437

© design basics inc. 1991

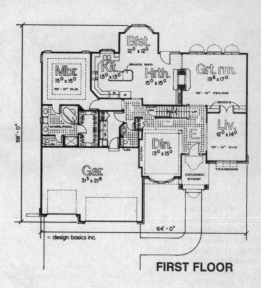

© design basics inc.

FIRST FLOOR

Units	Single
Price Code	G
Total Finished	2,814 sq. ft.
First Finished	2,073 sq. ft.
Second Finished	741 sq. ft.
Garage Unfinished	668 sq. ft.
Dimensions	64'x58'
Foundation	Basement
Bedrooms	4
Full Baths	2
Half Baths	1
First Ceiling	8'
Primary Roof Pitch	8:12
Max Ridge Height	28'6"
Roof Framing	Stick
Exterior Walls	2x4

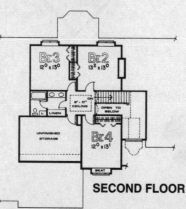

SECOND FLOOR

Order Today! 1-800-235-5700 or order online at
www.familyhomeplans.com

FIRST FLOOR

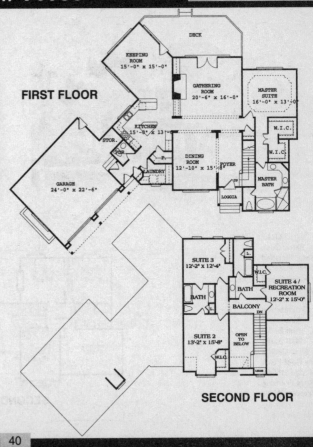

MASTER SUITE 15'-6" x 20'-0"
MASTER BATH
BREAKFAST/ SUN ROOM 18'-0" x 11'-0"
COVERED PORCH 22'-4" x 9'-2"
W.I.C.
LAUNDRY
STOR.
P.
KITCHEN 19'-0" x 13'-0"
FAMILY ROOM 21'-6" x 14'-6"
BUTLERS PANTRY
STOOP
PDR.
GARAGE 21'-4" x 31'-0"
DINING ROOM 14'-4" x 16'-0"
LIVING ROOM 14'-4" x 16'-0"
FOYER
COVERED PORCH

SECOND FLOOR

ATTIC
OPEN TO BELOW
BALCONY
SUITE 2 16'-6" x 14'-6"
W.I.C.
STOR.
BATH
W.I.C.
BATH
W.I.C.
RECREATION ROOM 13'-8" x 26'-10"
SUITE 4 14'-4" x 14'-0"
OPEN TO BELOW
SUITE 3 14'-4" x 16'-0"

New Design — HOT OFF THE DRAWING BOARD

Units	Single
Price Code	K
Total Finished	4,019 sq. ft.
First Finished	2,647 sq. ft.
Second Finished	1,372 sq. ft.
Bonus Unfinished	453 sq. ft.
Garage Unfinished	686 sq. ft.
Dimensions	72'10"x71'8"
Foundation	Basement, Crawl space
Bedrooms	4
Full Baths	3
Half Baths	1
First Ceiling	9'
Second Ceiling	9'
Primary Roof Pitch	12:10
Secondary Roof Pitch	12:14
Max Ridge Height	38'
Roof Framing	Stick
Exterior Walls	2x4

FIRST FLOOR

KEEPING ROOM 15'-0" x 15'-0"
DECK
GATHERING ROOM 20'-6" x 16'-0"
MASTER SUITE 16'-0" x 13'-0"
KITCHEN 15'-8" x 13'
W.I.C.
STOR.
PDR.
DINING ROOM 12'-10" x 15'
FOYER
W.I.C.
P.
LAUNDRY
GARAGE 24'-0" x 22'-6"
LOGGIA
MASTER BATH

New Design — HOT OFF THE DRAWING BOARD

SECOND FLOOR

SUITE 3 12'-2" x 12'-4"
W.I.C.
SUITE 4 / RECREATION ROOM 12'-2" x 15'-0"
BATH
BATH
BALCONY
SUITE 2 13'-2" x 15'-8"
OPEN TO BELOW
W.I.C.

Units	Single
Price Code	G
Total Finished	2,986 sq. ft.
First Finished	2,060 sq. ft.
Second Finished	926 sq. ft.
Garage Unfinished	665 sq. ft.
Deck Unfinished	294 sq. ft.
Dimensions	86'x65'5"
Foundation	Crawl space
Bedrooms	4
Full Baths	2
Half Baths	1
First Ceiling	10'
Second Ceiling	9'
Primary Roof Pitch	12:10
Secondary Roof Pitch	12:8
Max Ridge Height	34'
Roof Framing	Stick
Exterior Walls	2x4

Plan # 97433

FIRST FLOOR

Fam. rm. 13⁰ x 17⁰

Bfst. 10⁰ x 12²

SNACK BAR

Kit. 10⁷ x 12²

Sto. 9⁸ x 8⁴

Par. 13⁰ x 10⁰

DN

E.

UP

Din. 13⁰ x 10⁰

W D

Gar. 21⁴ x 21⁰

COVERED PORCH

38'-0"

56'-0"

© design basics inc.

Units	Single
Price Code	D
Total Finished	2,119 sq. ft.
First Finished	1,086 sq. ft.
Second Finished	1,033 sq. ft.
Bonus Unfinished	215 sq. ft.
Garage Unfinished	547 sq. ft.
Dimensions	56'x38'
Foundation	Basement
Bedrooms	4
Full Baths	2
Half Baths	1
First Ceiling	8'
Primary Roof Pitch	6:12
Secondary Roof Pitch	9:12
Max Ridge Height	24'8"
Roof Framing	Stick
Exterior Walls	2x4

Br. 4 10⁰ x 11⁰

Br. 2 11⁰ x 11⁰

DN

Mbr. 13⁰ x 15⁰

Br. 3 10⁷ x 10⁰

Sto. 10⁰ x 15⁸ UNFINISHED

OPEN TO BELOW

SECOND FLOOR

New Design — HOT OFF THE DRAWING BOARD

Plan # 97424

FIRST FLOOR

SNACK BAR

Fam. rm. 16⁰ x 16⁰

Bfst. 10⁰ x 11⁶

Kit. 9⁴ x 11⁰

DN PANT.

Gar. 21⁰ x 25³

Liv. rm. 12⁰ x 13⁰

E. UP

Din. 12⁰ x 10⁰

W D

STOOP

30'-0"

57'-4"

© design basics inc.

Units	Single
Price Code	E
Total Finished	2,345 sq. ft.
First Finished	1,000 sq. ft.
Second Finished	1,345 sq. ft.
Garage Unfinished	568 sq. ft.
Dimensions	57'4"x30'
Foundation	Basement
	Slab
Bedrooms	4
Full Baths	2
Half Baths	1
3/4 Baths	1
First Ceiling	8'
Primary Roof Pitch	8:12
Secondary Roof Pitch	10:12
Max Ridge Height	27'6"
Roof Framing	Stick
Exterior Walls	2x4

Br 4 12⁰ x 11²

WHIRL-POOL LIN

Mbr. 14⁰ x 16⁰ 9'-0" CEILING

Sit. 9⁰ x 10⁰

TRANSOM

DN

DRESSING

Br 3 12⁰ x 12⁰

OPEN TO BELOW

Br 2 12⁰ x 13⁰

ENT. CENTER

SECOND FLOOR

New Design — HOT OFF THE DRAWING BOARD

Plan # 96957

New Design

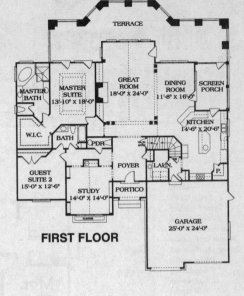

FIRST FLOOR

MASTER BATH	
MASTER SUITE 13'-10" x 18'-0"	
GREAT ROOM 18'-0" x 24'-0"	DINING ROOM 11'-8" x 16'-0"
SCREEN PORCH	
W.I.C.	BATH
PDR.	KITCHEN 14'-6" x 20'-6"
GUEST SUITE 2 15'-0" x 12'-6"	FOYER LAUN. P.
STUDY 14'-0" x 14'-0"	PORTICO
	GARAGE 25'-0" x 24'-0"

TERRACE

Units	Single
Price Code	L
Total Finished	4,360 sq. ft.
First Finished	2,546 sq. ft.
Lower Finished	1,814 sq. ft.
Garage Unfinished	653 sq. ft.
Dimensions	66'4"x80'8"
Foundation	Basement
Bedrooms	3
Full Baths	3
Half Baths	1
First Ceiling	10'
Lower Ceiling	9'
Primary Roof Pitch	12:9
Secondary Roof Pitch	12:4
Max Ridge Height	42'
Roof Framing	Stick
Exterior Walls	2x4

COVERED TERRACE

SUITE 3 14'-0" x 11'-10"	BATH
	14'-6" x 6'-6"
	BAR 10'-0" x 15'-0"
W.I.C.	RECREATION ROOM 19'-6" x 21'-0"
STOR. / WORKSHOP	HOME THEATER 16'-0" x 16'-10"
	MECH. / STOR. 18'-10" x 8'-0"
	EXERCISE ROOM 13'-6" x 19'-0"

LOWER FLOOR

Plan # 96951

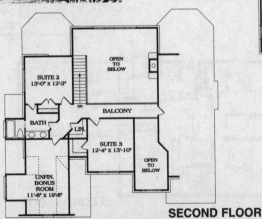

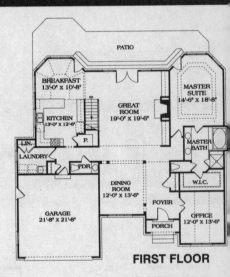

FIRST FLOOR

PATIO

BREAKFAST 13'-0" x 10'-8"	
KITCHEN 13'-0" x 12'-6"	GREAT ROOM 19'-0" x 19'-6"
	MASTER SUITE 14'-6" x 18'-8"
LIN.	P.
LAUNDRY	MASTER BATH
PDR.	DINING ROOM 12'-0" x 13'-6"
	W.I.C.
GARAGE 21'-8" x 21'-8"	FOYER
	PORCH
	OFFICE 12'-0" x 13'-6"

Units	Single
Price Code	F
Total Finished	2,674 sq. ft.
First Finished	2,022 sq. ft.
Second Finished	652 sq. ft.
Bonus Unfinished	285 sq. ft.
Garage Unfinished	488 sq. ft.
Dimensions	58'4"x54'5"
Foundation	Crawl space
Bedrooms	3
Full Baths	2
Half Baths	1
First Ceiling	9'
Second Ceiling	9'
Primary Roof Pitch	10:12
Secondary Roof Pitch	12:12
Max Ridge Height	34'6"
Roof Framing	Stick
Exterior Walls	2x4

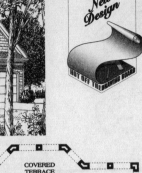

SUITE 2 13'-0" x 12'-2"	OPEN TO BELOW
	DN
BATH	BALCONY
LIN.	
	SUITE 3 12'-4" x 13'-10"
UNFIN. BONUS ROOM 11'-8" x 19'-8"	OPEN TO BELOW

SECOND FLOOR

New Design

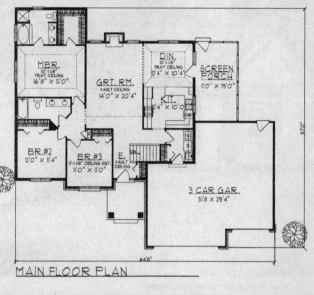

Rear Elevation

New Design

Units	Single
Price Code	B
Total Finished	1,591 sq. ft.
Main Finished	1,591 sq. ft.
Basement Unfinished	1,591 sq. ft.
Dimensions	64'8"x57'
Foundation	Basement
Bedrooms	3
Full Baths	2
Main Ceiling	11'
Primary Roof Pitch	8:12
Secondary Roof Pitch	8:12
Max Ridge Height	24'8"
Roof Framing	Truss
Exterior Walls	2x6

MAIN FLOOR PLAN

New Design

Units	Single
Price Code	H
Total Finished	3,141 sq. ft.
First Finished	1,728 sq. ft.
Second Finished	1,413 sq. ft.
Basement Unfinished	970 sq. ft.
Garage Unfinished	429 sq. ft.
Dimensions	47'2"x65'5"
Foundation	Basement
Bedrooms	4
Full Baths	3
Half Baths	1
First Ceiling	10'
Second Ceiling	9'
Primary Roof Pitch	12:12
Max Ridge Height	43'6"
Roof Framing	Stick
Exterior Walls	2x4

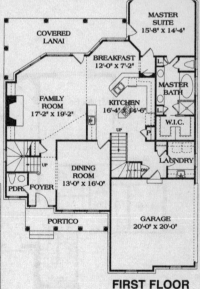

FIRST FLOOR

SECOND FLOOR

Photography by Donna & Ron Kolb — Exposures Unlimited

Units	Single
Price Code	D
Total Finished	2,082 sq. ft.
First Finished	1,524 sq. ft.
Second Finished	558 sq. ft.
Bonus Unfinished	267 sq. ft.
Basement Unfinished	1,460 sq. ft.
Dimensions	60'x50'4''
Foundation	Basement
Bedrooms	3
Full Baths	2
Half Baths	1
First Ceiling	8'
Second Ceiling	8'
Primary Roof Pitch	12:8
Secondary Roof Pitch	12:12
Max Ridge Height	26'
Roof Framing	Truss
Exterior Walls	2x4

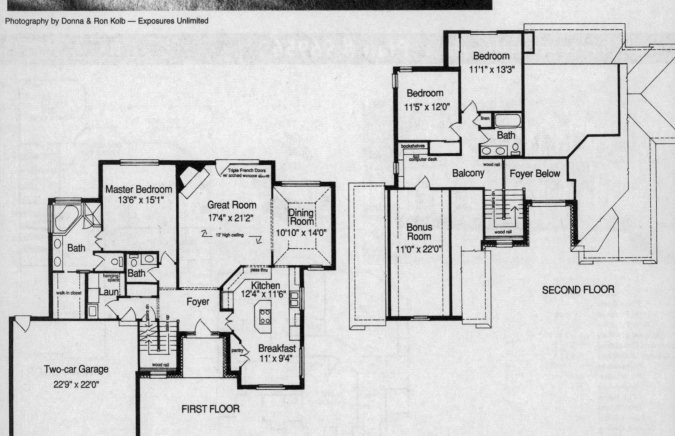

44

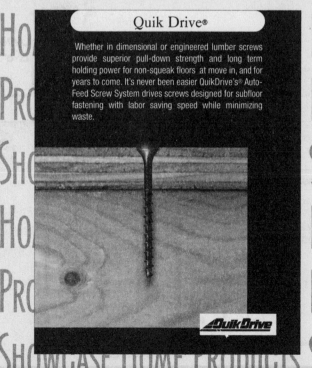

Units	Single
Price Code	E
Total Finished	2,392 sq. ft.
Upper Finished	1,196 sq. ft.
Lower Finished	1,196 sq. ft.
Dimensions	46'x26'
Foundation	Slab
Bedrooms	4
Full Baths	2
Half Baths	1
Primary Roof Pitch	5:12
Max Ridge Height	24'
Roof Framing	Stick
Exterior Walls	2x6

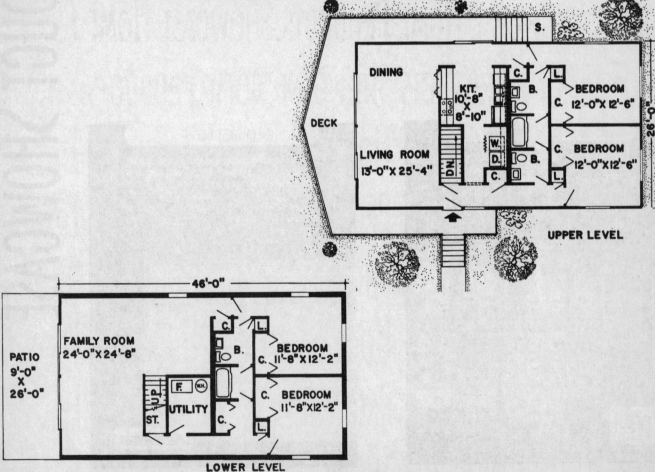

UPPER LEVEL

- DECK
- DINING
- KIT. 10'-8" X 8'-10"
- LIVING ROOM 13'-0" X 25'-4"
- BEDROOM 12'-0" X 12'-6"
- BEDROOM 12'-0" X 12'-6"
- 26'-0"
- S.

LOWER LEVEL

- 46'-0"
- PATIO 9'-0" X 26'-0"
- FAMILY ROOM 24'-0" X 24'-8"
- UTILITY
- ST.
- BEDROOM 11'-8" X 12'-2"
- BEDROOM 11'-8" X 12'-2"

Units	Single
Price Code	B
Total Finished	1,560 sq. ft.
First Finished	1,061 sq. ft.
Second Finished	499 sq. ft.
Basement Unfinished	1,061 sq. ft.
Porch Unfinished	339 sq. ft.
Dimensions	44'x34'
Foundation	Basement
	Crawl space
	Slab
Bedrooms	3
Full Baths	2
Half Baths	1
First Ceiling	8'
Second Ceiling	8'
Primary Roof Pitch	12:12
Secondary Roof Pitch	4.75:12
Max Ridge Height	26'
Roof Framing	Stick
Exterior Walls	2x4, 2x6

Rear Elevation

FIRST FLOOR

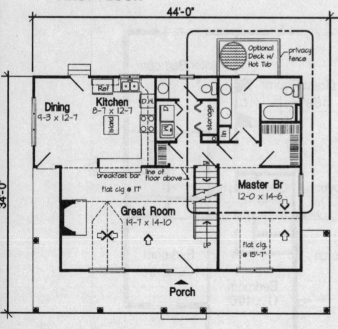

44'-0"

34'-0"

Dining 9-3 x 12-7

Kitchen 8-7 x 12-7
Ref
Island

Optional Deck w/ Hot Tub
privacy fence

storage

breakfast bar
line of floor above
flat clg @ 17'

Master Br 12-0 x 14-6

Great Room 19-7 x 14-10

DN

UP

flat clg. @ 15'-7"

Porch

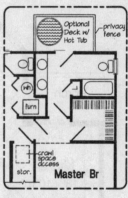

Alternate Foundation Plan

Optional Deck w/ Hot Tub
privacy fence

furn

crawl space access

stor.

Master Br

SECOND FLOOR

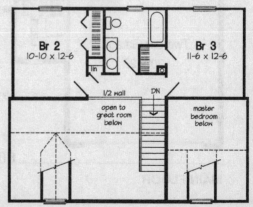

Br 2 10-10 x 12-6

Br 3 11-6 x 12-6

1/2 wall

DN

open to great room below

master bedroom below

Units	Single
Price Code	B
Total Finished	1,508 sq. ft.
Main Finished	1,508 sq. ft.
Basement Unfinished	1,439 sq. ft.
Garage Unfinished	440 sq. ft.
Dimensions	60'x47'
Foundation	Basement
Bedrooms	3
Full Baths	2
Main Ceiling	8'
Primary Roof Pitch	12:8
Secondary Roof Pitch	12:12
Max Ridge Height	21'9''
Roof Framing	Truss
Exterior Walls	2x4

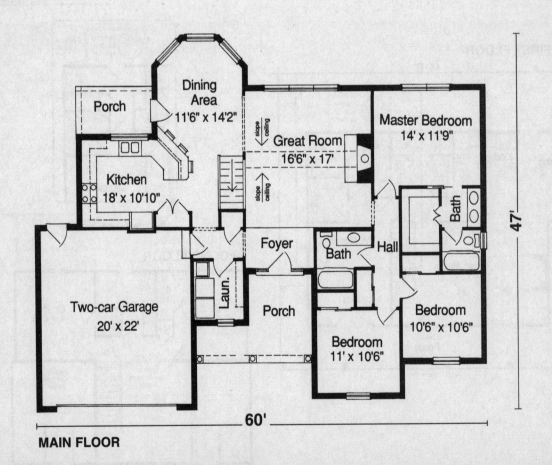

Porch

Dining Area
11'6" x 14'2"

Kitchen
18' x 10'10"

Great Room
16'6" x 17'
slope ceiling
slope ceiling

Master Bedroom
14' x 11'9"

Bath

47'

Foyer

Bath

Hall

Two-car Garage
20' x 22'

Laun.

Porch

Bedroom
10'6" x 10'6"

Bedroom
11' x 10'6"

60'

MAIN FLOOR

Plan # 92673

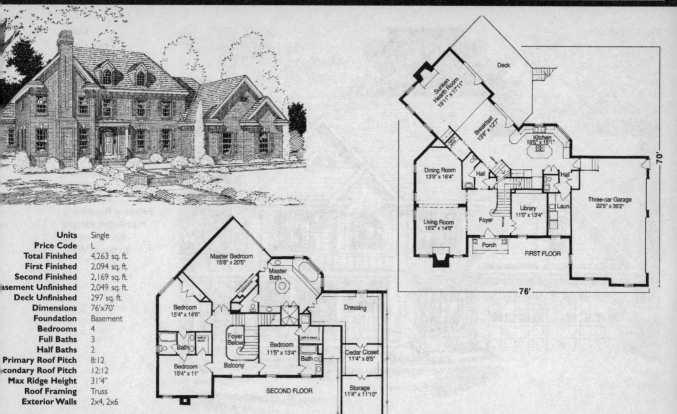

Units	Single
Price Code	L
Total Finished	4,263 sq. ft.
First Finished	2,094 sq. ft.
Second Finished	2,169 sq. ft.
Basement Unfinished	2,049 sq. ft.
Deck Unfinished	297 sq. ft.
Dimensions	76'x70'
Foundation	Basement
Bedrooms	4
Full Baths	3
Half Baths	2
Primary Roof Pitch	8:12
Secondary Roof Pitch	12:12
Max Ridge Height	31'4"
Roof Framing	Truss
Exterior Walls	2x4, 2x6

Plan # 93708

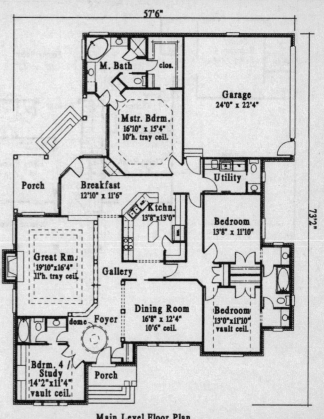

Main Level Floor Plan

Units	Single
Price Code	F
Total Finished	2,579 sq. ft.
Main Finished	2,579 sq. ft.
Garage Unfinished	536 sq. ft.
Dimensions	57'6"x73'2"
Foundation	Crawl space, Slab
Bedrooms	3
Full Baths	3
Half Baths	1
Primary Roof Pitch	9:12
Secondary Roof Pitch	4:12
Max Ridge Height	25'
Roof Framing	Stick
Exterior Walls	2x4

Order Today! 1-800-235-5700 or order online at
www.familyhomeplans.com

Units	Single
Price Code	D
Total Finished	2,128 sq. ft.
First Finished	1,257 sq. ft.
Second Finished	871 sq. ft.
Bonus Unfinished	444 sq. ft.
Basement Unfinished	1,275 sq. ft.
Garage Unfinished	462 sq. ft.
Dimensions	61'x40'6"
Foundation	Basement
	Crawl space
Bedrooms	4
Full Baths	3
Half Baths	1
Primary Roof Pitch	10:12
Max Ridge Height	32'
Roof Framing	Stick
Exterior Walls	2x4

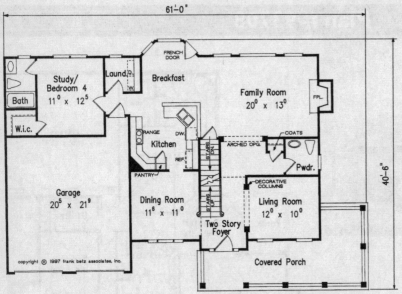

FIRST FLOOR

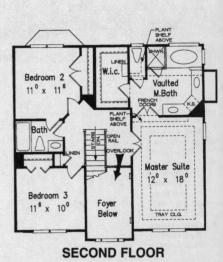

SECOND FLOOR

Units	Single
Price Code	H
Total Finished	3,063 sq. ft.
First Finished	2,035 sq. ft.
Second Finished	1,028 sq. ft.
Basement Unfinished	2,035 sq. ft.
Garage Unfinished	530 sq. ft.
Dimensions	56'x62'6''
Foundation	Basement, Crawl space
Bedrooms	4
Full Baths	3
Half Baths	1
First Ceiling	9'
Second Ceiling	8'
Vaulted Ceiling	13'6'' - 15'
Primary Roof Pitch	12:12
Secondary Roof Pitch	8:12
Max Ridge Height	33'9''
Roof Framing	Stick
Exterior Walls	2x4

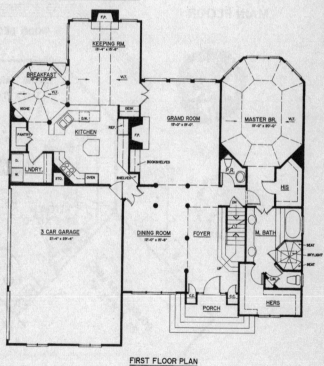

FIRST FLOOR PLAN

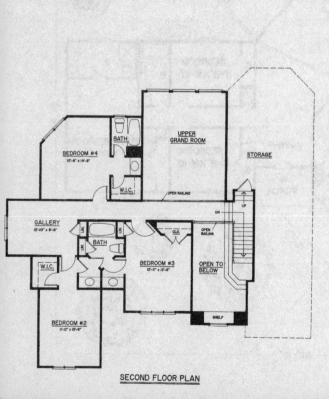

SECOND FLOOR PLAN

Units	Single
Price Code	C
Total Finished	1,783 sq. ft.
Main Finished	1,783 sq. ft.
Garage Unfinished	576 sq. ft.
Dimensions	82'10"x58'
Foundation	Slab
Bedrooms	3
Full Baths	1
3/4 Baths	1
Main Ceiling	8'
Primary Roof Pitch	5:12
Max Ridge Height	16'
Roof Framing	Stick
Exterior Walls	2x4

MAIN FLOOR

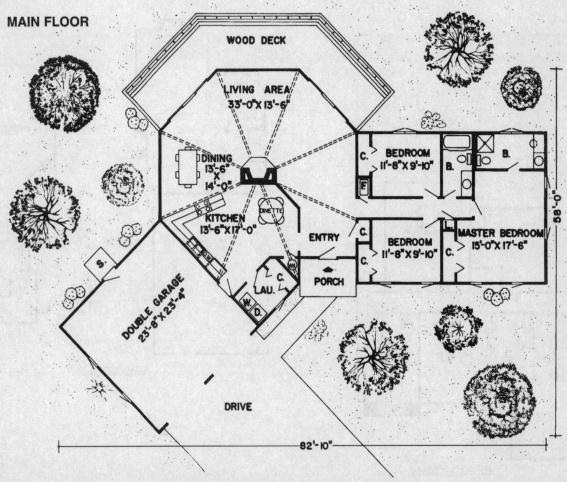

WOOD DECK

LIVING AREA
33'-0" X 13'-6"

DINING
13'-6" X 14'-0"

KITCHEN
13'-6" X 17'-0"

DINETTE

ENTRY

PORCH

LAU.

W. D.

S.

DOUBLE GARAGE
23'-8" X 23'-4"

DRIVE

BEDROOM
11'-8" X 9'-10"

C.

F

B.

B.

BEDROOM
11'-8" X 9'-10"

C.

C.

MASTER BEDROOM
15'-0" X 17'-6"

C.

58'-0"

82'-10"

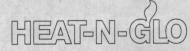

Plan # 94116

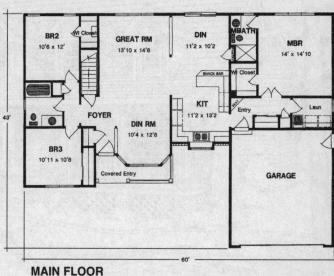

Units	Single
Price Code	B
Total Finished	1,546 sq. ft.
Main Finished	1,546 sq. ft.
Basement Unfinished	1,530 sq. ft.
Garage Unfinished	440 sq. ft.
Dimensions	60'x43'
Foundation	Basement
Bedrooms	3
Full Baths	1
3/4 Baths	1
Main Ceiling	9'2"
Primary Roof Pitch	10:12
Max Ridge Height	23'
Roof Framing	Truss
Exterior Walls	2x4

MAIN FLOOR

Plan # 98457

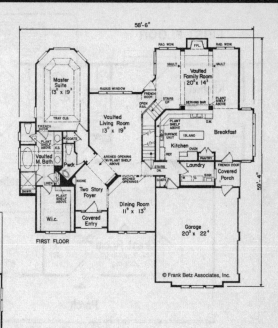

© Frank Betz Associates, Inc.

Units	Single
Price Code	F
Total Finished	2,686 sq. ft.
First Finished	1,883 sq. ft.
Second Finished	803 sq. ft.
Basement Unfinished	1,883 sq. ft.
Garage Unfinished	495 sq. ft.
Dimensions	58'6"x59'4"
Foundation	Basement, Crawl space
Bedrooms	4
Full Baths	3
Half Baths	1
Primary Roof Pitch	12:12
Max Ridge Height	33'
Roof Framing	Stick
Exterior Walls	2x4

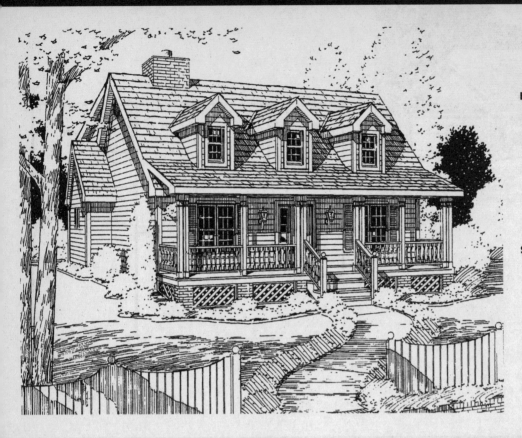

Units	Single
Price Code	B
Total Finished	1,560 sq. ft.
First Finished	1,061 sq. ft.
Second Finished	499 sq. ft.
Basement Unfinished	1,061 sq. ft.
Porch Unfinished	240 sq. ft.
Dimensions	40'x34'
Foundation	Basement
	Crawl space
	Slab
Bedrooms	3
Full Baths	2
Half Baths	1
First Ceiling	8'
Second Ceiling	8'
Primary Roof Pitch	12:12
Secondary Roof Pitch	5:12
Max Ridge Height	26'
Roof Framing	Stick
Exterior Walls	2x4, 2x6

Rear Elevatio

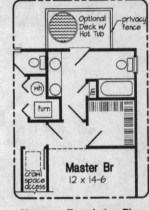

Alternate Foundation Plan

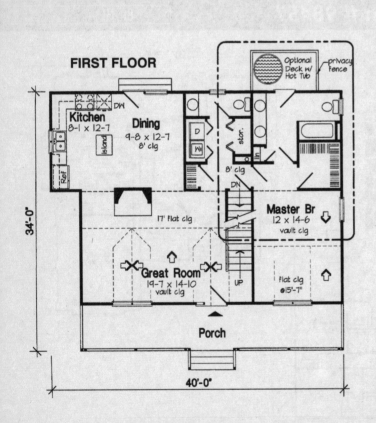

FIRST FLOOR

Optional Deck w/ Hot Tub

privacy fence

Kitchen
8-1 x 12-7

Dining
9-8 x 12-7
8' clg

DW

Island

Ref

stor.

8' clg

DN

Master Br
12 x 14-6
vault clg

17' flat clg

Great Room
19-7 x 14-10
vault clg

UP

flat clg
@15'-7"

Porch

34'-0"

40'-0"

SECOND FLOOR

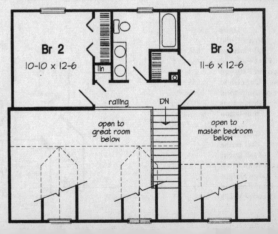

Br 2
10-10 x 12-6

Br 3
11-6 x 12-6

railing

DN

open to great room below

open to master bedroom below

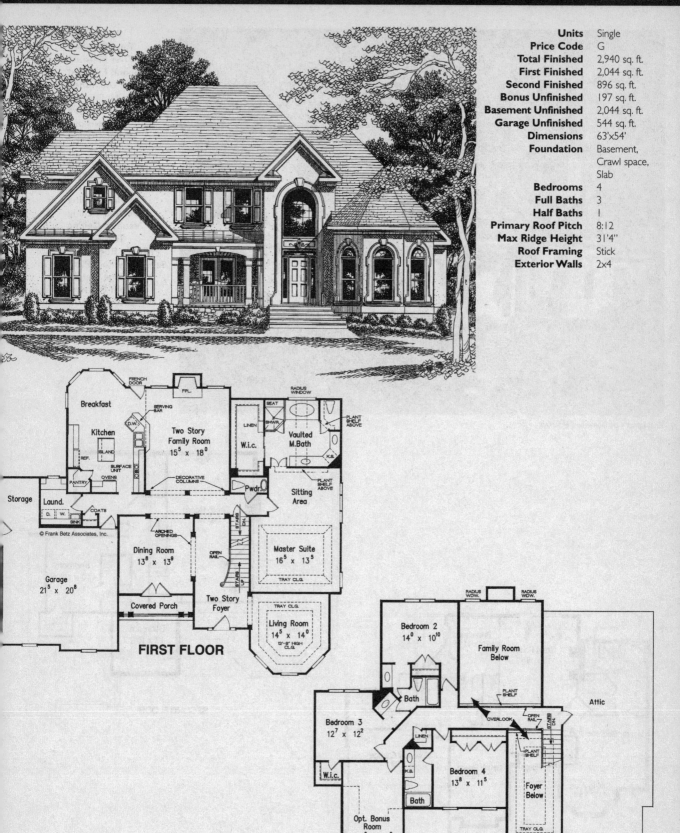

Units	Single
Price Code	G
Total Finished	2,940 sq. ft.
First Finished	2,044 sq. ft.
Second Finished	896 sq. ft.
Bonus Unfinished	197 sq. ft.
Basement Unfinished	2,044 sq. ft.
Garage Unfinished	544 sq. ft.
Dimensions	63'x54'
Foundation	Basement, Crawl space, Slab
Bedrooms	4
Full Baths	3
Half Baths	1
Primary Roof Pitch	8:12
Max Ridge Height	31'4"
Roof Framing	Stick
Exterior Walls	2x4

FIRST FLOOR

Breakfast
Kitchen
ISLAND
REF.
PANTRY
OVENS
SURFACE UNIT
D.W.
SERVING BAR
FPL.
FRENCH DOOR
Two Story Family Room 15⁵ x 18⁰
LINEN
W.i.c.
SEAT
SHWR.
RADIUS WINDOW
PLANT SHELF ABOVE
Vaulted M.Bath
K.S.
DECORATIVE COLUMNS
Pwdr.
PLANT SHELF ABOVE
Sitting Area
Storage
Laund.
D. W.
SINK
COATS
© Frank Betz Associates, Inc.
ARCHED OPENINGS
STAIRS DN.
OPEN RAIL
STAIRS
Dining Room 13⁸ x 13⁹
Master Suite 16⁵ x 13⁵
TRAY CLG.
Garage 21⁵ x 20⁸
Covered Porch
Two Story Foyer
TRAY CLG.
Living Room 14⁵ x 14⁰
12'-8" HIGH CLG.

SECOND FLOOR

Bedroom 2 14⁰ x 10¹⁰
RADIUS WDW. RADIUS WDW.
Family Room Below
Bath
PLANT SHELF
Attic
Bedroom 3 12⁷ x 12²
OVERLOOK
OPEN RAIL
STAIRS DN.
LINEN
W.i.c.
K.S.
PLANT SHELF
Bedroom 4 13⁸ x 11⁵
Foyer Below
Bath
Opt. Bonus Room 11⁰ x 17⁰
TRAY CLG.

Photography by Domenic Centofanti

Price Code	E
Total Finished	2,403 sq. ft.
First Finished	1,710 sq. ft.
Second Finished	693 sq. ft.
Basement Unfinished	1,620 sq. ft.
Garage Unfinished	467 sq. ft.
Porch Unfinished	43 sq. ft.
Dimensions	63'4"x48'
Foundation	Basement, Slab
Bedrooms	4
Full Baths	3
Half Baths	1
First Ceiling	8'
Second Ceiling	8'
Vaulted Ceiling	11'
Tray Ceiling	17'
Primary Roof Pitch	12:8
Secondary Roof Pitch	12:12
Max Ridge Height	20'
Roof Framing	Truss
Exterior Walls	2x4

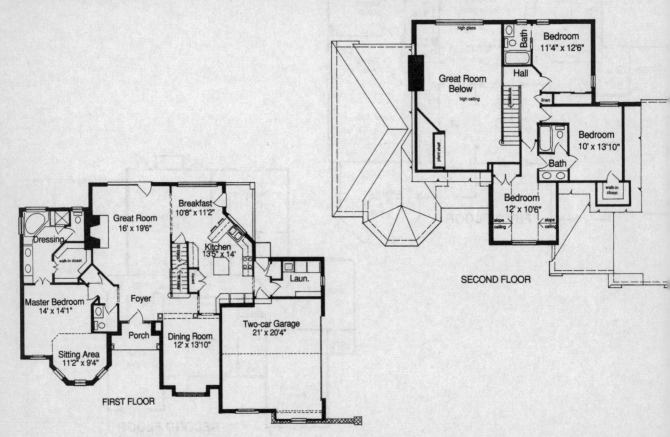

SECOND FLOOR

FIRST FLOOR

Units	Single
Price Code	G
Total Finished	2,806 sq. ft.
First Finished	1,952 sq. ft.
Second Finished	854 sq. ft.
Basement Unfinished	1,952 sq. ft.
Garage Unfinished	460 sq. ft.
Dimensions	56'6''x50'6''
Foundation	Basement
	Crawl space
Bedrooms	4
Full Baths	2
Half Baths	1
First Ceiling	9'2''
Second Ceiling	8'2''
Primary Roof Pitch	12:12
Max Ridge Height	32'3''
Roof Framing	Stick
Exterior Walls	2x4

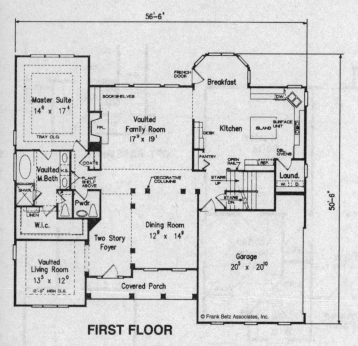

FIRST FLOOR

© Frank Betz Associates, Inc.

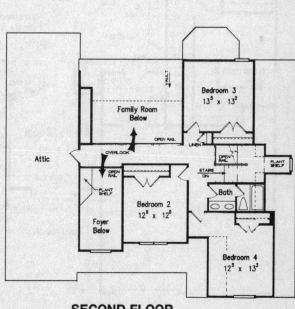

SECOND FLOOR

Units	Single
Price Code	B
Total Finished	1,544 sq. ft.
Main Finished	1,544 sq. ft.
Bonus Unfinished	284 sq. ft.
Basement Unfinished	1,544 sq. ft.
Garage Unfinished	440 sq. ft.
Dimensions	54'x47'6"
Foundation	Basement, Crawl space
Bedrooms	3
Full Baths	2
First Ceiling	9'2"
Bonus Ceiling	8'2"
Primary Roof Pitch	12:12
Max Ridge Height	26'6"
Roof Framing	Stick
Exterior Walls	2x4

Bedroom 2 10⁰ x 11⁰

Bath

Breakfast

FRENCH DOOR

FPL.

VAULT

D.W.

RANGE

Kitchen

SERVING BAR

REF.

Master Suite 13⁰ x 15⁰

TRAY CLG.

Vaulted Family Room 15⁰ x 18⁸

13'-0" HIGH CLG.

STAIRS UP

Bedroom 3 10⁰ x 11⁰

Laund.

W. D.

PANTRY

DECORATIVE COLUMN

Foyer 13'-0" HIGH CLG.

COATS

Vaulted Master Bath

LINEN

SHWR.

Dining Room 11² x 11⁹

13'-0" HIGH CLG.

Covered Porch

PLANT SHELF ABOVE

W.i.c.

© Frank Betz Associates, Inc.

Garage 21⁵ x 19⁸

MAIN FLOOR

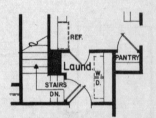

OPT. BASEMENT STAIR LOCATIO

REF.

PANTRY

Laund.

STAIRS DN.

W. D.

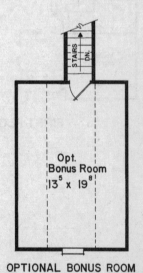

STAIRS DN.

Opt. Bonus Room 13⁵ x 19⁸

OPTIONAL BONUS ROOM

Units	Single
Price Code	H
Total Finished	3,143 sq. ft.
First Finished	2,253 sq. ft.
Second Finished	890 sq. ft.
Basement Unfinished	2,253 sq. ft.
Garage Unfinished	630 sq. ft.
Dimensions	61'6''x64'
Foundation	Basement
Bedrooms	4
Full Baths	3
Half Baths	1
First Ceiling	9'
Second Ceiling	8'
Primary Roof Pitch	12:12
Secondary Roof Pitch	7:12
Max Ridge Height	36'6''
Roof Framing	Stick
Exterior Walls	2x4

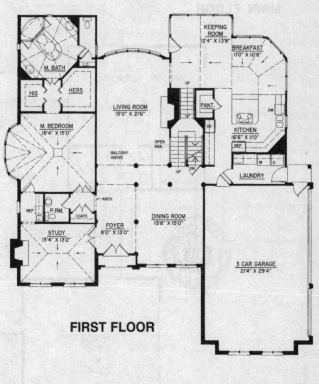

FIRST FLOOR

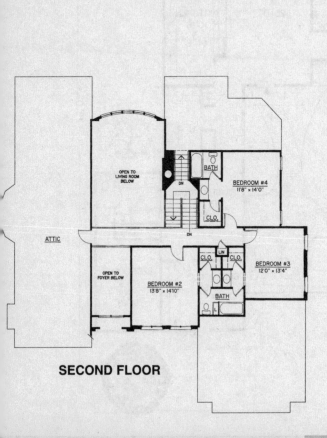

SECOND FLOOR

Units	Single
Price Code	D
Total Finished	2,194 sq. ft.
MainFinished	2,194 sq. ft.
Garage Unfinished	576 sq. ft.
Dimensions	76'x75'
Foundation	Crawl space
Bedrooms	3
Full Baths	1
3/4 Baths	1
Main Ceiling	8'
Primary Roof Pitch	4:12
Max Ridge Height	15'
Roof Framing	Stick
Exterior Walls	2x6

MAIN FLOOR

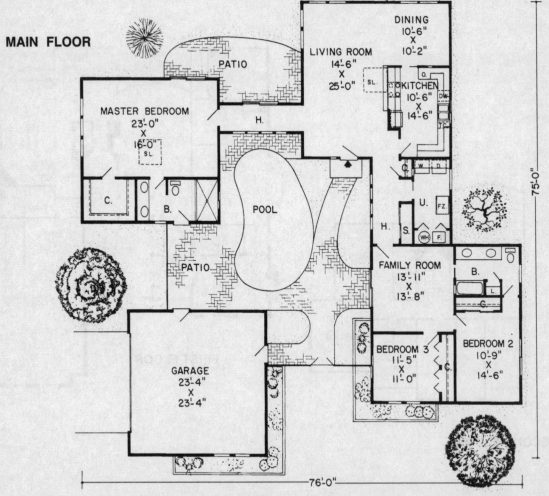

Plan # 92674

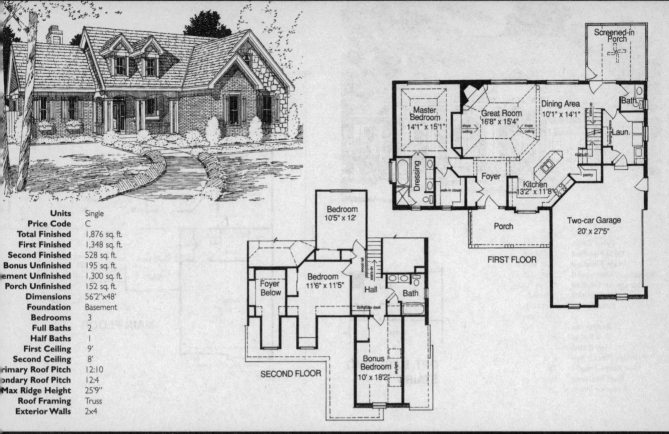

FIRST FLOOR

- Screened-in Porch
- Master Bedroom 14'1" x 15'1"
- Great Room 16'8" x 15'4"
- Dining Area 10'1" x 14'1"
- Bath
- Laun.
- Dressing
- Foyer
- Kitchen 13'2" x 11'8"
- pantry
- Porch
- Two-car Garage 20' x 27'5"

SECOND FLOOR

- Bedroom 10'5" x 12'
- Bedroom 11'6" x 11'5"
- Foyer Below
- Hall
- Bath
- Bonus Bedroom 10' x 18'2"

Units	Single
Price Code	C
Total Finished	1,876 sq. ft.
First Finished	1,348 sq. ft.
Second Finished	528 sq. ft.
Bonus Unfinished	195 sq. ft.
ement Unfinished	1,300 sq. ft.
Porch Unfinished	152 sq. ft.
Dimensions	56'2"x48'
Foundation	Basement
Bedrooms	3
Full Baths	2
Half Baths	1
First Ceiling	9'
Second Ceiling	8'
rimary Roof Pitch	12:10
ondary Roof Pitch	12:4
Max Ridge Height	25'9"
Roof Framing	Truss
Exterior Walls	2x4

Plan # 98464

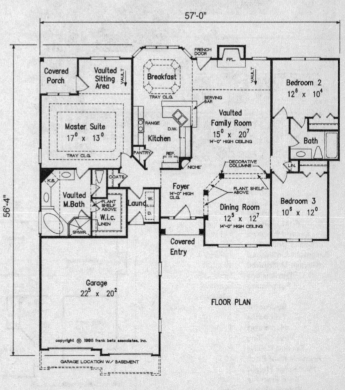

FLOOR PLAN

57'-0"

56'-4"

- Covered Porch
- Vaulted Sitting Area
- Breakfast
- French Door
- FP.
- Bedroom 2 12'6" x 10'4"
- Master Suite 17'0" x 13'0"
- TRAY CLG.
- Kitchen
- Vaulted Family Room 15'0" x 20'7" 14'-0" HIGH CEILING
- Bath
- Vaulted M.Bath
- W.i.c.
- Laund.
- Foyer 14'-0" HIGH CLG.
- Dining Room 12'5" x 12'7" 14'-0" HIGH CEILING
- Bedroom 3 10'8" x 12'0"
- Covered Entry
- Garage 22'5" x 20'2"

copyright © 1995 frank betz associates, inc.

GARAGE LOCATION W./ BASEMENT

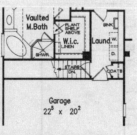

- Vaulted M.Bath
- W.I.C.
- Laund.
- Garage 22'5" x 20'2"

OPT. BASEMENT STAIR LOCATION

Units	Single
Price Code	C
Total Finished	1,779 sq. ft.
Main Finished	1,779 sq. ft.
ement Unfinished	1,818 sq. ft.
Garage Unfinished	499 sq. ft.
Dimensions	57'x56'4"
Foundation	Basement
	Crawl space
Bedrooms	3
Full Baths	2
Main Ceiling	9'
rimary Roof Pitch	10:12
Max Ridge Height	24'6"
Roof Framing	Stick
Exterior Walls	2x4

Units	Single
Price Code	D
Total Finished	2,201 sq. ft.
Main Finished	2,201 sq. ft.
Basement Unfinished	2,201 sq. ft.
Garage Unfinished	452 sq. ft.
Dimensions	59'6"x62'
Foundation	Basement
	Crawl space
Bedrooms	3
Full Baths	2
Half Baths	1
Primary Roof Pitch	8:12
Max Ridge Height	25'
Roof Framing	Stick
Exterior Walls	2x4

OPT. BASEMENT STAIRS

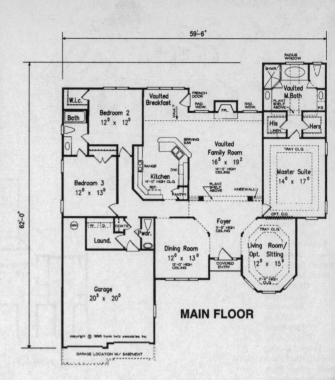

MAIN FLOOR

Units	Single
Price Code	C
Total Finished	1,995 sq. ft.
First Finished	1,071 sq. ft.
Second Finished	924 sq. ft.
Bonus Unfinished	280 sq. ft.
Basement Unfinished	1,071 sq. ft.
Garage Unfinished	480 sq. ft.
Dimensions	55'10"x38'6"
Foundation	Basement
	Crawl space
Bedrooms	3
Full Baths	2
Half Baths	1
First Ceiling	9'
Second Ceiling	8'
Primary Roof Pitch	10:12
Max Ridge Height	31'3"
Roof Framing	Stick
Exterior Walls	2x4

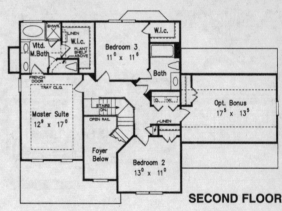

SECOND FLOOR

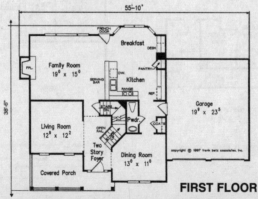

FIRST FLOOR

Photography by John Ehrenclou

Units	Single
Price Code	D
Total Finished	2,015 sq. ft.
Main Finished	1,280 sq. ft.
Upper Finished	735 sq. ft.
Porch Unfinished	80 sq. ft.
Dimensions	32'x40'
Foundation	Crawl space
Bedrooms	3
Full Baths	2
Half Baths	1
Main Ceiling	8'
Upper Ceiling	8'
Primary Roof Pitch	6:12
Secondary Roof Pitch	10:12
Max Ridge Height	32'
Roof Framing	Stick
Exterior Walls	2x6

Rear Elevation

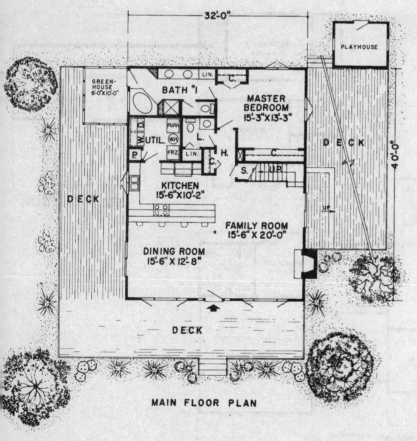

MAIN FLOOR PLAN

32'-0"

GREEN-HOUSE 8'-0"x10'-0"

BATH #1

LIN.

C.

MASTER BEDROOM 15'-3"x13'-3"

UTIL. W/D FURN WH FRZ P LIN L H. C. S. UP

DECK

KITCHEN 15'-6"x10'-2"

FAMILY ROOM 15'-6" X 20'-0"

DINING ROOM 15'-6" X 12'-8"

DECK

DECK

40'-0"

PLAYHOUSE

UP

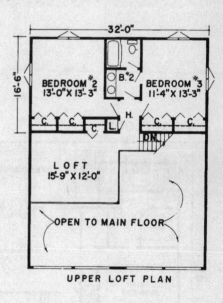

UPPER LOFT PLAN

32'-0"

16'-6"

B.#2

BEDROOM #2 13'-0" X 13'-3"

BEDROOM #3 11'-4" X 13'-3"

C. C. C. L H. C. C.

LOFT 15'-9" X 12'-0"

DN.

OPEN TO MAIN FLOOR

Units	Single
Price Code	G
Total Finished	2,759 sq. f
First Finished	1,927 sq. f
Second Finished	832 sq. ft.
Bonus Unfinished	624 sq. ft.
Basement Unfinished	1,674 sq. f
Dimensions	79'4''x46'
Foundation	Basement
	Crawl spac
	Slab
Bedrooms	3
Full Baths	3
Half Baths	2
First Ceiling	9'
Primary Roof Pitch	12:12
Secondary Roof Pitch	5:12
Max Ridge Height	28'
Roof Framing	Stick
Exterior Walls	2x4

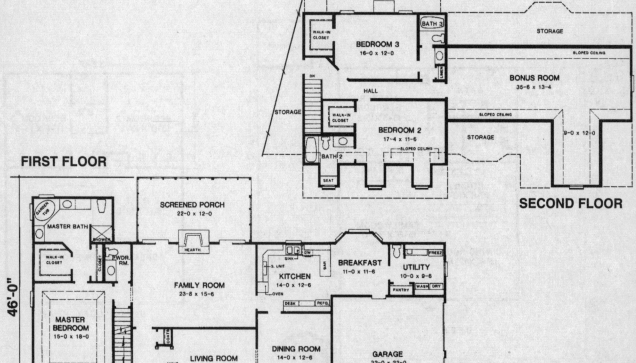

FIRST FLOOR

SECOND FLOOR

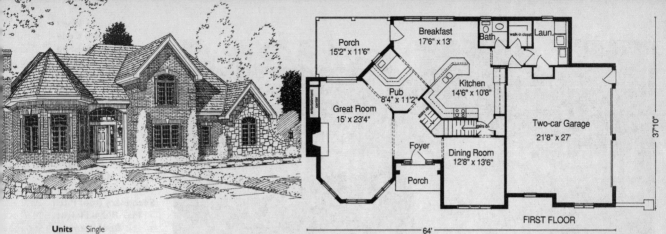

FIRST FLOOR

- Porch 15'2" x 11'6"
- Breakfast 17'6" x 13'
- Bath
- walk-in closet
- Laun.
- Pub 8'4" x 11'2"
- Kitchen 14'6" x 10'8"
- Great Room 15' x 23'4"
- Two-car Garage 21'8" x 27'
- Foyer
- Dining Room 12'8" x 13'6"
- Porch

64'
37'10"

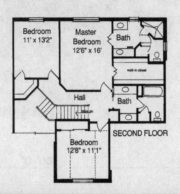

SECOND FLOOR

- Bedroom 11' x 13'2"
- Master Bedroom 12'6" x 16'
- Bath
- walk-in closet
- Hall
- Bath
- Bedroom 12'8" x 11'1"

Units	Single
Price Code	D
Total Finished	2,205 sq. ft.
First Finished	1,192 sq. ft.
Second Finished	1,013 sq. ft.
Basement Unfinished	1,157 sq. ft.
Porch Unfinished	48 sq. ft.
Dimensions	64'x37'10"
Foundation	Basement
Bedrooms	3
Full Baths	2
Half Baths	1
Primary Roof Pitch	8:12
Secondary Roof Pitch	12:12
Max Ridge Height	26'9"
Roof Framing	Stick
Exterior Walls	2x4

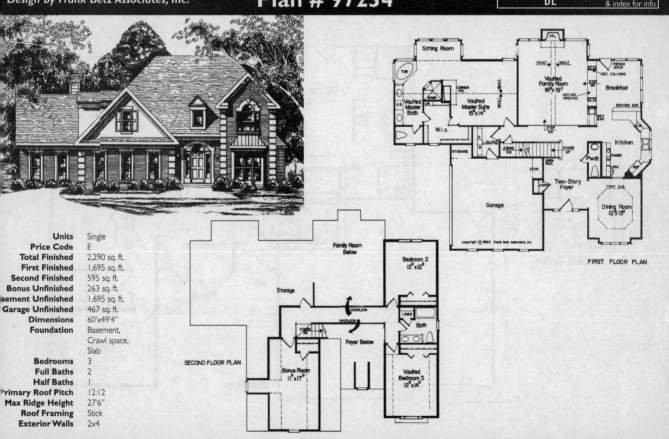

FIRST FLOOR PLAN

- Sitting Room
- Vaulted Family Room 16' x 19'
- French Door
- Dec. Columns
- Breakfast
- Serving Bar
- Vaulted Master Bath
- Vaulted Master Suite 15' x 14'
- W.i.c.
- Laund.
- Kitchen
- Pwdr.
- Two-Story Foyer
- Garage
- Dining Room 12' x 13'
- Tray Ceiling

copyright © 1990 frank betz associates, inc.

SECOND FLOOR PLAN

- Family Room Below
- Storage
- Bedroom 2 12' x 12'
- Overlook
- Foyer Below
- Bath
- Bonus Room 11' x 17'
- Vaulted Bedroom 3 12' x 14'

Units	Single
Price Code	E
Total Finished	2,290 sq. ft.
First Finished	1,695 sq. ft.
Second Finished	595 sq. ft.
Bonus Unfinished	263 sq. ft.
Basement Unfinished	1,695 sq. ft.
Garage Unfinished	467 sq. ft.
Dimensions	60'x49'4"
Foundation	Basement, Crawl space, Slab
Bedrooms	3
Full Baths	2
Half Baths	1
Primary Roof Pitch	12:12
Max Ridge Height	27'6"
Roof Framing	Stick
Exterior Walls	2x4

Photography by John Ehrenclou

Units	Single
Price Code	B
Total Finished	1,738 sq.
Main Finished	1,738 sq.
Basement Unfinished	1,083 sq.
Garage Unfinished	796 sq. ft.
Dimensions	66'x52'
Foundation	Basement
	Crawl spa
	Slab
Bedrooms	2
Full Baths	2
Main Ceiling	8'
Primary Roof Pitch	8:12
Secondary Roof Pitch	10:12
Max Ridge Height	24'6"
Roof Framing	Stick
Exterior Walls	2x4, 2x6

Rear Eleva

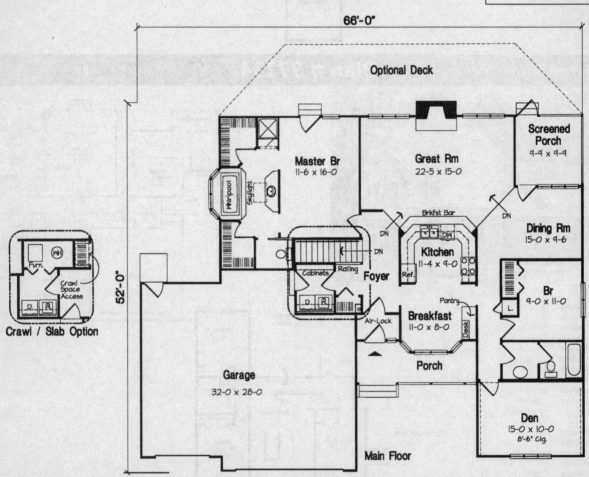

Crawl / Slab Option

Furn.   WH
Crawl Space Access

66'-0"

52'-0"

Optional Deck

Master Br
11-6 x 16-0

Whirlpool   Skylight

Great Rm
22-5 x 15-0

Screened Porch
9-9 x 9-9

DN

Dining Rm
15-0 x 9-6

Brkfst Bar

DN

Kitchen
11-4 x 9-0

Ref.

Cabinets   Railing

Foyer

Pantry

Br
9-0 x 11-0

L

Desk

Air-Lock

Breakfast
11-0 x 8-0

Garage
32-0 x 28-0

Porch

Den
15-0 x 10-0
8'-6" Clg.

Main Floor

Units	Single
Price Code	C
Total Finished	1,784 sq. ft.
Main Finished	1,784 sq. ft.
Garage Unfinished	491 sq. ft.
Dimensions	58'x64'8"
Foundation	Slab
Bedrooms	3
Full Baths	2
Primary Roof Pitch	6:12
Max Ridge Height	21'
Roof Framing	Truss
Exterior Walls	8" Concrete block

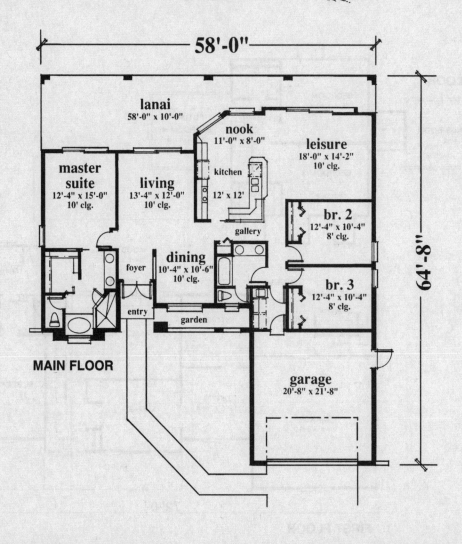

MAIN FLOOR

58'-0"

64'-8"

lanai
58'-0" x 10'-0"

nook
11'-0" x 8'-0"

leisure
18'-0" x 14'-2"
10' clg.

master suite
12'-4" x 15'-0"
10' clg.

living
13'-4" x 12'-0"
10' clg.

kitchen
12' x 12'

br. 2
12'-4" x 10'-4"
8' clg.

gallery

dining
10'-4" x 10'-6"
10' clg.

foyer

br. 3
12'-4" x 10'-4"
8' clg.

entry

garden

garage
20'-8" x 21'-8"

Units	Single
Price Code	E
Total Finished	2,297 sq. f
First Finished	1,580 sq. f
Second Finished	717 sq. ft.
Bonus Unfinished	410 sq. ft.
Basement Unfinished	1,342 sq. f
Garage Unfinished	484 sq. ft.
Deck Unfinished	288 sq. ft.
Porch Unfinished	144 sq. ft.
Dimensions	72'x40'
Foundation	Basement
	Crawl spa
Bedrooms	3
Full Baths	2
Half Baths	1
First Ceiling	8'
Second Ceiling	8'
Vaulted Ceiling	11'4"
Primary Roof Pitch	12:12
Secondary Roof Pitch	5:12
Max Ridge Height	25'6"
Roof Framing	Stick
Exterior Walls	2x4

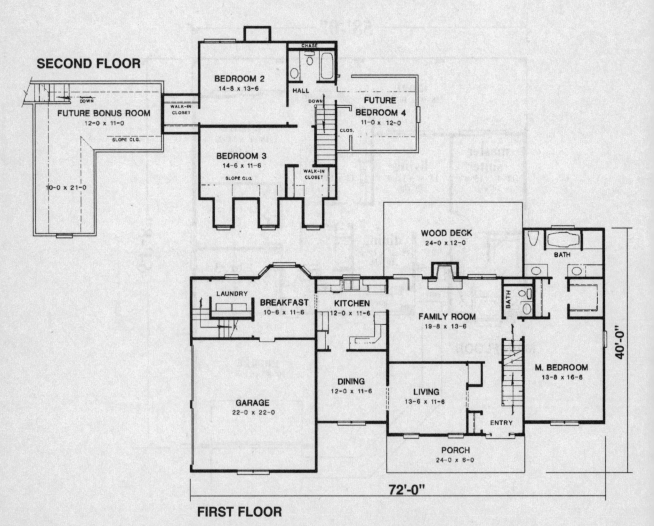

SECOND FLOOR

FUTURE BONUS ROOM
12-0 x 11-0
SLOPE CLG.

10-0 x 21-0

BEDROOM 2
14-8 x 13-6

WALK-IN CLOSET

CHASE

HALL

DOWN

FUTURE BEDROOM 4
11-0 x 12-0

CLOS.

BEDROOM 3
14-6 x 11-6
SLOPE CLG.

WALK-IN CLOSET

WOOD DECK
24-0 x 12-0

BATH

LAUNDRY

BREAKFAST
10-6 x 11-6

KITCHEN
12-0 x 11-6

FAMILY ROOM
19-8 x 13-6

BATH

GARAGE
22-0 x 22-0

DINING
12-0 x 11-6

LIVING
13-6 x 11-6

ENTRY

M. BEDROOM
13-8 x 16-8

PORCH
24-0 x 6-0

40'-0"

72'-0"

FIRST FLOOR

Units	Single
Price Code	E
Total Finished	2,408 sq. ft.
First Finished	1,294 sq. ft.
Second Finished	1,114 sq. ft.
Basement Unfinished	1,294 sq. ft.
Garage Unfinished	458 sq. ft.
Porch Unfinished	100 sq. ft.
Dimensions	57'8''x44'2''
Foundation	Basement
Bedrooms	4
Full Baths	2
Half Baths	1
First Ceiling	9'
Second Ceiling	8'
Vaulted Ceiling	12'
Primary Roof Pitch	9:12
Secondary Roof Pitch	12:12
Max Ridge Height	31'
Roof Framing	Truss
Exterior Walls	2x4

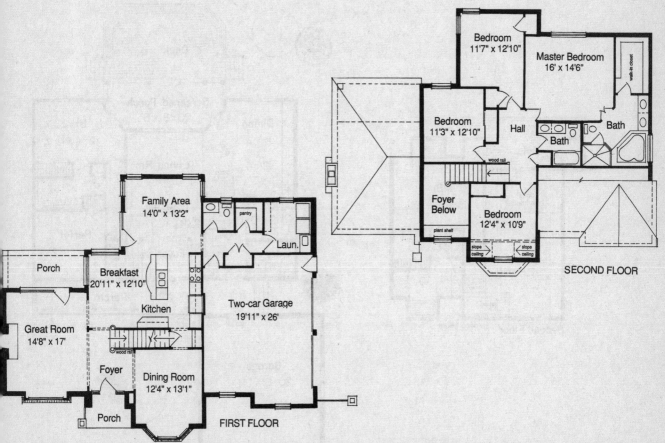

Photography supplied by The Meredith Corporation

Units	Single
Price Code	B
Total Finished	1,695 sq.
First Finished	1,290 sq.
Second Finished	405 sq.
Garage Unfinished	513 sq.
Porch Unfinished	152 sq.
Dimensions	50'8"x6
Foundation	Baseme
	Crawl sp
Bedrooms	2
Full Baths	2
First Ceiling	9'
Second Ceiling	8'
Primary Roof Pitch	10:12
Max Ridge Height	29'
Roof Framing	Stick/Tr
Exterior Walls	2x4

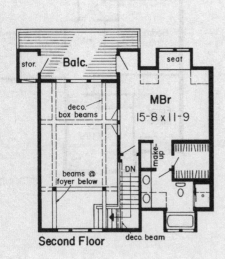

Second Floor

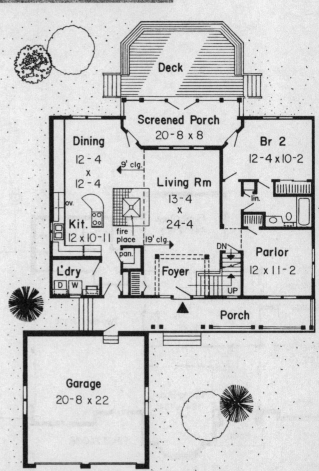

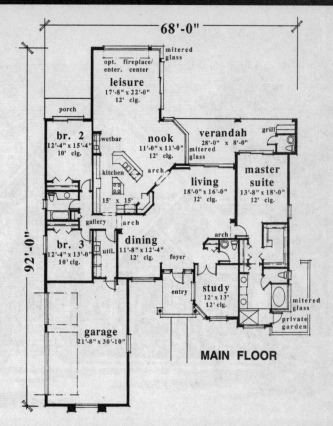

Units	Single
Price Code	G
Total Finished	2,894 sq. ft.
Main Finished	2,894 sq. ft.
Garage Unfinished	734 sq. ft.
Dimensions	68'x92'
Foundation	Slab
Bedrooms	3
Full Baths	2
Half Baths	1
Primary Roof Pitch	6:12
Max Ridge Height	25'6"
Roof Framing	Stick

68'-0"

92'-0"

leisure
17'-8" x 22'-0"
12' clg.

opt. fireplace/ enter. center

mitered glass

porch

br. 2
12'-4" x 15'-4"
10' clg.

wetbar

nook
11'-0" x 11'-0"
12' clg.

verandah
28'-0" x 8'-0"
mitered glass

grill

kitchen

15' x 15'

arch

living
18'-0" x 16'-0"
12' clg.

master suite
13'-8" x 18'-0"
12' clg.

gallery

arch

br. 3
12'-4" x 13'-0"
10' clg.

util.

dining
11'-8" x 12'-4"
12' clg.

foyer

arch

entry

study
12' x 13'
12' clg.

mitered glass

private garden

garage
21'-8" x 30'-10"

MAIN FLOOR

Unfinished Basement

STAIRS UP

COATS

Garage
21² x 21⁵

copyright ©1994 frank betz associates, inc.

LOWER LEVEL PLAN

Units	Single
Price Code	B
Total Finished	1,609 sq. ft.
Upper Finished	1,509 sq. ft.
Lower Finished	100 sq. ft.
Basement Unfinished	954 sq. ft.
Garage Unfinished	484 sq. ft.
Dimensions	49'x34'4"
Foundation	Basement
Bedrooms	3
Full Baths	2
Primary Roof Pitch	10:12
Max Ridge Height	28'
Roof Framing	Stick
Exterior Walls	2x4

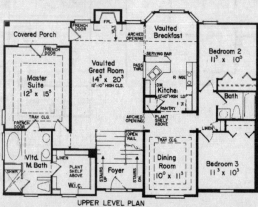

Covered Porch

FRENCH DOOR

FPL

VLT

ARCHED OPENING

Vaulted Breakfast

FRENCH DOOR

SERVING BAR

PASS THRU

Vaulted Great Room
14³ x 20³
12'-10" HIGH CLG.

Bedroom 2
11³ x 10⁰

Master Suite
12³ x 15⁵

DW
RANGE

Kitchen
12'-10" HIGH CLG.

PLANT SHELF ABOVE

PANTRY

Bath

FRENCH DOOR

ARCHED OPENING

OPEN RAIL

TRAY CLG.

Vltd. M. Bath

PLANT SHELF ABOVE

Foyer

STAIRS UP

STAIRS DN

Dining Room
10⁰ x 11³

LINEN

TRAY CLG.

Bedroom 3
11³ x 10³

SHWR.

Wi.c.

UPPER LEVEL PLAN

Units	Single
Price Code	H
Total Finished	3,027 sq. ft.
First Finished	1,468 sq. ft.
Second Finished	1,559 sq. ft.
Basement Unfinished	1,468 sq. ft.
Garage Unfinished	816 sq. ft.
Dimensions	52'4"x55'4'
Foundation	Basement
	Crawl space
Bedrooms	4
Full Baths	3
Primary Roof Pitch	10:12
Max Ridge Height	35'9"
Roof Framing	Stick
Exterior Walls	2x4

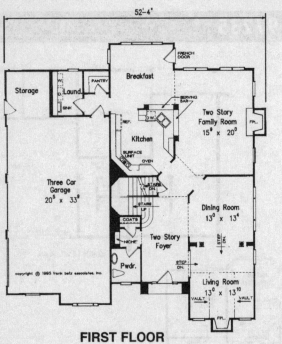

FIRST FLOOR

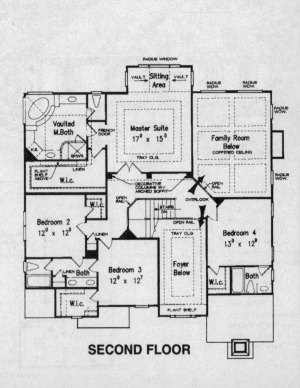

SECOND FLOOR

72

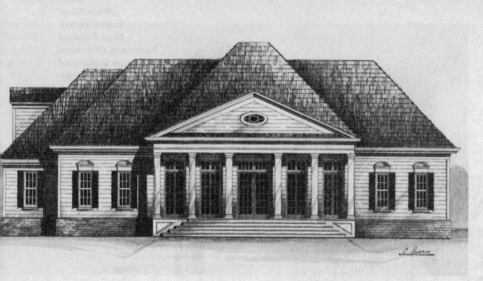

Units	Single
Price Code	E
Total Finished	2,460 sq. ft.
First Finished	1,684 sq. ft.
Second Finished	776 sq. ft.
Bonus Unfinished	550 sq. ft.
Basement Unfinished	1,684 sq. ft.
Garage Unfinished	470 sq. ft.
Porch Unfinished	246 sq. ft.
Dimensions	64'x46'
Foundation	Basement, Slab
Bedrooms	4
Full Baths	3
Half Baths	1
First Ceiling	9'
Vaulted Ceiling	10'
Tray Ceiling	10'
Primary Roof Pitch	10:12
Max Ridge Height	31'
Roof Framing	Stick
Exterior Walls	2x4

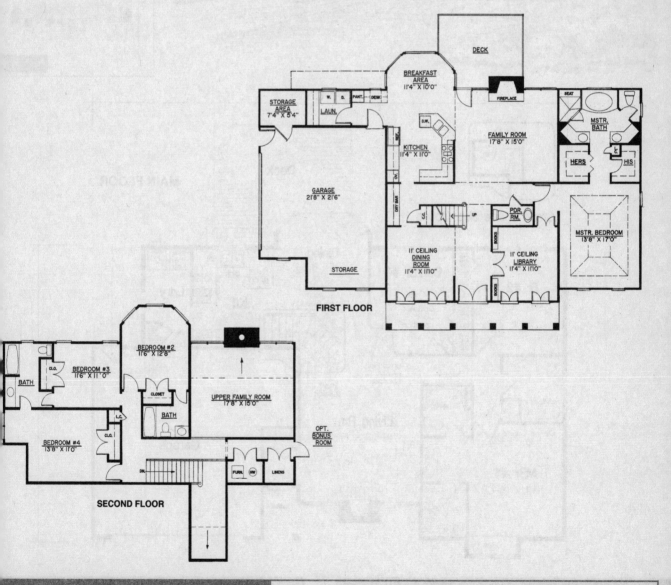

FIRST FLOOR

SECOND FLOOR

Rear Elevation

Units	Single
Price Code	A
Total Finished	1,359 sq. ft
Main Finished	1,359 sq. ft
Basement Unfinished	1,359 sq. ft
Garage Unfinished	501 sq. ft.
Dimensions	58'x34'4''
Foundation	Basement
	Crawl space
	Slab
Bedrooms	3
Full Baths	2
Main Ceiling	8'
Primary Roof Pitch	6:12
Secondary Roof Pitch	12:12
Max Ridge Height	18'6''
Roof Framing	Stick
Exterior Walls	2x4, 2x6

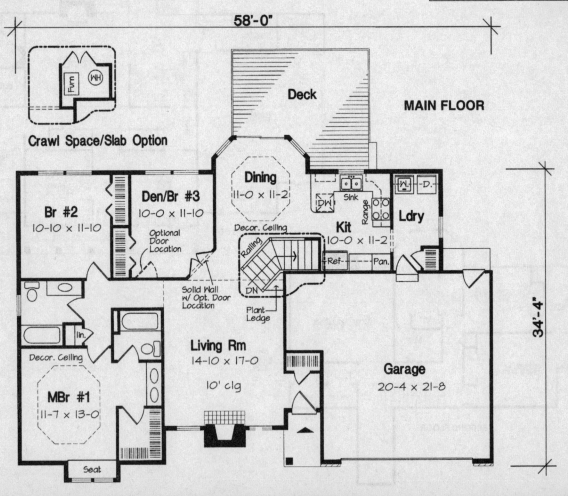

MAIN FLOOR

58'-0"

34'-4"

Crawl Space/Slab Option

Fur WH

Deck

Dining 11-0 x 11-2

Decor. Ceiling

DW Sink Range

Kit 10-0 x 11-2

Ldry W. D.

Ref Pan.

Br #2 10-10 x 11-10

Den/Br #3 10-0 x 11-10

Optional Door Location

Railing

DN

Plant Ledge

Solid Wall w/ Opt. Door Location

lin.

Decor. Ceiling

MBr #1 11-7 x 13-0

Seat

Living Rm 14-10 x 17-0

10' clg

Garage 20-4 x 21-8

Units	Single
Price Code	E
Total Finished	2,386 sq. ft.
First Finished	1,223 sq. ft.
Second Finished	1,163 sq. ft.
Bonus Unfinished	204 sq. ft.
Basement Unfinished	1,223 sq. ft.
Garage Unfinished	400 sq. ft.
Dimensions	50'x48'
Foundation	Basement, Crawl space
Bedrooms	4
Full Baths	2
Half Baths	1
First Ceiling	9'
Second Ceiling	8'
Primary Roof Pitch	10:12
Max Ridge Height	32'6"
Roof Framing	Stick
Exterior Walls	2x4

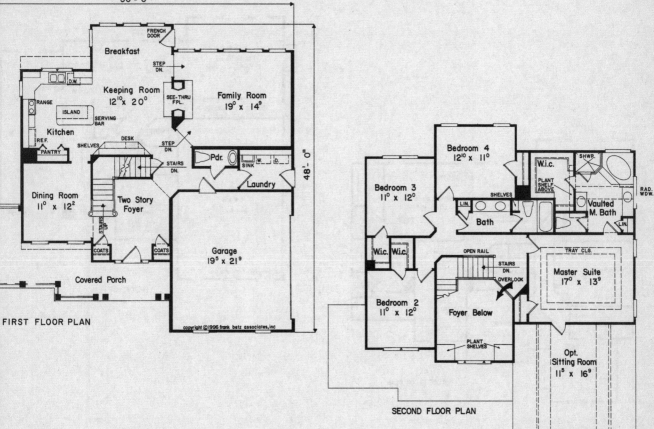

FIRST FLOOR PLAN

SECOND FLOOR PLAN

copyright ©1996 frank betz associates, inc

Units	Single
Price Code	H
Total Finished	3,165 sq. ft
First Finished	1,533 sq. ft
Second Finished	1,632 sq. ft
Basement Unfinished	1,583 sq. ft
Garage Unfinished	640 sq. ft.
Dimensions	58'4''×50'
Foundation	Basement, Crawl space
Bedrooms	5
Full Baths	4
First Ceiling	9'
Second Ceiling	8'
Primary Roof Pitch	10:12
Max Ridge Height	34'4''
Roof Framing	Stick
Exterior Walls	2x4

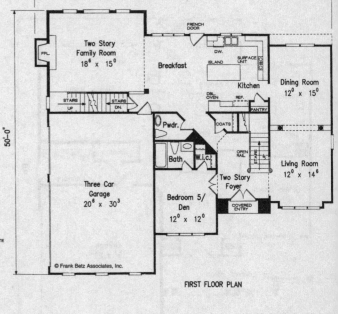

FIRST FLOOR PLAN

© Frank Betz Associates, Inc.

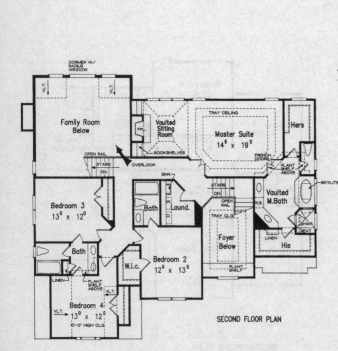

SECOND FLOOR PLAN

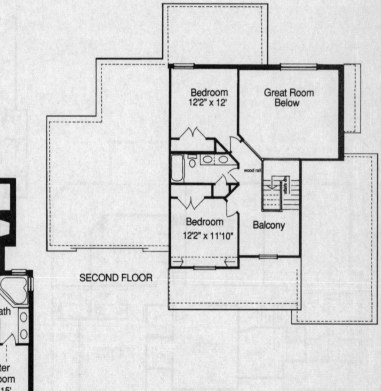

Units	Single
Price Code	D
Total Finished	2,017 sq. ft.
First Finished	1,432 sq. ft.
Second Finished	585 sq. ft.
Basement Unfinished	1,432 sq. ft.
Porch Unfinished	141 sq. ft.
Dimensions	58'x44'4''
Foundation	Basement
Bedrooms	3
Full Baths	2
Half Baths	1
Primary Roof Pitch	8:12
Secondary Roof Pitch	12:12
Max Ridge Height	29'10''
Roof Framing	Truss
Exterior Walls	2x4

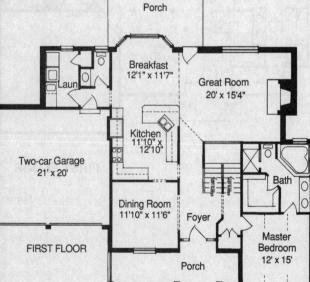

FIRST FLOOR

Porch

Breakfast 12'1" x 11'7"

Great Room 20' x 15'4"

Laun

Kitchen 11'10" x 12'10"

Two-car Garage 21' x 20'

Bath

Dining Room 11'10" x 11'6"

Foyer

Master Bedroom 12' x 15'

Porch

SECOND FLOOR

Bedroom 12'2" x 12'

Great Room Below

wood rail

Bedroom 12'2" x 11'10"

Balcony

Units	Single
Price Code	F
Total Finished	2,522 sq. ft.
First Finished	1,704 sq. ft.
Second Finished	818 sq. ft.
Basement Unfinished	1,704 sq. ft.
Dimensions	54'x51'
Foundation	Basement
Bedrooms	4
Full Baths	2
Half Baths	1
First Ceiling	9'
Second Ceiling	8'
Primary Roof Pitch	12:12
Max Ridge Height	31'
Roof Framing	Stick
Exterior Walls	2x4

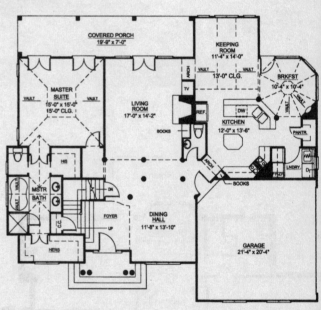

FIRST FLOOR

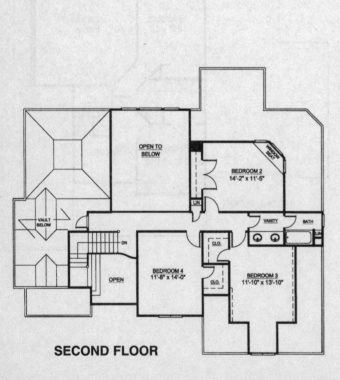

SECOND FLOOR

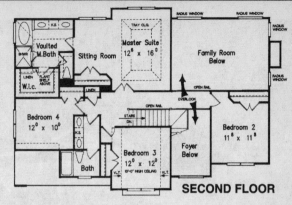

SECOND FLOOR

Units	Single
Price Code	E
Total Finished	2,477 sq. ft.
First Finished	1,258 sq. ft.
Second Finished	1,219 sq. ft.
Basement Unfinished	1,258 sq. ft.
Garage Unfinished	473 sq. ft.
Dimensions	55'4"x37'
Foundation	Basement
	Crawl space
Bedrooms	4
Full Baths	2
Half Baths	1
First Ceiling	9'
Second Ceiling	8'
Primary Roof Pitch	10:12
Max Ridge Height	32'
Roof Framing	Stick
Exterior Walls	2x4

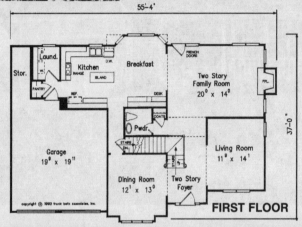

FIRST FLOOR

Units	Single
Price Code	E
Total Finished	2,445 sq. ft.
Main Finished	2,445 sq. ft.
Garage Unfinished	630 sq. ft.
Deck Unfinished	234 sq. ft.
Porch Unfinished	32 sq. ft.
Dimensions	65'x68'8''
Foundation	Slab
Bedrooms	4
Full Baths	3
Half Baths	1
Main Ceiling	9'-12'
Primary Roof Pitch	12:12
Max Ridge Height	32'
Roof Framing	Stick
Exterior Walls	2x4

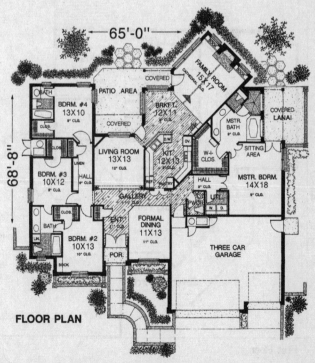

FLOOR PLAN

Photography by Laurie Solomon

Units	Single
Price Code	C
Total Finished	1,763 sq. ft.
First Finished	909 sq. ft.
Second Finished	854 sq. ft.
Basement Unfinished	899 sq. ft.
Garage Unfinished	491 sq. ft.
Dimensions	48'x44'
Foundation	Basement
	Crawl space
	Slab
Bedrooms	3
Full Baths	2
Half Baths	1
First Ceiling	8'
Second Ceiling	8'
Tray Ceiling	9'
Primary Roof Pitch	8:12
Secondary Roof Pitch	12:12
Max Ridge Height	29'
Roof Framing	Stick
Exterior Walls	2x4, 2x6

Rear Elevation

Opt. Slab/ Crawl Space

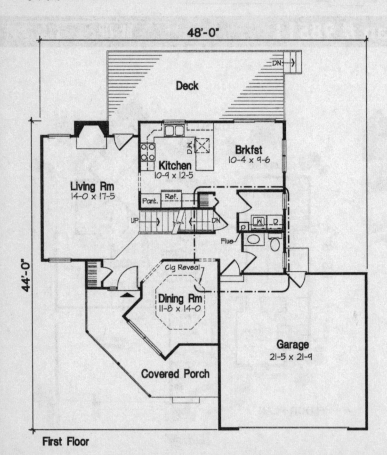

48'-0"

44'-0"

Deck

Living Rm
14-0 x 17-5

Kitchen
10-9 x 12-5

Brkfst
10-4 x 9-6

Pant.   Ref.

UP   DN

Flue

Clg Reveal

Dining Rm
11-8 x 14-0

Garage
21-5 x 21-9

Covered Porch

First Floor

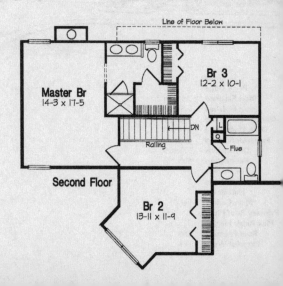

Line of Floor Below

Master Br
14-3 x 17-5

Br 3
12-2 x 10-1

DN

Railing

Flue

Second Floor

Br 2
13-11 x 11-9

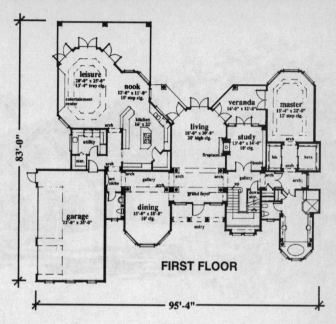

SECOND FLOOR

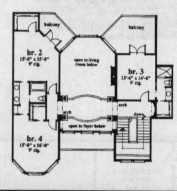

FIRST FLOOR

83'-0"

95'-4"

Units	Single
Price Code	L
Total Finished	4,759 sq. ft.
First Finished	3,546 sq. ft.
Second Finished	1,213 sq. ft.
Garage Unfinished	822 sq. ft.
Deck Unfinished	239 sq. ft.
Porch Unfinished	719 sq. ft.
Dimensions	95'4x83'
Foundation	Slab
Bedrooms	4
Full Baths	2
Half Baths	1
3/4 Baths	1
First Ceiling	10'
Second Ceiling	9'
Primary Roof Pitch	10:12
Max Ridge Height	37'8"
Roof Framing	Truss
Exterior Walls	2x6

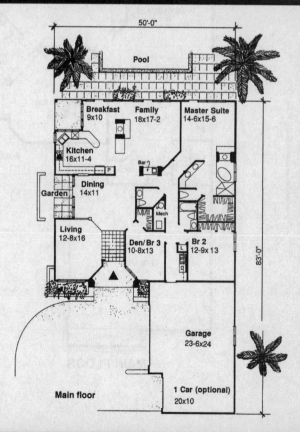

Main floor

Units	Single
Price Code	D
Total Finished	2,235 sq. ft.
Main Finished	2,235 sq. ft.
Garage Unfinished	776 sq. ft.
Dimensions	50'x83'
Foundation	Slab
Bedrooms	2
Full Baths	2
Half Baths	1
Primary Roof Pitch	6:12
Max Ridge Height	21'6"
Roof Framing	Truss
Exterior Walls	2x4

Units	Single
Price Code	E
Main Finished	2,389 sq. ft.
First Finished	2,389 sq. ft.
Garage Unfinished	543 sq. ft.
Porch Unfinished	208 sq. ft.
Dimensions	75'2''x61'4''
Foundation	Crawl space
	Slab
Bedrooms	4
Full Baths	2
Half Baths	1
Primary Roof Pitch	8:12
Secondary Roof Pitch	12:12
Max Ridge Height	22'
Roof Framing	Stick
Exterior Walls	2x4

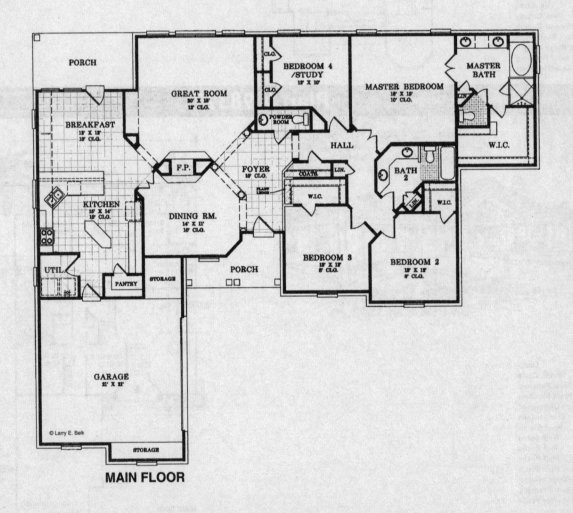

MAIN FLOOR

© Larry E. Belk

Photography by John Ehrenclou

Units	Single
Price Code	A
Total Finished	1,307 sq. ft.
Main Finished	1,307 sq. ft.
Basement Unfinished	1,298 sq. ft.
Garage Unfinished	462 sq. ft.
Dimensions	50'x40'
Foundation	Basement
	Crawl space
	Slab
Bedrooms	3
Full Baths	2
Main Ceiling	8'
Primary Roof Pitch	6:12
Secondary Roof Pitch	12:12
Max Ridge Height	19'
Roof Framing	Stick
Exterior Walls	2x6

Rear Elevation

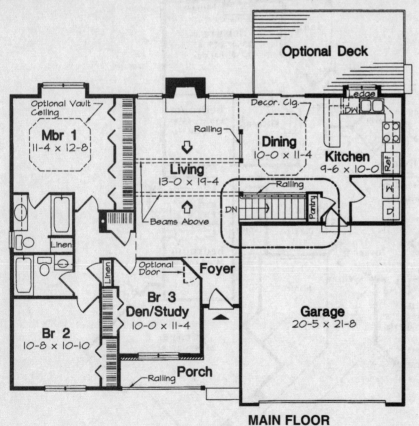

Optional Deck

Optional Vault Ceiling

Mbr 1
11-4 x 12-8

Railing

Decor. Clg.

Ledge

DW

Dining
10-0 x 11-4

Kitchen
9-6 x 10-0

Ref

Living
13-0 x 19-4

Railing

Beams Above

DN

Pantry

Linen

Optional Door

Foyer

Br 3 Den/Study
10-0 x 11-4

Linen

Br 2
10-8 x 10-10

Garage
20-5 x 21-8

Railing **Porch**

MAIN FLOOR

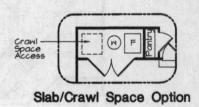

Crawl Space Access

W F

Pantry

Slab/Crawl Space Option

Photography supplied by The Sater Design Group

Units	Single
Price Code	I
Total Finished	3,477 sq. ft.
Main Finished	3,477 sq. ft.
Garage Unfinished	771 sq. ft.
Porch Unfinished	512 sq. ft.
Dimensions	95'x88'8"
Foundation	Slab
Bedrooms	3
Full Baths	2
Half Baths	I
3/4 Baths	I
Main Ceiling	14'
Vaulted Ceiling	14'
Tray Ceiling	12'
Primary Roof Pitch	8:12
Max Ridge Height	35'6"
Roof Framing	Stick

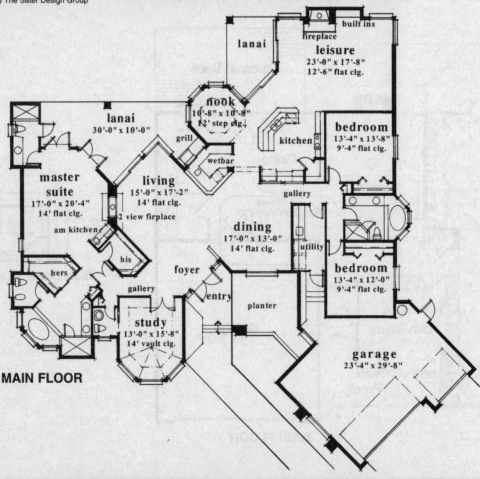

MAIN FLOOR

Units	Single
Price Code	E
Total Finished	2,311 sq. ft.
First Finished	2,311 sq. ft.
Bonus Unfinished	425 sq. ft.
Basement Unfinished	2,311 sq. ft.
Garage Unfinished	500 sq. ft.
Dimensions	61'x65'4"
Foundation	Basement
	Crawl space
Bedrooms	3
Full Baths	2
Half Baths	1
Primary Roof Pitch	10:12
Max Ridge Height	26'8"
Roof Framing	Stick
Exterior Walls	2x4

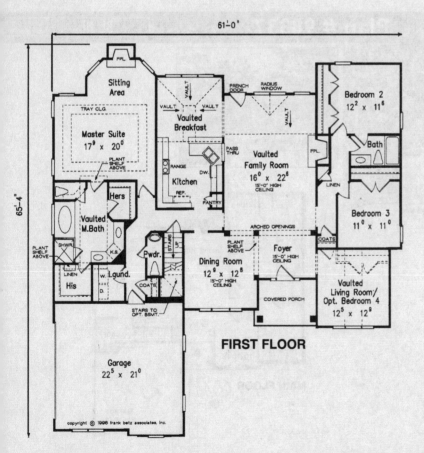

FIRST FLOOR

Sitting Area

TRAY CLG.

Master Suite 17⁹ x 20⁰

PLANT SHELF ABOVE

Vaulted Breakfast

Vaulted M.Bath

Hers

RANGE

Kitchen

REF.

PANTRY

Vaulted Family Room 16⁰ x 22⁶ 15'-0" HIGH CEILING

FPL.

FRENCH DOOR   RADIUS WINDOW   VAULT

Bedroom 2 12² x 11⁶

Bath

LINEN

Bedroom 3 11⁰ x 11⁰

SHWR.   K.B.

LINEN

His

W. LAUND.   D.

Pwdr.

COATS

STAIRS

STAIRS TO OPT. BSMT.

Dining Room 12⁹ x 12⁸ 15'-0" HIGH CEILING

PLANT SHELF ABOVE

ARCHED OPENINGS

Foyer 15'-0" HIGH CEILING

COATS

COVERED PORCH

Vaulted Living Room/ Opt. Bedroom 4 12⁵ x 12⁹

Garage 22⁵ x 21⁰

copyright © 1998 frank betz associates, inc.

61'-0"

65'-4"

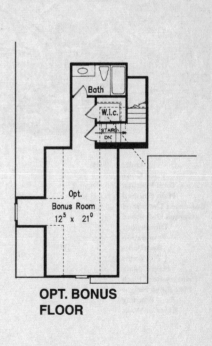

OPT. BONUS FLOOR

Bath

W.I.c.

STAIRS DN.

Opt. Bonus Room 12⁵ x 21⁰

Whirlpool ® HOME ■ Appliances

www.whirlpool.com
1.800.253.1301

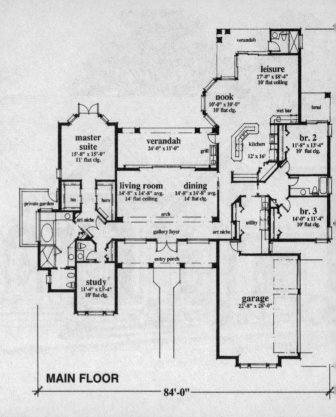

Units	Single
Price Code	G
Total Finished	2,978 sq. ft.
Main Finished	2,978 sq. ft.
Garage Unfinished	702 sq. ft.
Dimensions	84'x90'
Foundation	Slab
Bedrooms	3
Full Baths	2
Half Baths	1
3/4 Baths	1
Primary Roof Pitch	8:12
Max Ridge Height	36'6"
Roof Framing	Stick
Exterior Walls	8" concrete block

MAIN FLOOR

84'-0"

Rear Elevation

Units	Single
Price Code	B
Total Finished	1,633 sq. ft.
Main Finished	1,633 sq. ft.
Basement Unfinished	1,633 sq. ft.
Garage Unfinished	450 sq. ft.
Dimensions	52'4"x57'4"
Foundation	Basement
Bedrooms	3
Full Baths	2
Main Ceiling	8'
Primary Roof Pitch	8:12
Max Ridge Height	20'
Roof Framing	Truss
Exterior Walls	2x6

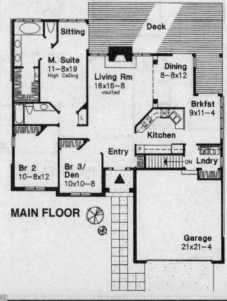

MAIN FLOOR

Units	Single
Price	Code 1
Total Finished	3,262 sq. ft.
First Finished	1,418 sq. ft.
Second Finished	1,844 sq. ft.
Basement Unfinished	1,418 sq. ft.
Garage Unfinished	820 sq. ft.
Dimensions	63'x41'
Foundation	Basement Crawl space
Bedrooms	4
Full Baths	3
Half Baths	1
First Ceiling	9'
Second Ceiling	8'
Primary Roof Pitch	10:12
Max Ridge Height	33'
Roof Framing	Stick
Exterior Walls	2x4

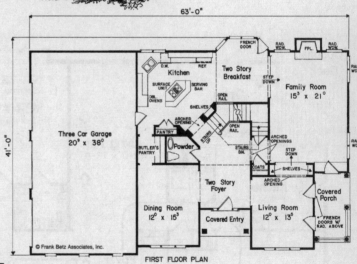

FIRST FLOOR PLAN

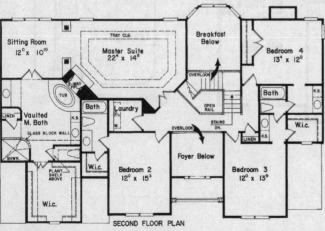

SECOND FLOOR PLAN

Weather Shield
Windows & Doors

www.weathershield.com

Weather Shield Windows and Doors offers project planning guides for your remodeling or new home project. FREE. *Specify "Remodeling" or "New Home" Planning Guide by calling*

1-800-477-6808

Photography supplied by Gauthier Roofing and Siding

Units	Single
Price Code	A
Total Finished	1,456 sq. ft.
First Finished	1,456 sq. ft.
Basement Unfinished	1,448 sq. ft.
Garage Unfinished	452 sq. ft.
Dimensions	50'x45'4''
Foundation	Basement
	Crawl space
	Slab
Bedrooms	3
Full Baths	2
First Ceiling	8'
Primary Roof Pitch	6:12
Secondary Roof Pitch	8:12
Max Ridge Height	19'
Roof Framing	Stick
Exterior Walls	2x6

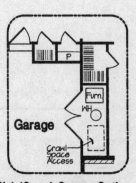

Rear Elevation

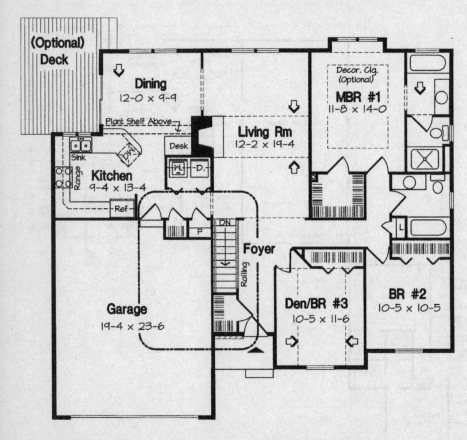

(Optional) Deck

Dining 12-0 x 9-9

Plant Shelf Above

Sink

Range

Kitchen 9-4 x 13-4

Ref

Desk

Living Rm 12-2 x 19-4

Decor. Clg. (Optional)

MBR #1 11-8 x 14-0

Foyer

DN

Railing

P

Garage 19-4 x 23-6

Den/BR #3 10-5 x 11-6

BR #2 10-5 x 10-5

First Floor Plan

Slab/Crawl Space Option

P

Garage

Furn.

WH

Crawl Space Access

Units	Single
Price Code	F
Total Finished	2,643 sq. ft.
First Finished	2,015 sq. ft.
Second Finished	628 sq. ft.
Bonus Unfinished	315 sq. ft.
Basement Unfinished	2,015 sq. ft.
Garage Unfinished	518 sq. ft.
Dimensions	56'x52'6''
Foundation	Basement, Crawl space
Bedrooms	4
Full Baths	3
Primary Roof Pitch	12:12
Max Ridge Height	29'6''
Roof Framing	Stick
Exterior Walls	2x4

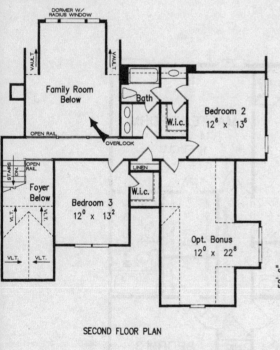

SECOND FLOOR PLAN

DORMER W/ RADIUS WINDOW

Family Room Below

Bath

W.i.c.

Bedroom 2
12⁶ x 13⁶

OPEN RAIL

OVERLOOK

LINEN

W.i.c.

OPEN RAIL

STAIRS DN.

Foyer Below

Bedroom 3
12⁰ x 13²

Opt. Bonus
12⁰ x 22⁸

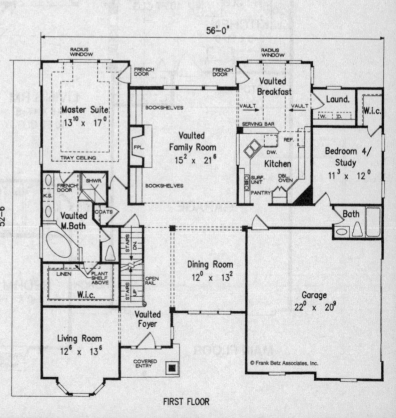

FIRST FLOOR

56'–0"

52'–6"

RADIUS WINDOW

FRENCH DOOR

FRENCH DOOR

RADIUS WINDOW

Vaulted Breakfast

Laund.

W.i.c.

Master Suite
13¹⁰ x 17⁰

BOOKSHELVES

VAULT

VAULT

SERVING BAR

TRAY CEILING

Vaulted Family Room
15² x 21⁶

FPL

Kitchen

SURF. UNIT

DW.

REF.

DBL. OVEN

Bedroom 4/ Study
11³ x 12⁰

BOOKSHELVES

PANTRY

K.S.

FRENCH DOOR

SHWR

Vaulted M.Bath

COATS

Bath

LINEN

PLANT SHELF ABOVE

W.i.c.

OPEN RAIL

Dining Room
12⁰ x 13²

Garage
22⁰ x 20⁹

Vaulted Foyer

Living Room
12⁶ x 13⁶

COVERED ENTRY

© Frank Betz Associates, Inc.

Units	Single
Price Code	A
Total Finished	1,310 sq. ft.
Main Finished	1,310 sq. ft.
Garage Unfinished	449 sq. ft.
Dimensions	49'10''x40'6''
Foundation	Crawl space
	Slab
Bedrooms	3
Full Baths	2
Primary Roof Pitch	7:12
Secondary Roof Pitch	12;12
Max Ridge Height	22'
Roof Framing	Stick
Exterior Walls	2x4

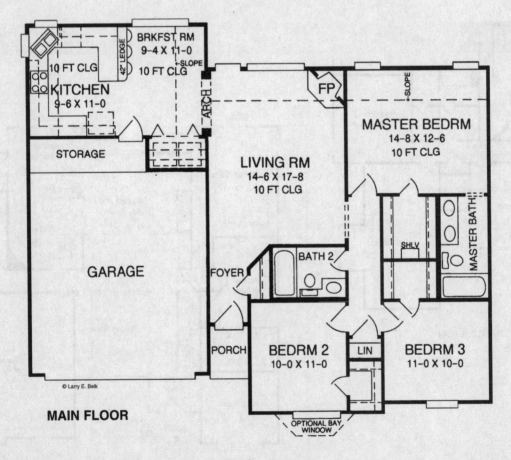

BRKFST RM
9-4 X 11-0
10 FT CLG

42" LEDGE

SLOPE

10 FT CLG

KITCHEN
9-6 X 11-0

STORAGE

ARCH

FP

SLOPE

MASTER BEDRM
14-8 X 12-6
10 FT CLG

LIVING RM
14-6 X 17-8
10 FT CLG

SHLV

MASTER BATH

GARAGE

FOYER

BATH 2

BEDRM 2
10-0 X 11-0

LIN

BEDRM 3
11-0 X 10-0

PORCH

© Larry E. Belk

OPTIONAL BAY WINDOW

MAIN FLOOR

Design by Perfect Plan

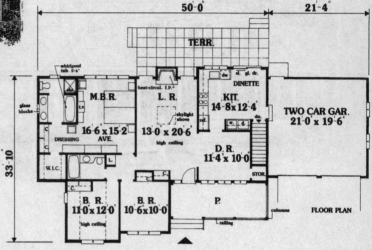

Units	Single
Price Code	A
Total Finished	1,367 sq. ft.
Main Finished	1,367 sq. ft.
Basement Unfinished	1,267 sq. ft.
Garage Unfinished	431 sq. ft.
Dimensions	71'4"x33'10"
Foundation	Basement
	Slab
Bedrooms	3
Full Baths	2
Main Ceiling	8'
Vaulted Ceiling	11'
Primary Roof Pitch	7.5:12
Max Ridge Height	20'
Roof Framing	Stick
Exterior Walls	2x6

Design by Corley Plan Service

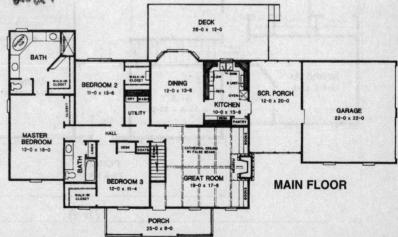

Units	Single
Price Code	C
Total Finished	1,811 sq. ft.
Main Finished	1,811 sq. ft.
Basement Unfinished	1,811 sq. ft.
Garage Unfinished	484 sq. ft.
Deck Unfinished	336 sq. ft.
Porch Unfinished	390 sq. ft.
Dimensions	89'6"x44'4"
Foundation	Basement
	Crawl space
	Slab
Bedrooms	3
Full Baths	2
Main Ceiling	8'
Primary Roof Pitch	6:12
Max Ridge Height	16'4"
Roof Framing	Stick
Exterior Walls	2x4

MAIN FLOOR

Order Today! 1-800-235-5700 or order online at
www.familyhomeplans.com

Units	Single
Price Code	E
Total Finished	2,344 sq. ft.
Main Finished	2,344 sq. ft.
Basement Unfinished	2,344 sq. ft.
Garage Unfinished	498 sq. ft.
Deck Unfinished	531 sq. ft.
Porch Unfinished	288 sq. ft.
Dimensions	78'8"x56'4"
Foundation	Basement Crawl space Slab
Bedrooms	3
Full Baths	2
Primary Roof Pitch	7:12
Secondary Roof Pitch	4:12
Max Ridge Height	20'8"
Roof Framing	Stick
Exterior Walls	2x4

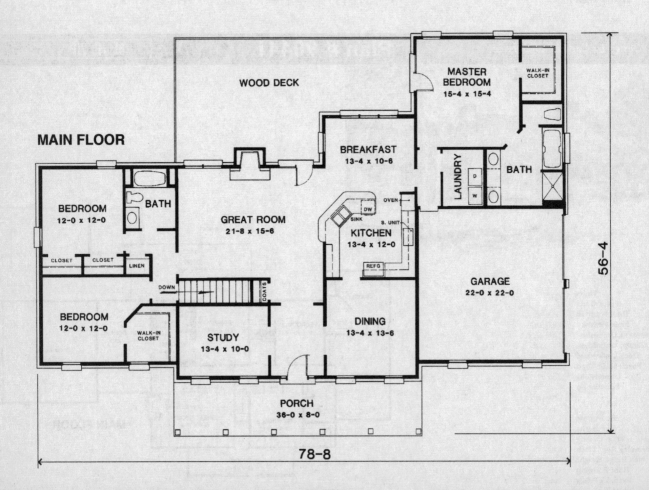

MAIN FLOOR

WOOD DECK

MASTER BEDROOM
15-4 x 15-4

WALK-IN CLOSET

BREAKFAST
13-4 x 10-6

BEDROOM
12-0 x 12-0

BATH

GREAT ROOM
21-8 x 15-6

LAUNDRY

BATH

KITCHEN
13-4 x 12-0

OVEN

S. UNIT

CLOSET CLOSET LINEN

DOWN

COATS

REFG

GARAGE
22-0 x 22-0

BEDROOM
12-0 x 12-0

WALK-IN CLOSET

STUDY
13-4 x 10-0

DINING
13-4 x 13-6

56-4

PORCH
36-0 x 8-0

78-8

Units	Single
Price Code	C
Total Finished	1,853 sq. ft.
First Finished	1,342 sq. ft.
Second Finished	511 sq. ft.
Garage Unfinished	1,740 sq. ft.
Dimensions	44'x40'
Foundation	Post
Bedrooms	3
Full Baths	2
First Ceiling	8'
Second Ceiling	8'
Primary Roof Pitch	12:12
Max Ridge Height	37'
Roof Framing	Stick
Exterior Walls	2x6

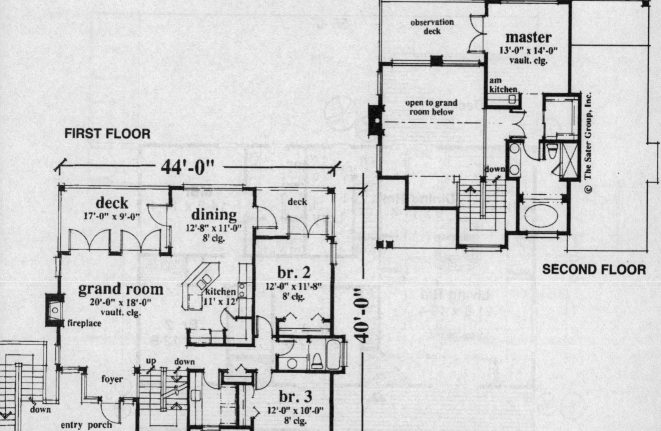

FIRST FLOOR

44'-0"

40'-0"

deck
17'-0" x 9'-0"

dining
12'-8" x 11'-0"
8' clg.

deck

grand room
20'-0" x 18'-0"
vault. clg.

fireplace

kitchen
11' x 12'

br. 2
12'-0" x 11'-8"
8' clg.

up   down

foyer

down

entry porch

br. 3
12'-0" x 10'-0"
8' clg.

SECOND FLOOR

observation deck

master
13'-0" x 14'-0"
vault. clg.

open to grand room below

am kitchen

down

© The Sater Group, Inc.

Units	Single
Price Code	C
Total Finished	1,792 sq. ft.
Main Finished	1,792 sq. ft.
Basement Unfinished	818 sq. ft.
Garage Unfinished	857 sq. ft.
Dimensions	56'x32'
Foundation	Basement
Bedrooms	3
Full Baths	2
Main Ceiling	8'
Primary Roof Pitch	6:12
Secondary Roof Pitch	3:12
Max Ridge Height	25'
Roof Framing	Stick
Exterior Walls	2x4, 2x6

Rear Elevatio

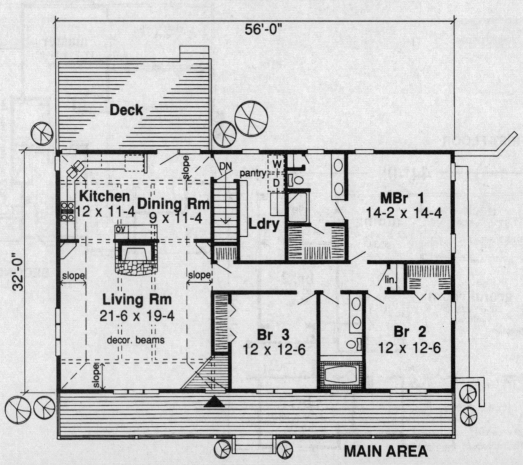

56'-0"

Deck

Kitchen
12 x 11-4

Dining Rm
9 x 11-4

pantry

W
D

Ldry

DN

MBr 1
14-2 x 14-4

32'-0"

slope

slope

slope

ov

Living Rm
21-6 x 19-4

decor. beams

lin.

Br 3
12 x 12-6

Br 2
12 x 12-6

slope

MAIN AREA

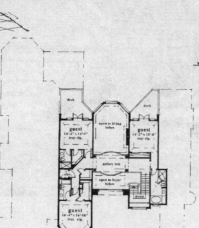

FIRST FLOOR

Units	Single
Price Code	L
Total Finished	6,312 sq. ft.
First Finished	4,760 sq. ft.
Second Finished	1,552 sq. ft.
Garage Unfinished	802 sq. ft.
Deck Unfinished	360 sq. ft.
Porch Unfinished	483 sq. ft.
Dimensions	98'×103'8''
Foundation	Slab
Bedrooms	5
Full Baths	4
Half Baths	1
3/4 Baths	2
First Ceiling	10'
Primary Roof Pitch	8:12
Max Ridge Height	42'8''
Roof Framing	Stick
Exterior Walls	2x6, 2x8

SECOND FLOOR

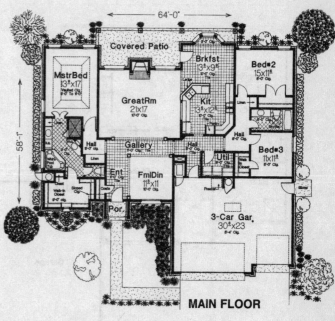

MAIN FLOOR

Units	Single
Price Code	D
Total Finished	2,167 sq. ft.
Main Finished	2,167 sq. ft.
Garage Unfinished	690 sq. ft.
Deck Unfinished	162 sq. ft.
Porch Unfinished	22 sq. ft.
Dimensions	64'×58'1''
Foundation	Slab
Bedrooms	3
Full Baths	2
Main Ceiling	8'-10'
Primary Roof Pitch	10:12
Max Ridge Height	26'3''
Roof Framing	Stick
Exterior Walls	2x4

Units	Single
Price Code	E
Total Finished	2,257 sq. ft.
First Finished	1,540 sq. ft.
Second Finished	717 sq. ft.
Basement Unfinished	1,545 sq. ft.
Garage Unfinished	503 sq. ft.
Porch Unfinished	144 sq. ft.
Dimensions	57'x56'8"
Foundation	Basement Crawl space Slab
Bedrooms	4
Full Baths	2
Half Baths	1
First Ceiling	9'
Second Ceiling	8'
Primary Roof Pitch	10:12
Max Ridge Height	33'6"
Roof Framing	Truss

SECOND FLOOR

Bedroom #3
12-0 x 12-0

(Open to Below)

Bedroom #2
13-0 x 12-0

Bedroom #4
13-6 x 10-8

FIRST FLOOR

57'-0"

Master Bedroom
13-9 x 15-6

Great Room
19-8 x 15-10
(Open to Above)

Nook
12-4 x 8-0

Kitchen
12-4 x 10-6

M. Bath

Foyer

Dining Room
14-3 x 11-0

Laun.

Covered Porch

Garage
20-7 x 21-8

OPTIONAL CRAWL / SLAB PLAN

Units	Single
Price Code	E
Total Finished	2,312 sq. ft.
First Finished	2,312 sq. ft.
Garage Unfinished	608 sq. ft.
Porch Unfinished	601 sq. ft.
Dimensions	65'x74'6"
Foundation	Slab
Bedrooms	3
Full Baths	2
Roof Framing	Truss

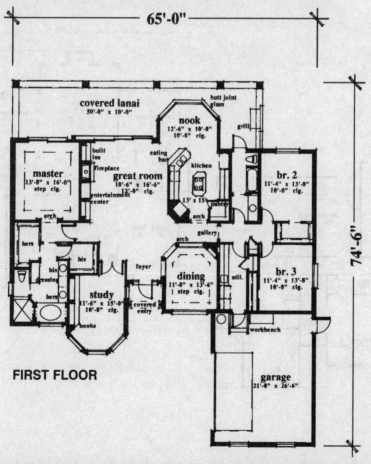

65'-0"

74'-6"

covered lanai
50'-0" x 10'-0"

nook
12'-6" x 10'-0"
10'-0" clg.

butt joint glass

grill

master
13'-8" x 16'-0"
step clg.

built ins

fireplace

entertainment center

great room
18'-6" x 16'-6"
12'-0" clg.

eating bar

kitchen

13' x 15'

pantry

arch

br. 2
11'-4" x 13'-8"
10'-0" clg.

gallery

arch

hers

his

his

dressing

hers

books

study
11'-6" x 15'-0"
10'-0" clg.

arch

foyer

covered entry

dining
11'-0" x 13'-6"
step clg.

util.

br. 3
11'-4" x 13'-8"
10'-0" clg.

workbench

garage
21'-0" x 26'-6"

FIRST FLOOR

Units	Single
Price Code	H
Total Finished	3,219 sq. ft.
First Finished	1,665 sq. ft.
Second Finished	1,554 sq. ft.
Basement Unfinished	1,665 sq. ft.
Garage Unfinished	462 sq. ft.
Dimensions	58'6"x44'10"
Foundation	Basement, Crawl space
Bedrooms	5
Full Baths	4
First Ceiling	9'
Second Ceiling	8'
Primary Roof Pitch	12:12
Max Ridge Height	33'
Roof Framing	Stick
Exterior Walls	2x4

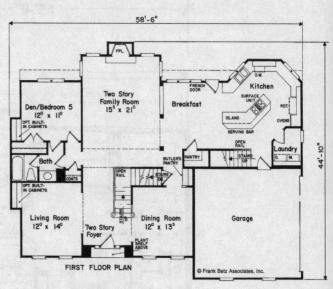

FIRST FLOOR PLAN

© Frank Betz Associates, Inc.

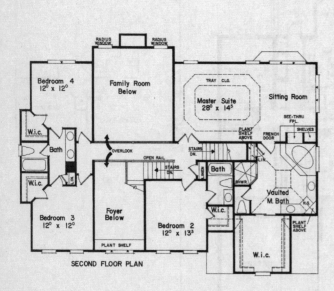

SECOND FLOOR PLAN

Plan # 93063

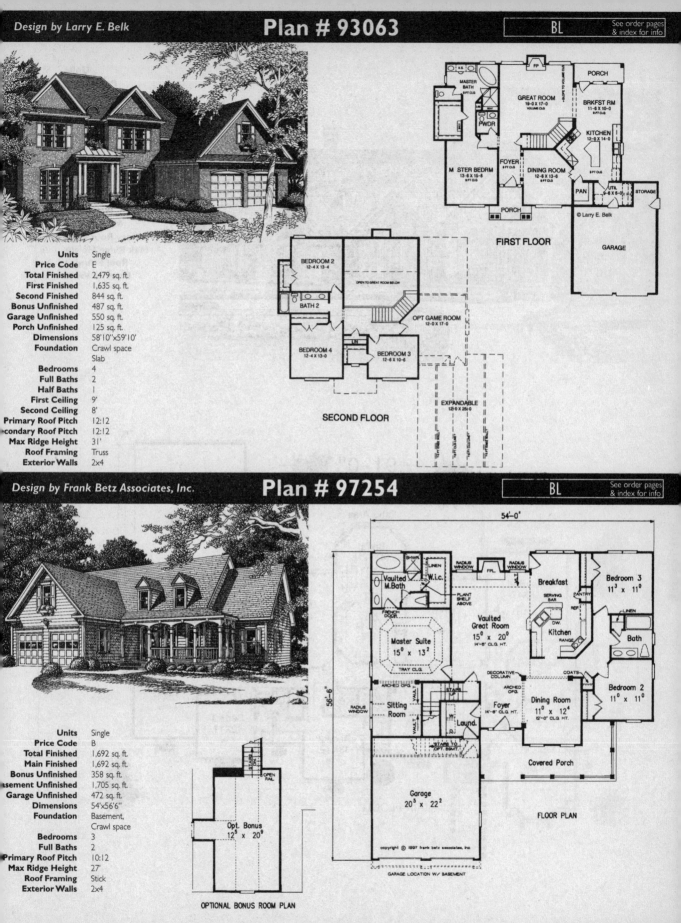

FIRST FLOOR

- MASTER BATH 8FT CLG
- GREAT ROOM 19-0 X 17-0 VOLUME CLG
- PORCH
- PWDR
- BRKFST RM 11-6 X 10-0
- KITCHEN 12-0 X 14-0 8FT CLG
- FOYER 8FT CLG
- M STER BEDRM 13-6 X 15-8 9FT CLG
- DINING ROOM 12-6 X 13-6 8FT CLG
- PAN
- UTIL 9-6 X 6-0
- STORAGE
- PORCH
- GARAGE
- © Larry E. Belk

SECOND FLOOR

- BEDROOM 2 12-4 X 13-4
- BATH 2
- OPEN TO GREAT ROOM BELOW
- OPT GAME ROOM 12-0 X 17-0
- BEDROOM 4 12-4 X 13-0
- LIN
- BEDROOM 3 12-6 X 10-6
- EXPANDABLE 12-0 X 25-0

Units	Single
Price Code	E
Total Finished	2,479 sq. ft.
First Finished	1,635 sq. ft.
Second Finished	844 sq. ft.
Bonus Unfinished	487 sq. ft.
Garage Unfinished	550 sq. ft.
Porch Unfinished	125 sq. ft.
Dimensions	58'10"x59'10'
Foundation	Crawl space Slab
Bedrooms	4
Full Baths	2
Half Baths	1
First Ceiling	9'
Second Ceiling	8'
Primary Roof Pitch	12:12
Secondary Roof Pitch	12:12
Max Ridge Height	31'
Roof Framing	Truss
Exterior Walls	2x4

Plan # 97254

54'-0"

56'-6"

FLOOR PLAN

- Vaulted M.Bath
- LINEN
- W.I.C.
- RADIUS WINDOW
- FPL.
- RADIUS WINDOW
- Breakfast
- Bedroom 3 11³ x 11⁰
- FRENCH DOOR
- PLANT SHELF ABOVE
- Vaulted Great Room 15⁰ x 20⁰ 14'-6" CLG. HT.
- SERVING BAR
- PANTRY
- DW.
- REF.
- LINEN
- Bath
- Master Suite 15⁰ x 13² TRAY CLG.
- Kitchen
- RANGE
- DECORATIVE COLUMN
- COATS
- Bedroom 2 11⁰ x 11⁰
- ARCHED OPG.
- RADIUS WINDOW
- Sitting Room
- STAIRS
- WALL
- W.
- Laund.
- ARCHED OPG.
- Foyer 14'-6" CLG. HT.
- Dining Room 11⁰ x 12⁴ 12'-0" CLG. HT.
- STAIRS TO OPT. BSMT.
- Garage 20⁵ x 22²
- Covered Porch
- copyright © 1997 frank betz associates, inc.
- GARAGE LOCATION W/ BASEMENT

OPTIONAL BONUS ROOM PLAN

- STAIR DN
- OPEN RAIL
- Opt. Bonus 12⁵ x 20⁹

Units	Single
Price Code	B
Total Finished	1,692 sq. ft.
Main Finished	1,692 sq. ft.
Bonus Unfinished	358 sq. ft.
Basement Unfinished	1,705 sq. ft.
Garage Unfinished	472 sq. ft.
Dimensions	54'x56'6"
Foundation	Basement, Crawl space
Bedrooms	3
Full Baths	2
Primary Roof Pitch	10:12
Max Ridge Height	27'
Roof Framing	Stick
Exterior Walls	2x4

Units	Single
Price Code	I
Total Finished	3,352 sq. ft.
Main Finished	3,352 sq. ft.
Garage Unfinished	672 sq. ft.
Deck Unfinished	462 sq. ft.
Porch Unfinished	60 sq. ft.
Dimensions	91'x71'9''
Foundation	Slab
Bedrooms	4
Full Baths	3
Half Baths	I
Main Ceiling	9'-11'
Primary Roof Pitch	12:12
Max Ridge Height	28'2''
Roof Framing	Stick
Exterior Walls	2x4

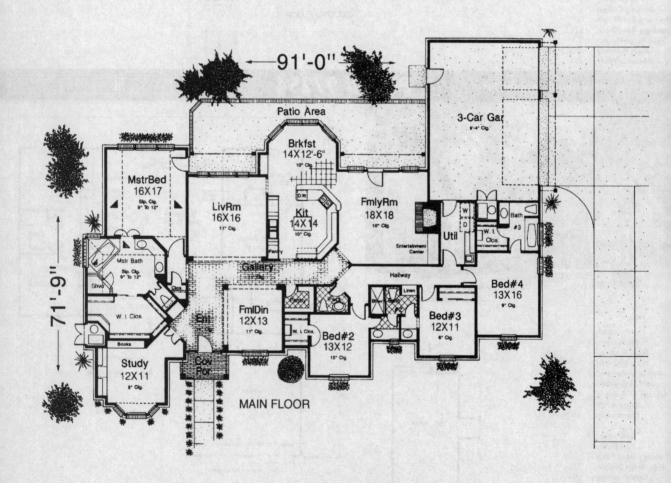

91'-0"

71'-9"

Patio Area

3-Car Gar
9'-4" Clg.

Brkfst
14X12'-6"
10" Clg.

MstrBed
16X17
Slp. Clg.
9" To 12'

LivRm
16X16
11" Clg.

Kit
14X14
10" Clg.

FmlyRm
18X18
10" Clg.

D.W.

Pantry

W
D

Util

Bath
#3

W.I.
Clos.

Mstr Bath
Slp. Clg.
9" To 12'

Shwr

Entertainment
Center

Bed#4
13X16
9' Clg.

W. I. Clos.

Clos.

Gallery

Hallway

Linen

Bed#3
12X11
6' Clg.

Shwr Bath

Ent

FmlDin
12X13
11" Clg.

Bath

W. I. Clos.

Bed#2
13X12
10" Clg.

Books

Study
12X11
9' Clg.

Cov
Por

MAIN FLOOR

Weather Shield
Windows & Doors

www.weathershield.com

Weather Shield Windows and Doors offers project planning guides for your remodeling or new home project. FREE. Specify "Remodeling" or "New Home" Planning Guide by calling
1-800-477-6808

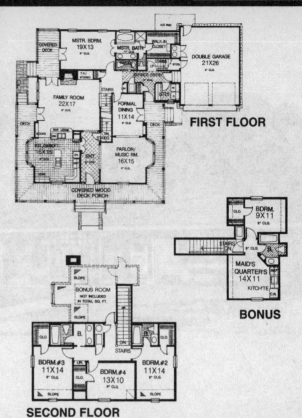

FIRST FLOOR

BONUS

SECOND FLOOR

Units	Single
Price Code	G
Total Finished	2,772 sq. ft.
First Finished	2,023 sq. ft.
Second Finished	749 sq. ft.
Bonus Unfinished	450 sq. ft.
Garage Unfinished	546 sq. ft.
Deck Unfinished	755 sq. ft.
Dimensions	77'2"x57'11"
Foundation	Basement
	Slab
Bedrooms	4
Full Baths	3
Half Baths	1
First Ceiling	9'
Second Ceiling	9'
Primary Roof Pitch	16:12
Max Ridge Height	33'
Roof Framing	Stick
Exterior Walls	2x4

Photography by John Ehrenclou

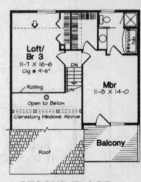

SECOND FLOOR

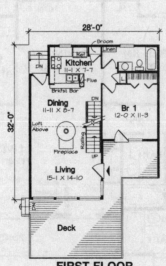

FIRST FLOOR

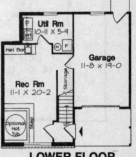

LOWER FLOOR

Units	Single
Price Code	B
Total Finished	1,710 sq. ft.
First Finished	728 sq. ft.
Second Finished	573 sq. ft.
Lower Finished	409 sq. ft.
Garage Unfinished	244 sq. ft.
Dimensions	28'x32'
Foundation	Basement
Bedrooms	3
Full Baths	2
First Ceiling	8'
Second Ceiling	8'
Primary Roof Pitch	6:12
Max Ridge Height	33'
Roof Framing	Stick
Exterior Walls	2x4, 2x6

Units	Single
Price Code	A
Total Finished	1,243 sq. ft.
First Finished	1,243 sq. ft.
Basement Unfinished	1,103 sq. ft.
Garage Unfinished	490 sq. ft.
Dimensions	66'4''x30'4''
Foundation	Basement
	Slab
Bedrooms	3
Full Baths	2
Primary Roof Pitch	4.5:12
Max Ridge Height	16'
Roof Framing	Stick
Exterior Walls	2x4

MAIN FLOOR

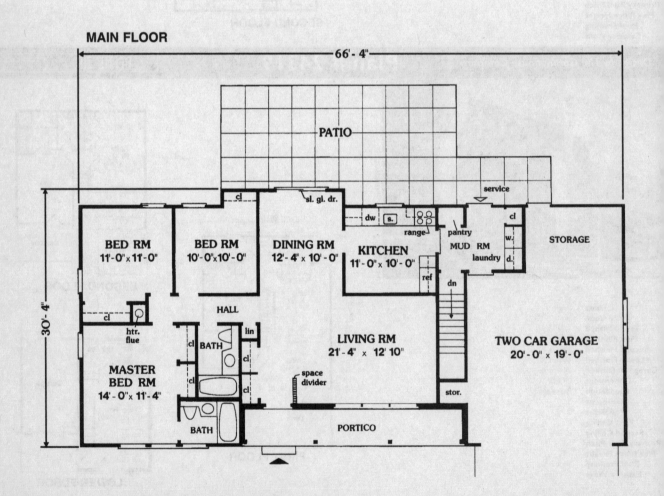

66'- 4"

30'- 4"

PATIO

cl
sl. gl. dr.
service
dw
s.
range
pantry
cl
w.
STORAGE
d.

BED RM
11'-0" x 11'-0"

BED RM
10'-0"x10'-0"

DINING RM
12'-4" x 10'-0"

KITCHEN
11'-0" x 10'-0"

MUD RM
laundry

cl
htr.
flue

HALL

BATH
cl
lin
cl
ref

cl
LIVING RM
21'-4" x 12' 10"

dn

TWO CAR GARAGE
20'-0" x 19'-0"

MASTER
BED RM
14'-0"x 11'-4"

cl
space
divider

stor.

BATH

PORTICO

Plan # 98588

BL   See order pages & index for info

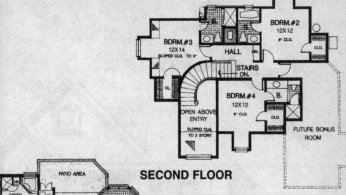

SECOND FLOOR

Units	Single
Price Code	H
Total Finished	3,219 sq. ft.
First Finished	2,337 sq. ft.
Second Finished	882 sq. ft.
Garage Unfinished	640 sq. ft.
Deck Unfinished	240 sq. ft.
Porch Unfinished	120 sq. ft.
Dimensions	70'x63'2"
Foundation	Basement
	Slab
Bedrooms	4
Full Baths	3
Half Baths	1
Primary Roof Pitch	12:12
Max Ridge Height	32'6"
Roof Framing	Stick
Exterior Walls	2x4

FIRST FLOOR

Plan # 93087

BL ML   See order pages & index for info

FIRST FLOOR

© Larry E. Belk

Units	Single
Price Code	F
Total Finished	2,721 sq. ft.
First Finished	1,930 sq. ft.
Second Finished	791 sq. ft.
Garage Unfinished	525 sq. ft.
Dimensions	64'2"x62'
Foundation	Basement
	Crawl space
	Slab
Bedrooms	4
Full Baths	3
Primary Roof Pitch	10:12
Secondary Roof Pitch	12:12
Max Ridge Height	29'6"
Roof Framing	Stick
Exterior Walls	2x4

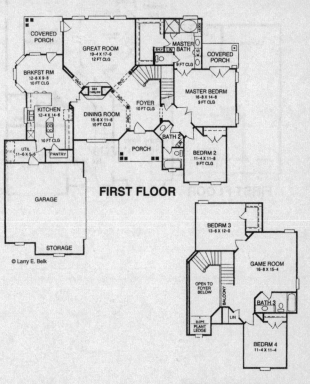

SECOND FLOOR

Units	Single
Price Code	E
Total Finished	2,482 sq. ft.
First Finished	1,205 sq. ft.
Second Finished	1,277 sq. ft.
Basement Unfinished	1,128 sq. ft.
Garage Unfinished	528 sq. ft.
Dimensions	53'6''x39'4''
Foundation	Basement
	Crawl spac
Bedrooms	4
Full Baths	2
Half Baths	1
Primary Roof Pitch	10:12
Max Ridge Height	33'
Roof Framing	Stick
Exterior Walls	2x4

FIRST FLOOR

53'-6'

39'-4"

Storage

Covered Porch

Laun.

PANTRY

FRENCH DOOR

Breakfast

SERVING BAR

FPL.

Two Story Family Room
14' x 18'

REF.

Kitchen

SURFACE UNIT

DBL OVENS

STAIRS DN

COATS

Pwdr.

Garage
20' x 21'

Dining Room
11³ x 14⁵

Two Story Foyer

Living Room
11⁵ x 12⁴

copyright © 1995 frank betz associates, inc.

SECOND FLOOR

Sitting Room

Master Suite
14³ x 17⁵

Bedroom 2
12⁶ x 12¹

Bath

RADIUS WDW.

RADIUS WDW.

Family Room Below

PLANT SHELF ABOVE

TRAY CLG.

OPEN RAIL

STAIRS DN

OVERLOOK

Vaulted M.Bath

LINEN

Bedroom 3
11³ x 13³

Foyer Below

Bedroom 4
11⁵ x 12¹⁰

W.I.C.

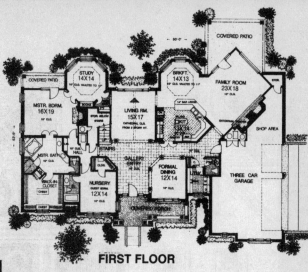

FIRST FLOOR

Units	Single
Price Code	L
Total Finished	4,166 sq. ft.
First Finished	3,168 sq. ft.
Second Finished	998 sq. ft.
Bonus Unfinished	320 sq. ft.
Garage Unfinished	810 sq. ft.
Deck Unfinished	290 sq. ft.
Porch Unfinished	180 sq. ft.
Dimensions	90'x63'5''
Foundation	Basement
	Crawl space
	Slab
Bedrooms	4
Full Baths	3
Half Baths	1
Primary Roof Pitch	12:12
Secondary Roof Pitch	16:12
Max Ridge Height	36'
Roof Framing	Stick
Exterior Walls	2x4

SECOND FLOOR

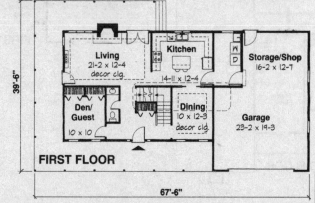

Photography supplied by Victora Palag

Rear Elevation

OPT. CRAWLSPACE FOUNDATION

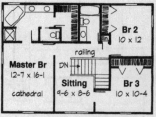

SECOND FLOOR

Units	Single
Price Code	C
Total Finished	1,978 sq. ft.
First Finished	1,034 sq. ft.
Second Finished	944 sq. ft.
Basement Unfinished	984 sq. ft.
Garage Unfinished	675 sq. ft.
Dimensions	67'6''x39'6''
Foundation	Basement
	Crawl space
	Slab
Bedrooms	3
Full Baths	2
Half Baths	1
First Ceiling	9'
Second Ceiling	8'
Primary Roof Pitch	8:12
Secondary Roof Pitch	4:12
Max Ridge Height	29'
Roof Framing	Stick
Exterior Walls	2x4, 2x6

FIRST FLOOR

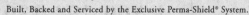

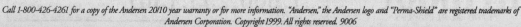

Units	Single
Price Code	I
Total Finished	3,395 sq. ft.
First Finished	2,467 sq. ft.
Second Finished	928 sq. ft.
Bonus Unfinished	296 sq. ft.
Basement Unfinished	2,467 sq. ft.
Garage Unfinished	566 sq. ft.
Dimensions	64'6"x62'10
Foundation	Basement
	Crawl space
	Slab
Bedrooms	4
Full Baths	3
Half Baths	1
First Ceiling	9'
Second Ceiling	8'
Primary Roof Pitch	12:12
Max Ridge Height	32'8"
Roof Framing	Stick
Exterior Walls	2x4

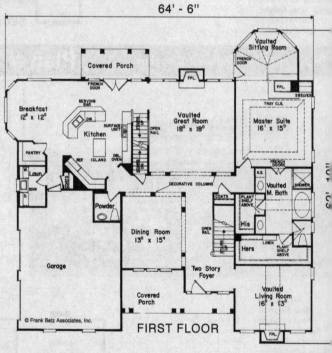

FIRST FLOOR

© Frank Betz Associates, Inc.

SECOND FLOOR

Units	Single
Price Code	A
Finished	786 sq. ft.
First Finished	786 sq. ft.
Deck Unfinished	580 sq. ft.
Dimensions	46'x22'
Foundation	Crawl space
Bedrooms	2
3/4 Baths	2
First Ceiling	8'
Vaulted Ceiling	16'
Primary Roof Pitch	8:12
Secondary Roof Pitch	5:12
Max Ridge Height 1	8'6"
Roof Framing	Truss
Exterior Walls	2x6

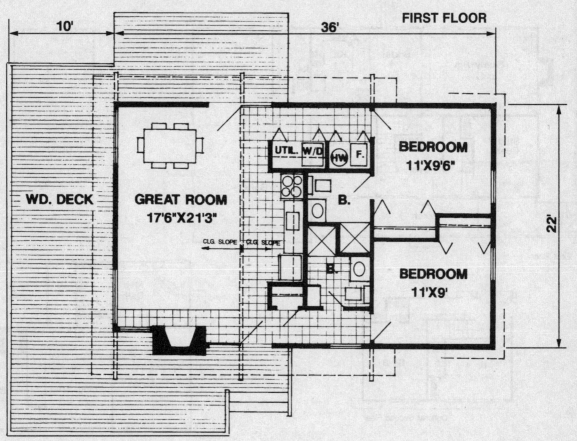

FIRST FLOOR

10' 36' 22'

WD. DECK

GREAT ROOM
17'6"X21'3"

CLG. SLOPE   CLG. SLOPE

UTIL. W/D HW F.

B.

BEDROOM
11'X9'6"

BEDROOM
11'X9'

Units	Single
Price Code	F
Total Finished	2,647 sq.
First Finished	1,378 sq.
Second Finished	1,269 sq.
Basement Unfinished	1,378 sq.
Garage Unfinished	717 sq. ft.
Dimensions	71'x45'
Foundation	Basement Crawl spa Slab
Bedrooms	3
Full Baths	2
3/4 Baths	2
First Ceiling	9'
Second Ceiling	8'
Primary Roof Pitch	6:12
Secondary Roof Pitch	8:12
Max Ridge Height	29'
Roof Framing	Stick
Exterior Walls	2x4

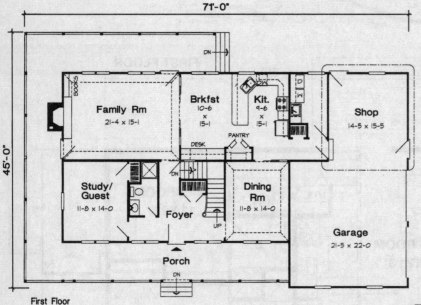

First Floor

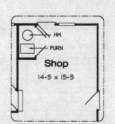

Crawl Space/Slab Option

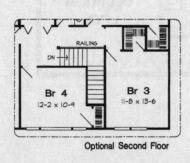

Optional Second Floor

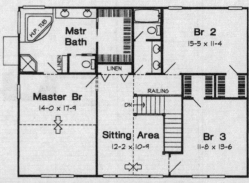

Second Floor

Plan # 94622

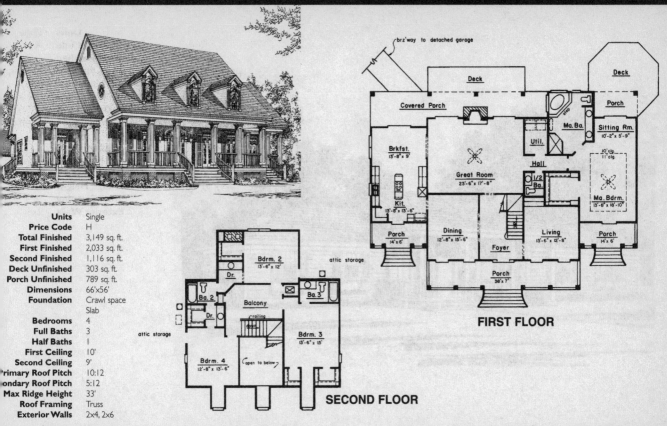

Units	Single
Price Code	H
Total Finished	3,149 sq. ft.
First Finished	2,033 sq. ft.
Second Finished	1,116 sq. ft.
Deck Unfinished	303 sq. ft.
Porch Unfinished	789 sq. ft.
Dimensions	66'x56'
Foundation	Crawl space
	Slab
Bedrooms	4
Full Baths	3
Half Baths	1
First Ceiling	10'
Second Ceiling	9'
Primary Roof Pitch	10:12
Secondary Roof Pitch	5:12
Max Ridge Height	33'
Roof Framing	Truss
Exterior Walls	2x4, 2x6

FIRST FLOOR

SECOND FLOOR

Plan # 98518

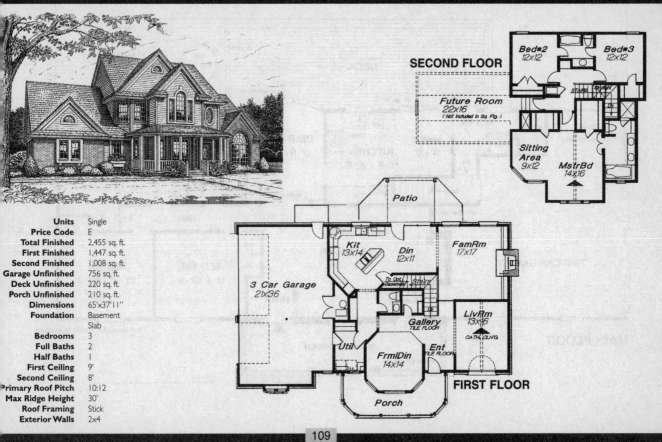

Units	Single
Price Code	E
Total Finished	2,455 sq. ft.
First Finished	1,447 sq. ft.
Second Finished	1,008 sq. ft.
Garage Unfinished	756 sq. ft.
Deck Unfinished	220 sq. ft.
Porch Unfinished	210 sq. ft.
Dimensions	65'x37'11"
Foundation	Basement
	Slab
Bedrooms	3
Full Baths	2
Half Baths	1
First Ceiling	9'
Second Ceiling	8'
Primary Roof Pitch	10:12
Max Ridge Height	30'
Roof Framing	Stick
Exterior Walls	2x4

SECOND FLOOR

FIRST FLOOR

Units	Single
Price Code	A
Total Finished	1,476 sq. f
Main Finished	1,476 sq. f
Basement Unfinished	1,361 sq. f
Garage Unfinished	548 sq. ft.
Dimensions	75'9"x34'6
Foundation	Basement
	Slab
Bedrooms	3
Full Baths	2
Primary Roof Pitch	5:12
Max Ridge Height	19'
Roof Framing	Stick
Exterior Walls	2x6

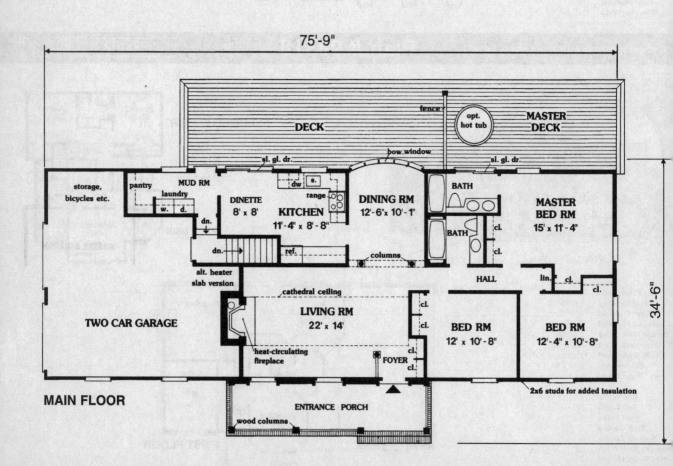

75'-9"

34'-6"

DECK

fence

opt. hot tub

MASTER DECK

bow window

sl. gl. dr.

sl. gl. dr.

storage, bicycles etc.

pantry

MUD RM

laundry

w. d.

dw

s.

range

BATH

MASTER BED RM
15' x 11'-4"

DINETTE
8' x 8'

KITCHEN
11'-4" x 8'-8"

DINING RM
12'-6"x 10'-1"

BATH

cl.

cl.

dn.

dn.

ref.

columns

HALL

lin.

cl.

cl.

alt. heater slab version

cathedral ceiling

cl.

cl.

LIVING RM
22' x 14'

BED RM
12' x 10'-8"

BED RM
12'-4" x 10'-8"

TWO CAR GARAGE

heat-circulating fireplace

cl.

FOYER

cl.

2x6 studs for added insulation

MAIN FLOOR

ENTRANCE PORCH

wood columns

Photography supplied by Ahmann Design, Inc.

Units	Single
Price Code	I
Total Finished	3,397 sq. ft.
Main Finished	2,385 sq. ft.
Second Finished	1,012 sq. ft.
Basement Unfinished	2,385 sq. ft.
Garage Unfinished	846 sq. ft.
Dimensions	79'x55'
Foundation	Basement
Bedrooms	4
Full Baths	3
Half Baths	I
Main Ceiling	7'-9.5'
Primary Roof Pitch	12:12
Secondary Roof Pitch	10:12
Max Ridge Height	32'
Roof Framing	Stick/Truss
Exterior Walls	2x6

* This plan is not to be built within a 75 mile radius of Cedar Rapids, IA.

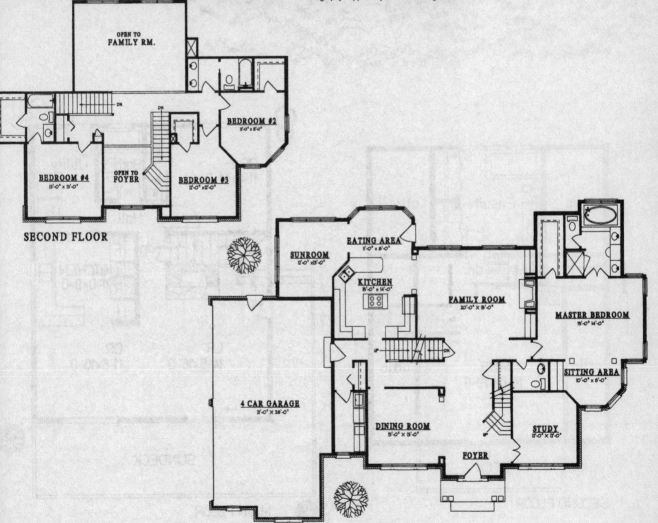

OPEN TO FAMILY RM.

BEDROOM #2
11'-0" x 11'-0"

BEDROOM #4
13'-0" x 15'-0"

OPEN TO FOYER

BEDROOM #3
11'-0" x 11'-0"

SECOND FLOOR

SUNROOM
12'-0" x 13'-0"

EATING AREA
11'-0" x 8'-0"

KITCHEN
15'-0" x 14'-0"

FAMILY ROOM
20'-0" x 15'-0"

MASTER BEDROOM
15'-0" x 14'-0"

SITTING AREA
10'-0" x 8'-0"

4 CAR GARAGE
21'-0" x 38'-0"

DINING ROOM
13'-0" x 13'-0"

STUDY
11'-0" x 12'-0"

FOYER

MAIN FLOOR

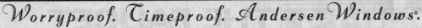

Units	Single
Price Code	A
Total Finished	1,360 sq.
Main Finished	864 sq. f
Second Finished	496 sq. f
Basement Unfinished	864 sq. f
Dimensions	27'x32'
Foundation	Basemen
Bedrooms	2
Full Baths	2
Primary Roof Pitch	10:12
Exterior Walls	2x6

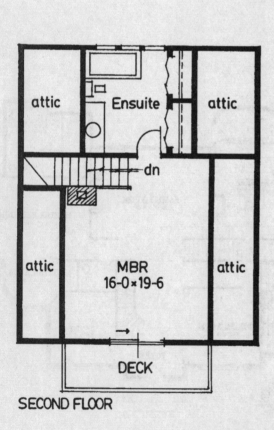

SECOND FLOOR

attic

Ensuite

attic

dn

attic

MBR
16-0×19-6

attic

DECK

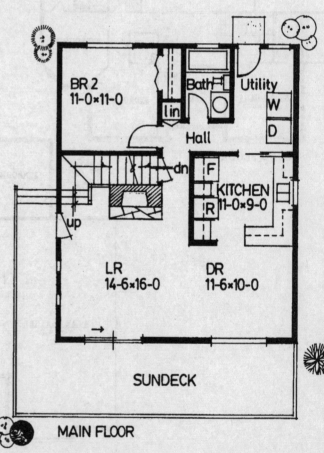

BR 2
11-0×11-0

Bath

Utility

W
D

lin

Hall

dn

F

KITCHEN
11-0×9-0

R

up

LR
14-6×16-0

DR
11-6×10-0

SUNDECK

MAIN FLOOR

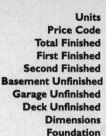

Units	Single
Price Code	I
Total Finished	3,485 sq. ft.
First Finished	2,012 sq. ft.
Second Finished	1,473 sq. ft.
Basement Unfinished	2,012 sq. ft.
Garage Unfinished	750 sq. ft.
Deck Unfinished	225 sq. ft.
Dimensions	80'x51'
Foundation	Basement
	Crawl space
	Slab
Bedrooms	4
Full Baths	3
First Ceiling	9'
Second Ceiling	8'
Primary Roof Pitch	8:12
Secondary Roof Pitch	10:12
Max Ridge Height	34'
Roof Framing	Truss
Exterior Walls	2x6

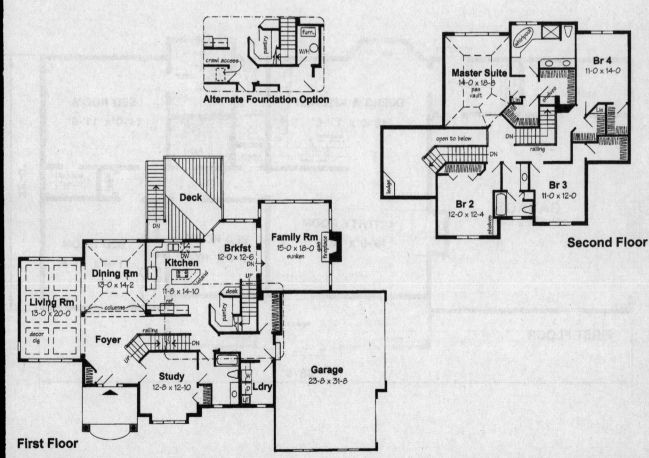

Alternate Foundation Option

Second Floor

First Floor

113

Units	Single
Price Code	A
Total Finished	1,300 sq. ft
First Finished	1,300 sq. ft
Garage Unfinished	576 sq. ft.
Porch Unfinished	166 sq. ft.
Dimensions	68'x28'
Foundation	Crawl spac Slab
Bedrooms	3
Full Baths	2
First Ceiling	8'
Primary Roof Pitch	7:12
Max Ridge Height	19'6"
Roof Framing	Truss
Exterior Walls	2x4

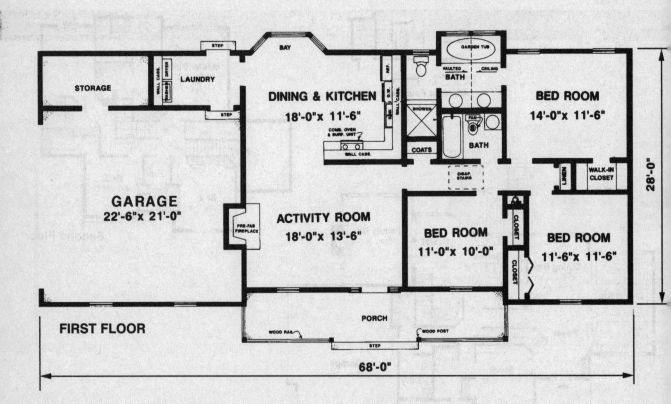

STORAGE

STEP

LAUNDRY

WASHER DRYER

WALL CABS.

STEP

BAY

DINING & KITCHEN
18'-0"x 11'-6"

COMB. OVEN & SURF. UNIT

WALL CABS.

REF.

D.W.

WALL CABS.

GARDEN TUB

BATH

VAULTED CEILING

SHOWER

FAN

BATH

COATS

COATS

BED ROOM
14'-0"x 11'-6"

LINEN

WALK-IN CLOSET

GARAGE
22'-6"x 21'-0"

PRE-FAB FIREPLACE

ACTIVITY ROOM
18'-0"x 13'-6"

DISAP. STAIRS

BED ROOM
11'-0"x 10'-0"

CLOSET

CLOSET

BED ROOM
11'-6"x 11'-6"

28'-0"

FIRST FLOOR

WOOD RAIL

PORCH

WOOD POST

STEP

68'-0"

Plan # 98596

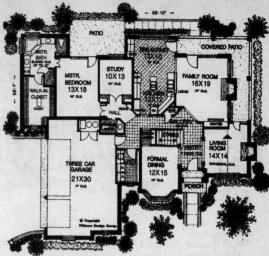

FIRST FLOOR

Units	Single
Price Code	H
Total Finished	3,062 sq. ft.
First Finished	2,115 sq. ft.
Second Finished	947 sq. ft.
Bonus Unfinished	195 sq. ft.
Garage Unfinished	635 sq. ft.
Deck Unfinished	210 sq. ft.
Porch Unfinished	32 sq. ft.
Dimensions	68'10"x58'1"
Foundation	Basement
	Crawl space
	Slab
Bedrooms	4
Full Baths	3
Half Baths	1
First Ceiling	10'
Second Ceiling	8'
Primary Roof Pitch	12:12
Max Ridge Height	32'6"
Roof Framing	Stick
Exterior Walls	2x4

SECOND FLOOR

Plan # 93133

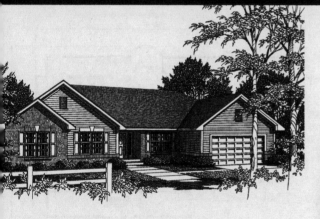

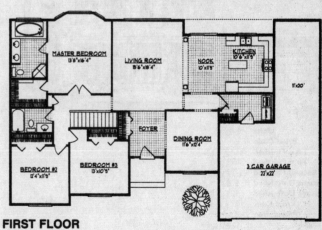

FIRST FLOOR

Units	Single
Price Code	C
Total Finished	1,761 sq. ft.
First Finished	1,761 sq. ft.
Basement Unfinished	1,761 sq. ft.
Garage Unfinished	658 sq. ft.
Dimensions	67'8"x42'8"
Foundation	Basement
Bedrooms	3
Full Baths	2
First Ceiling	8'
Vaulted Ceiling	14'
Primary Roof Pitch	8:12
Secondary Roof Pitch	8:12
Max Ridge Height	22'
Roof Framing	Truss
Exterior Walls	2x6

Plan # 97274

Units	Single
Price Code	A
Total Finished	1,432 sq. ft.
First Finished	1,432 sq. ft.
Basement Unfinished	1,454 sq. ft.
Garage Unfinished	440 sq. ft.
Dimensions	49'x52'4"
Foundation	Basement
	Crawl space
Bedrooms	3
Full Baths	2
Primary Roof Pitch	10:12
Max Ridge Height	24'2"
Roof Framing	Stick
Exterior Walls	2x4

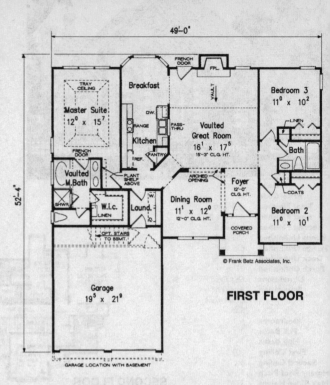

FIRST FLOOR

© Frank Betz Associates, Inc.

GARAGE LOCATION WITH BASEMENT

Plan # 98406

Units	Single
Price Code	B
Total Finished	1,600 sq. ft.
First Finished	828 sq. ft.
Second Finished	772 sq. ft.
Basement Unfinished	828 sq. ft.
Garage Unfinished	473 sq. ft.
Dimensions	52'4"x34'
Foundation	Basement
	Crawl space
	Slab
Bedrooms	3
Full Baths	2
Half Baths	1
First Ceiling	9'
Second Ceiling	8'
Primary Roof Pitch	12:12
Max Ridge Height	28'
Roof Framing	Stick
Exterior Walls	2x4

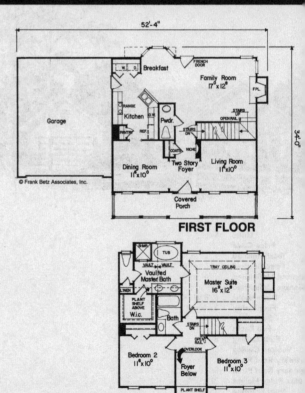

© Frank Betz Associates, Inc.

FIRST FLOOR

SECOND FLOOR

Units	Single
Price Code	F
Total Finished	2,748 sq. ft.
Main Finished	2,748 sq. ft.
Garage Unfinished	660 sq. ft.
Deck Unfinished	212 sq. ft.
Porch Unfinished	72 sq. ft.
Dimensions	75'x64'5''
Foundation	Slab
Bedrooms	4
Full Baths	3
Half Baths	1
Primary Roof Pitch	12:12
Max Ridge Height	31'6''
Roof Framing	Stick
Exterior Walls	2x4

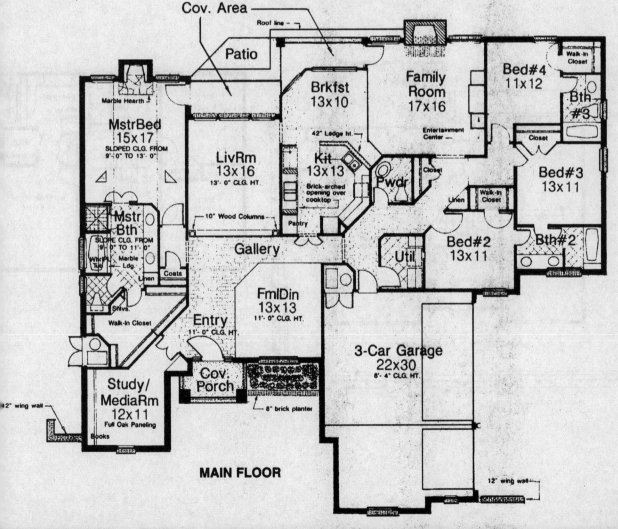

MAIN FLOOR

Cov. Area

Roof line

Patio

Marble Hearth

MstrBed 15x17
SLOPED CLG. FROM 9'-0" TO 13'-0"

Brkfst 13x10

Family Room 17x16

Bed#4 11x12

Walk-In Closet

Bth #3

Closet

42" Ledge ht.

Entertainment Center

LivRm 13x16
13'-0" CLG. HT.

Kit 13x13

Brick-arched opening over cooktop

Pwdr

Closet

Bed#3 13x11

Mstr Bth
SLOPE CLG. FROM 9'-0" TO 11'-0"

Whrlpl. Tub

Marble Ldg.

Linen

Coats

10" Wood Columns

Pantry

Linen

Walk-In Closet

Gallery

Walk-In Closet

Stvs.

Util.

Bed#2 13x11

Bth#2

FmlDin 13x13
11'-0" CLG. HT.

Entry 11'-0" CLG. HT.

3-Car Garage 22x30
8'-4" CLG. HT.

2" wing wall

Study/ MediaRm 12x11
Full Oak Paneling

Books

Cov. Porch

8" brick planter

12" wing wall

12" wing wall

Units	Single
Price Code	F
Total Finished	2,634 sq.
Main Finished	1,389 sq.
Second Finished	1,245 sq.
Basement Unfinished	1,389 sq.
Dimensions	57'x39'
Foundation	Basement
Bedrooms	3
Full Baths	2
3/4 Baths	1
Primary Roof Pitch	6:12
Secondary Roof Pitch	8:12
Max Ridge Height	27'
Roof Framing	Truss
Exterior Walls	2x6

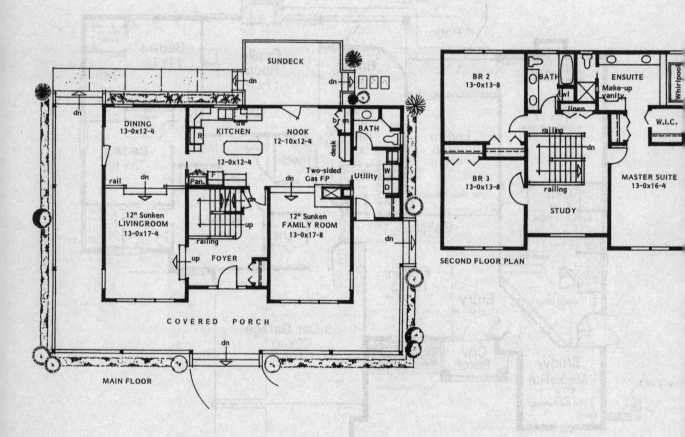

SUNDECK

DINING
13-0x12-4

KITCHEN
12-0x12-4

NOOK
12-10x12-4

BATH

desk

Two-sided
Gas FP

Utility

W
D

rail

Pan.

F

12" Sunken
LIVINGROOM
13-0x17-4

12" Sunken
FAMILY ROOM
13-0x17-8

railing

up

up   FOYER

COVERED   PORCH

MAIN FLOOR

SECOND FLOOR PLAN

BR 2
13-0x13-8

BATH

ENSUITE
Make-up
vanity

Whirlpool

linen

W.I.C.

railing

BR 3
13-0x13-8

STUDY

railing

MASTER SUITE
13-0x16-4

Plan # 99641

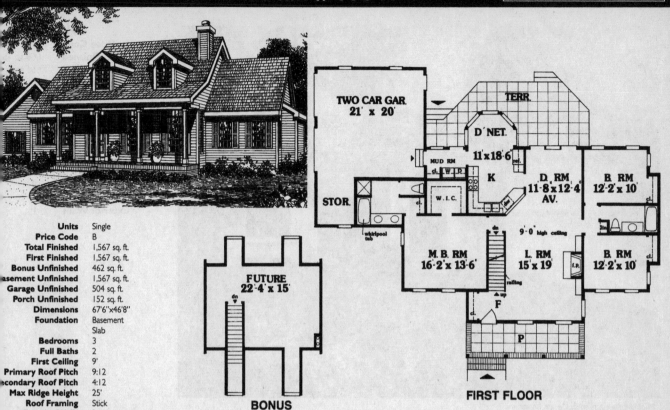

Units	Single
Price Code	B
Total Finished	1,567 sq. ft.
First Finished	1,567 sq. ft.
Bonus Unfinished	462 sq. ft.
Basement Unfinished	1,567 sq. ft.
Garage Unfinished	504 sq. ft.
Porch Unfinished	152 sq. ft.
Dimensions	67'6"x46'8"
Foundation	Basement
	Slab
Bedrooms	3
Full Baths	2
First Ceiling	9'
Primary Roof Pitch	9:12
Secondary Roof Pitch	4:12
Max Ridge Height	25'
Roof Framing	Stick
Exterior Walls	2x6

TWO CAR GAR. 21' x 20'

TERR.

D'NET. 11' x 18'-6

MUD RM

STOR.

K

W.I.C.

whirlpool tub

D. RM 11'-8 x 12'-4 AV.

B. RM 12'-2' x 10'

9'-0" high ceiling

M. B. RM 16'-2' x 13'-6'

L. RM 15' x 19'

B. RM 12'-2' x 10'

F

P

FIRST FLOOR

FUTURE 22'-4' x 15'

BONUS

Plan # 98534

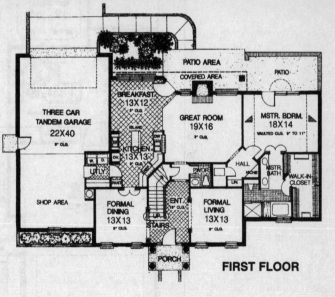

Units	Single
Price Code	G
Total Finished	2,959 sq. ft.
First Finished	1,848 sq. ft.
Second Finished	1,111 sq. ft.
Garage Unfinished	722 sq. ft.
Deck Unfinished	172 sq. ft.
Porch Unfinished	42 sq. ft.
Dimensions	73'4"x44'
Foundation	Crawl space
	Slab
Bedrooms	4
Full Baths	3
Half Baths	1
First Ceiling	9'
Second Ceiling	8'
Primary Roof Pitch	9:12
Max Ridge Height	32'
Roof Framing	Stick
Exterior Walls	2x4

PATIO AREA

COVERED AREA

PATIO

BREAKFAST 13X12

THREE CAR TANDEM GARAGE 22X40

GREAT ROOM 19X16

MSTR. BDRM. 18X14

KITCHEN 13X13

UTLY

HALL

MSTR. BATH

WALK-IN-CLOSET

SHOP AREA

FORMAL DINING 13X13

PWDR

FORMAL LIVING 13X13

ENT

STAIRS

PORCH

FIRST FLOOR

BDRM.#2 13X11

BDRM.#3 13X12

BALCONY

STAIRS DOWN

BDRM.#4 13X12

ENTRY BELOW

LOFT AREA 13X14

PLANT LEDGE

PORCH BELOW

SECOND FLOOR

Units	Single
Price Code	B
Total Finished	1,666 sq. ft.
First Finished	1,666 sq. ft.
Basement Unfinished	1,666 sq. ft.
Garage Unfinished	496 sq. ft.
Dimensions	55'4"x48'
Foundation	Basement
Bedrooms	3
Full Baths	2
Primary Roof Pitch	8:12
Secondary Roof Pitch	8:12
Max Ridge Height	22'9"
Roof Framing	Stick
Exterior Walls	2x4

Photography supplied by Design Basics, Inc.

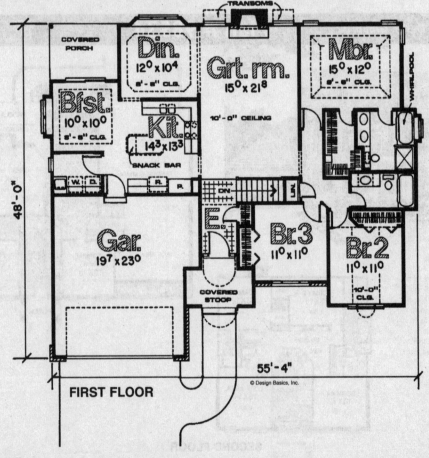

FIRST FLOOR

© Design Basics, Inc.

Units	Single
Price Code	C
Total Finished	1,815 sq. ft.
First Finished	1,073 sq. ft.
Second Finished	742 sq. ft.
Bonus Unfinished	336 sq. ft.
Basement Unfinished	1,073 sq. ft.
Garage Unfinished	495 sq. ft.
Dimensions	45'x40'
Foundation	Basement Crawl space
Bedrooms	3
Full Baths	2
Half Baths	1
Primary Roof Pitch	9:12
Max Ridge Height	30'
Roof Framing	Stick
Exterior Walls	2x4

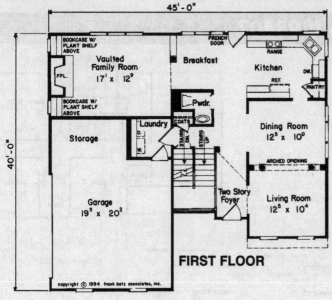

FIRST FLOOR

45'-0"

40'-0"

- BOOKCASE W/ PLANT SHELF ABOVE
- Vaulted Family Room 17¹ x 12⁹
- FPL.
- BOOKCASE W/ PLANT SHELF ABOVE
- Breakfast
- FRENCH DOOR
- RANGE
- Kitchen
- DW.
- REF.
- PANTRY
- Pwdr.
- Laundry
- COATS
- STAIRS DN.
- STAIRS UP
- Dining Room 12⁵ x 10⁰
- Storage
- ARCHED OPENING
- Garage 19⁵ x 20²
- Two Story Foyer
- Living Room 12⁵ x 10⁴

copyright © 1994 frank betz associates, inc.

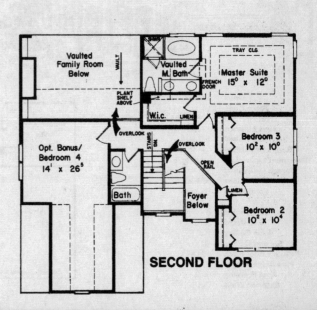

SECOND FLOOR

- Vaulted Family Room Below
- VAULT
- Vaulted M. Bath
- TRAY CLG.
- Master Suite 15⁰ x 12⁰
- FRENCH DOOR
- PLANT SHELF ABOVE
- W.i.c.
- LINEN
- Opt. Bonus/ Bedroom 4 14¹ x 26⁵
- OVERLOOK
- STAIRS DN.
- OVERLOOK
- OPEN RAIL
- Bedroom 3 10² x 10⁰
- Bath
- Foyer Below
- LINEN
- Bedroom 2 10² x 10⁴

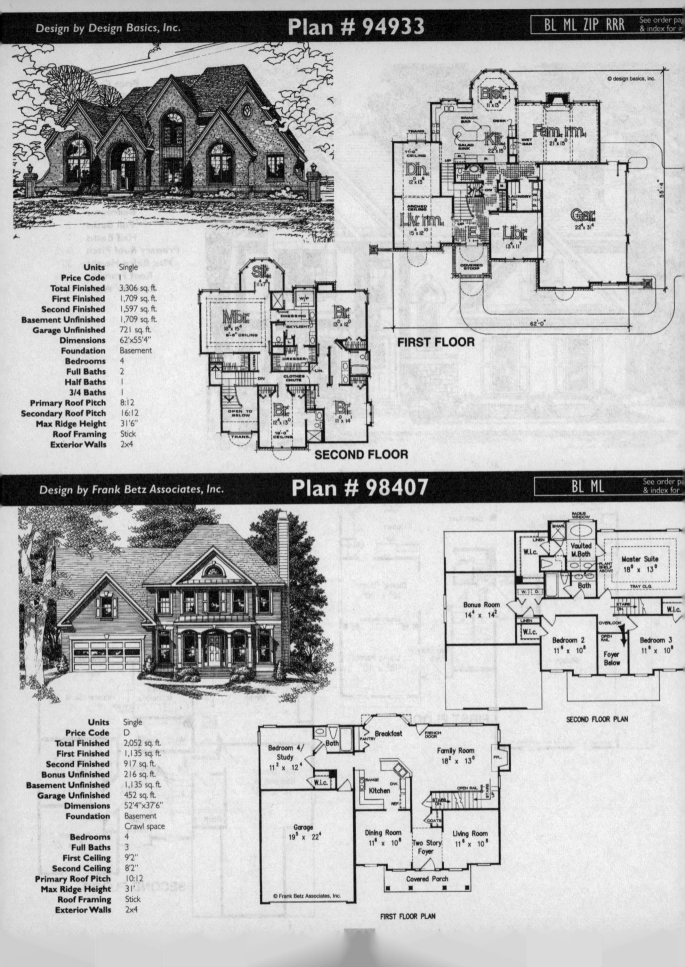

Plan # 94933

© design basics, inc.

FIRST FLOOR

Bfst. 11'x13'
Snack bar
Kit. 22'x15'
Fam. rm. 21'x15'
Desk
Salad sink
Wet bar
Din. 12'x13'
Gar. 22'x31'
Liv. rm. 15'x12'
Libr. 13'x11'
Covered Stoop
55'-4"
62'-0"

Mbr. 18'x15'4" 8'-0" ceiling
Slt. 11'x7'
Dressing
Skylight
Br. 13'x12'
Dresser
Clothes chute
Br. 12'x13' 13'-0" ceiling
Br. 11'x14'
Open to below
Trans.

SECOND FLOOR

Units	Single
Price Code	I
Total Finished	3,306 sq. ft.
First Finished	1,709 sq. ft.
Second Finished	1,597 sq. ft.
Basement Unfinished	1,709 sq. ft.
Garage Unfinished	721 sq. ft.
Dimensions	62'x55'4"
Foundation	Basement
Bedrooms	4
Full Baths	2
Half Baths	1
3/4 Baths	1
Primary Roof Pitch	8:12
Secondary Roof Pitch	16:12
Max Ridge Height	31'6"
Roof Framing	Stick
Exterior Walls	2x4

Plan # 98407

Radius Window
W.i.c.
Vaulted M.Bath
Master Suite 18'x13'
Bath
Tray clg.
Bonus Room 14'x14'2"
W.i.c.
Bedroom 2 11'6"x10'8"
Overlook
Open Rail
Bedroom 3 11'6"x10'8"
W.i.c.
Foyer Below

SECOND FLOOR PLAN

Bedroom 4/ Study 11'2"x12'4"
Bath
Pantry
Breakfast
French Door
Family Room 18'2"x13'0"
W.i.c.
Kitchen
Range
Open Rail Stairs
Garage 19'5"x22'4"
Dining Room 11'6"x10'8"
Two Story Foyer
Living Room 11'6"x10'8"
Covered Porch
© Frank Betz Associates, Inc.

FIRST FLOOR PLAN

Units	Single
Price Code	D
Total Finished	2,052 sq. ft.
First Finished	1,135 sq. ft.
Second Finished	917 sq. ft.
Bonus Unfinished	216 sq. ft.
Basement Unfinished	1,135 sq. ft.
Garage Unfinished	452 sq. ft.
Dimensions	52'4"x37'6"
Foundation	Basement Crawl space
Bedrooms	4
Full Baths	3
First Ceiling	9'2"
Second Ceiling	8'2"
Primary Roof Pitch	10:12
Max Ridge Height	31'
Roof Framing	Stick
Exterior Walls	2x4

Units	Single
Price Code	J
Total Finished	3,512 sq. ft.
Main Finished	2,658 sq. ft.
Upper Finished	854 sq. ft.
Garage Unfinished	660 sq. ft.
Deck Unfinished	190 sq. ft.
Porch Unfinished	62 sq. ft.
Dimensions	86'x58'1"
Foundation	Slab
Bedrooms	4
Full Baths	3
Half Baths	1
Main Ceiling	9'
Upper Ceiling	8'
Primary Roof Pitch	12:12
Max Ridge Height	28'6"
Roof Framing	Stick
Exterior Walls	2x4

86'-0"

58'-1"

Main Floor

Patio

Covered Patio

MstrBed 15²x17
Sloped Ceiling 9'-0" To 13'-0"

LivRm 14x14
11'-0" Clg

Din 12²x11²
9'-0" Clg Tile

Kit 12²x11²
9'-0" Clg

FamilyRm 19x15
9'-0" Vaulted Ceiling
T.V. & Books

Bed#2 11²x14²
9'-0" Vaulted Ceiling 9'-0" To 11'-0"

Chest

Skylite

Whirl-Pool Tub

Linen

Walk-In Closet 9'-0" Clg

Gallery 9'-0" Clg Tile

Hall

Walk-In Closet

Pwr

Util

Ent Sloped Clg 9'-0" To 13'-0" Tile

FmlDin 12²x11²
9'-0" Clg

Chest

Study 12²x12²
Vaulted Ceiling 9'-0" To 11'-0"

Cov Por

3-Car Gar 22x30
9'-0" Clg

Upper Floor
All Ceiling Height's 8'-0" Unless Noted.

BonusRm 14x10²
Not Included In Total Sq. Ft. (Unfinished)

Sloped Clg

Bed#3 12²x15
8'-0" Clg

Walk-In Closet

Sloped Clg

Balcony
Open To Entry Below

DN

PlayRm 12²x16²
Sloped Ceiling 8'-0" To 11'-0"

Linen

Bed#4 12²x11
8'-0" Clg
Sloped Clg

Cathedral Ceiling

Desk

Walk-In Closet

Attic Access

HEAT-N-GLO
No one builds a better fire

Units	Single
Price Code	A
Total Finished	1,472 sq. ft.
Main Finished	1,472 sq. ft.
Basement Unfinished	1,472 sq. ft.
Garage Unfinished	424 sq. ft.
Dimensions	48'x56'4"
Foundation	Basement
Bedrooms	3
Full Baths	2
Primary Roof Pitch	8:12
Secondary Roof Pitch	8:12
Max Ridge Height	19'8"
Roof Framing	Stick
Exterior Walls	2x6

* This plan is not to be built within a 20 mile radius of Iowa City, IA.

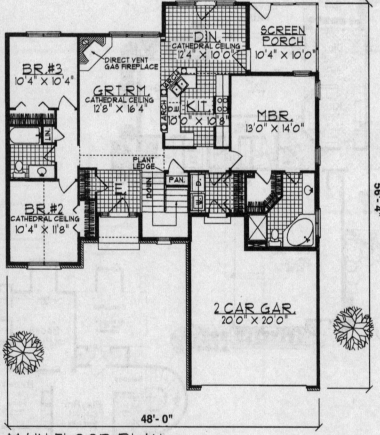

MAIN FLOOR PLAN

Units	Single
Price Code	E
Total Finished	2,311 sq. ft.
First Finished	2,311 sq. ft.
Garage Unfinished	657 sq. ft.
Dimensions	64'x57'2''
Foundation	Basement
Bedrooms	3
Full Baths	2
Half Baths	1
First Ceiling	8'
Primary Roof Pitch	6:12
Secondary Roof Pitch	8:12
Max Ridge Height	21'4''
Roof Framing	Stick
Exterior Walls	2x4

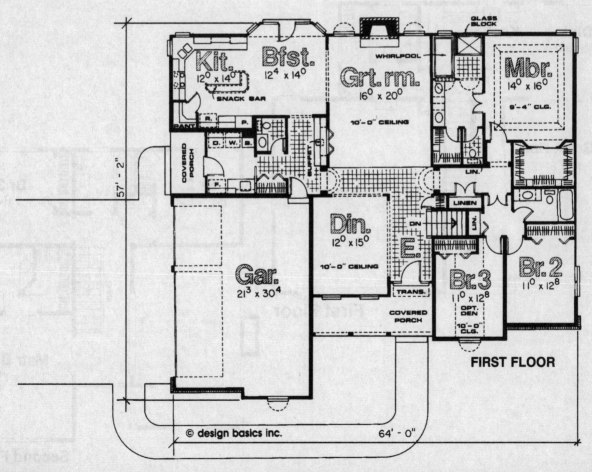

FIRST FLOOR

© design basics inc.

Rear Elevatio

Units	Single
Price Code	C
Total Finished	1,785 sq. ft.
First Finished	891 sq. ft.
Second Finished	894 sq. ft.
Basement Unfinished	891 sq. ft.
Garage Unfinished	534 sq. ft.
Dimensions	46'8''x35'8''
Foundation	Basement
	Crawl space
	Slab
Bedrooms	3
Full Baths	2
Half Baths	1
First Ceiling	8'
Second Ceiling	8'
Primary Roof Pitch	8:12
Max Ridge Height	28'
Roof Framing	Stick
Exterior Walls	2x4

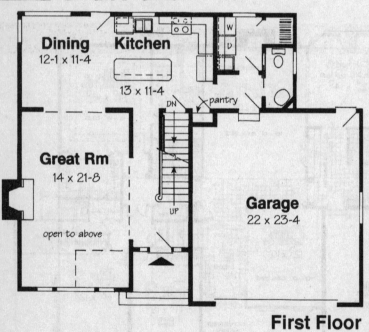

Dining 12-1 x 11-4

Kitchen 13 x 11-4

W D

DN pantry

Great Rm 14 x 21-8

open to above

UP

Garage 22 x 23-4

First Floor

Br 2 11-6 x 11-4

linen

Br 3 11 x 11-4

DN

railing

open to below

1/2 wall

Mstr Br 13-4 x 15

Second Floor

126

Units	Single
Price Code	A
Total Finished	1,345 sq. ft.
First Finished	1,325 sq. ft.
Staircase Finished	20 sq. ft.
Basement Unfinished	556 sq. ft.
Garage Unfinished	724 sq. ft.
Deck Unfinished	157 sq. ft.
Porch Unfinished	216 sq. ft.
Dimensions	52'x42'
Foundation	Basement
Bedrooms	3
Full Baths	2
First Ceiling	8'
Primary Roof Pitch	7:12
Max Ridge Height	19'
Roof Framing	Stick
Exterior Walls	2x4

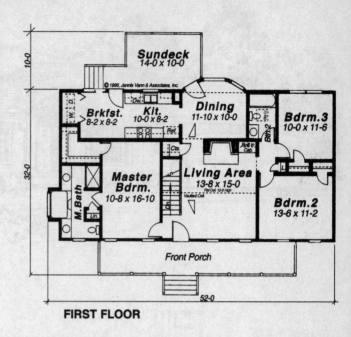

FIRST FLOOR

Units	Single
Price Code	B
Total Finished	1,702 sq. ft.
First Finished	1,238 sq. ft.
Second Finished	464 sq. ft.
Basement Unfinished	1,175 sq. ft.
Dimensions	34'x56'
Foundation	Basement
Bedrooms	3
Full Baths	1
3/4 Baths	1
Primary Roof Pitch	13.5:12
Max Ridge Height	26'6''
Roof Framing	Stick
Exterior Walls	2x6

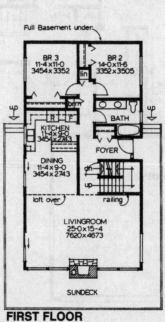

FIRST FLOOR

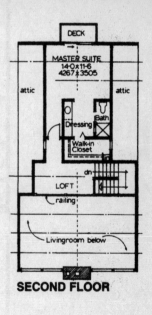

SECOND FLOOR

Order Today! 1-800-235-5700 or order online at
www.familyhomeplans.com

Units	Single
Price Code	A
Total Finished	1,423 sq. ft.
Main Finished	1,423 sq. ft.
Basement Unfinished	1,423 sq. ft.
Garage Unfinished	399 sq. ft.
Dimensions	54'x49'
Foundation	Basement
Bedrooms	3
Full Baths	1
3/4 Baths	1
Exterior Walls	2x6

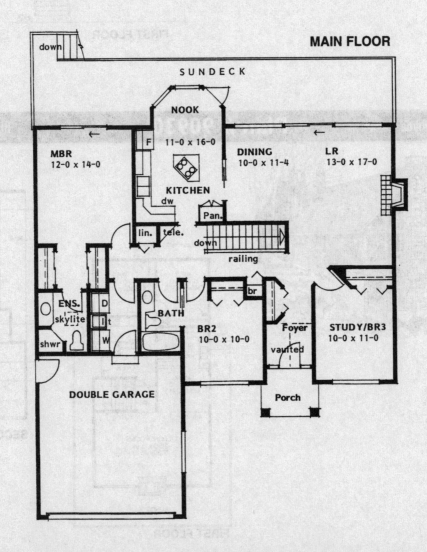

MAIN FLOOR

SUNDECK

NOOK
11-0 x 16-0

MBR
12-0 x 14-0

DINING
10-0 x 11-4

LR
13-0 x 17-0

KITCHEN
dw

Pan.

lin. tele.

down

railing

ENS.
skylite

D
lt
W

BATH

br

BR2
10-0 x 10-0

Foyer
vaulted

STUDY/BR3
10-0 x 11-0

shwr

DOUBLE GARAGE

Porch

Units	Single
Price Code	J
Total Finished	3,658 sq. ft.
First Finished	2,380 sq. ft.
Second Finished	1,086 sq. ft.
Staircase Finished	192 sq. ft.
Basement Unfinished	2,264 sq. ft.
Garage Unfinished	520 sq. ft.
Porch Unfinished	369 sq. ft.
Dimensions	85'x70'
Foundation	Basement
Bedrooms	4
Full Baths	3
Half Baths	1
First Ceiling	9'
Second Ceiling	8'
Primary Roof Pitch	12:12
Max Ridge Height	29'
Roof Framing	Stick
Exterior Walls	2x4

FIRST FLOOR

SECOND FLOOR

Units	Single
Price Code	F
Total Finished	2,578 sq. ft.
First Finished	1,245 sq. ft.
Second Finished	1,333 sq. ft.
Bonus Unfinished	192 sq. ft.
Basement Unfinished	1,245 sq. ft.
Garage Unfinished	614 sq. ft.
Dimensions	50'x46'
Foundation	Basement
	Crawl space
	Slab
Bedrooms	3
Full Baths	2
Half Baths	1
First Ceiling	9'
Second Ceiling	8'
Primary Roof Pitch	12:12
Secondary Roof Pitch	12:12
Max Ridge Height	35'
Roof Framing	Stick
Exterior Walls	2x4

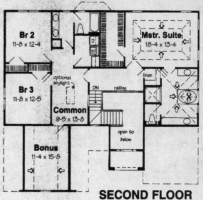

SECOND FLOOR

Crawl Space/ Slab Option

FIRST FLOOR

Order T...
V...

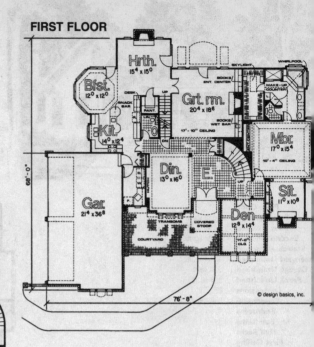

FIRST FLOOR

Hrth.
15⁴ x 15⁰

Bfst.
12⁰ x 12⁰

Grt. rm.
20⁴ x 18⁶

Kit.
14⁰ x 12⁴

Mbr.
17⁰ x 15⁴

Din.
13⁰ x 16⁰

Gar
21⁴ x 36⁸

Den
12⁸ x 14⁴

Sit.
11⁰ x 10⁸

76'-8"

© design basics, inc.

SECOND FLOOR

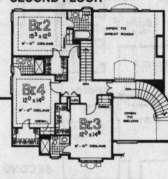

Br 2
15³ x 12⁰

OPEN TO
GREAT ROOM

Br 4
12⁰ x 14⁰

Br 3
12⁰ x 14⁶

OPEN TO
BELOW

Units	Single
Price Code	J
Total Finished	3,623 sq. ft.
First Finished	2,603 sq. ft.
Second Finished	1,020 sq. ft.
Basement Unfinished	2,603 sq. ft.
Garage Unfinished	801 sq. ft.
Dimensions	76'8"x68'
Foundation	Basement
Bedrooms	4
Full Baths	2
Half Baths	1
3/4 Baths	2
First Ceiling	9'
Primary Roof Pitch	8:12
Secondary Roof Pitch	12:12
Max Ridge Height	31'4"
Roof Framing	Stick
Exterior Walls	2x4

FIRST FLOOR

MASTER
BEDROOM
17'-4" x 18'-4"
9'-12' CH

MASTER
BATH
9' CH

BACK PORCH
9' CH

BREAKFAST
8'-0" x 11'-4"
9' CH

KITCHEN
9' CH

UTILITY
9' CH

MASTER
CLOSET
9' CH

SUN ROOM
11'-4" x 15'-0"
CATHEDRAL CLG
12' to 19' CH

FAMILY ROOM
15'-8" x 15'-0"
12' to 19' CH

PWDR
9' CH

2-CAR GARAGE
10'-4" CH

STORAGE

ENTRY

DINING ROOM
11'-4" x 13'-0"
9' CH

VERANDA
9' CH

66'-0"

SECOND FLOOR

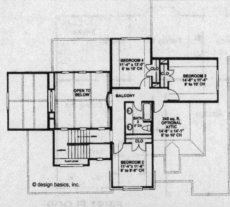

BEDROOM 4
11'-4" x 13'-0"
8' to 10' CH

BEDROOM 3
14'-4" x 11'-4"
8' to 10' CH

OPEN TO
BELOW

BALCONY

BATH
9' CH

245 sq. ft.
OPTIONAL
ATTIC
14'-4" x 14'-1"
8' to 10' CH

BEDROOM 2
11'-4" x 11'-4"
8' to 9'-8" CH

© design basics, inc.

Units	Single
Price Code	F
Total Finished	2,537 sq. ft.
First Finished	1,794 sq. ft.
Second Finished	743 sq. ft.
Dimensions	66'x55'11.5"
Foundation	Basement
	Slab
Bedrooms	4
Full Baths	2
Half Baths	1
Max Ridge Height	33'
Roof Framing	Stick
Exterior Walls	2x4

*Photography by John Ehrenclou

Units	Single
Price Code	B
Total Finished	1,668 sq. ft.
First Finished	1,057 sq. ft.
Second Finished	611 sq. ft.
Basement Unfinished	511 sq. ft.
Garage Unfinished	546 sq. ft.
Dimensions	40'4''x38'
Foundation	Basement
Bedrooms	3
Full Baths	2
Half Baths	1
First Ceiling	8'
Second Ceiling	8'
Primary Roof Pitch	12:12
Secondary Roof Pitch	5:12
Max Ridge Height	23'
Roof Framing	Stick
Exterior Walls	2x4

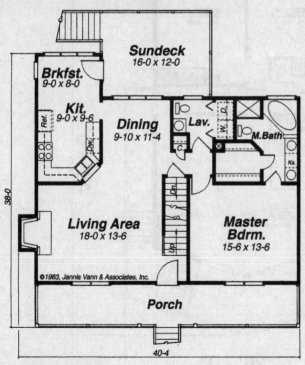

FIRST FLOOR

Sundeck 16-0 x 12-0
Brkfst. 9-0 x 8-0
Kit. 9-0 x 9-6
Ref.
Dw.
Dining 9-10 x 11-4
Lav.
W.D.
C.
M.Bath
Ks.
Living Area 18-0 x 13-6
Dn.
Up
Master Bdrm. 15-6 x 13-6
© 1983, Jannis Vann & Associates, Inc.
Porch
38-0
40-4

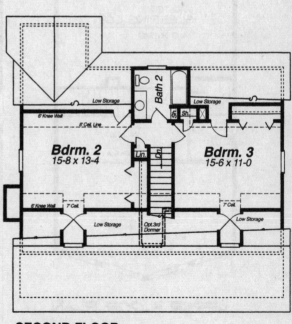

SECOND FLOOR

6' Knee Wall
8' Ceil. Line
Low Storage
Bath 2
Low Storage
Sh.
Sh.
Bdrm. 2 15-8 x 13-4
Lin.
Dn.
Bdrm. 3 15-6 x 11-0
6' Knee Wall
7' Ceil.
Low Storage
Opt.3rd Dormer
7' Ceil.
Low Storage

Units	Single
Price Code	A
Total Finished	1,354 sq. ft.
Main Finished	988 sq. ft.
Upper Finished	366 sq. ft.
Basement Unfinished	742 sq. ft.
Garage Unfinished	283 sq. ft.
Dimensions	26'x48'
Foundation	Basement
Bedrooms	3
Full Baths	1
3/4 Baths	1
Vaulted Ceiling	13'6"
Primary Roof Pitch	12:12
Max Ridge Height	32'
Roof Framing	Stick
Exterior Walls	2x6

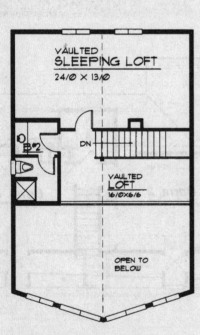

VAULTED
SLEEPING LOFT
24/0 X 13/0

B #2

DN

VAULTED
LOFT
16/0 X 6/6

OPEN TO
BELOW

UPPER FLOOR PLAN

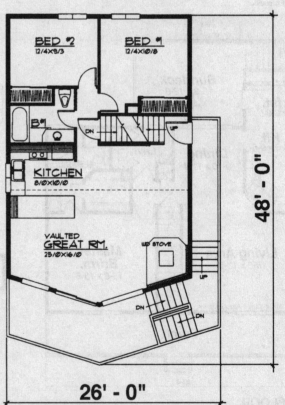

BED #2
12/4 X 9/3

BED #1
12/4 X 10/8

B #1

DN

UP

KITCHEN
8/0 X 10/0

VAULTED
GREAT RM.
25/0 X 16/0

STOVE

UP

UP

DN

DN

48' - 0"

26' - 0"

MAIN FLOOR PLAN

Plan # 99045

SECOND FLOOR

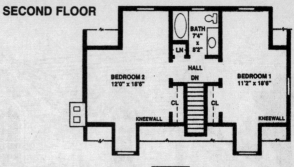

BATH 7'4" x 6'2"

LN

BEDROOM 2 12'0" x 18'6"

HALL

DN

BEDROOM 1 11'2" x 18'6"

CL CL

KNEEWALL

KNEEWALL

Units	Single
Price Code	C
Total Finished	1,767 sq. ft.
First Finished	1,108 sq. ft.
Second Finished	659 sq. ft.
Basement Unfinished	875 sq. ft.
Porch Unfinished	145 sq. ft.
Dimensions	67'x30'
Foundation	Basement
Bedrooms	3
Full Baths	2
Half Baths	1
Primary Roof Pitch	10:12
Max Ridge Height	21'
Roof Framing	Truss
Exterior Walls	2x4

DW

PANTRY

PR

REF

DINING ROOM 8'1" x 11'4"

WIC 6'2" x 7'2"

MASTER BATH 8'10" x 10'4"

2 CAR GARAGE 21'2" x 22'2"

HALL

KITCHEN 8'11" x 11'4"

RANGE

LN CL

CL

L W D

LAUNDRY 7'6" x 7'8"

CL

LIVING ROOM 13'2" x 20'2"

DN

UP

MASTER BEDROOM 13'2" x 13'8"

FIREPLACE

PORCH

FIRST FLOOR

Plan # 96505

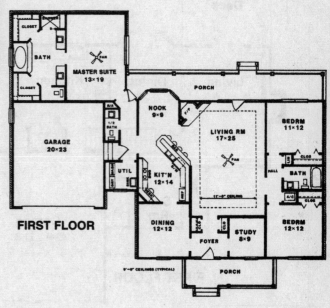

CLOSET

BATH

MASTER SUITE 13×19

FAN

PORCH

CLOSET

R/A

GARAGE 20×23

NOOK 9×9

1/2 BATH

LIVING RM 17×25

FAN

BEDRM 11×12

CLOS

UTIL

KIT'N 12×14

HALL

BATH

11'-0" CEILING

A/C

CLOS

Units	Single
Price Code	D
Total Finished	2,069 sq. ft.
First Finished	2,069 sq. ft.
Garage Unfinished	481 sq. ft.
Porch Unfinished	374 sq. ft.
Dimensions	70'x58'
Foundation	Crawl space
	Slab
Bedrooms	3
Full Baths	2
Half Baths	1
First Ceiling	9'
Primary Roof Pitch	8:12
Secondary Roof Pitch	4:12
Max Ridge Height	23'
Exterior Walls	2x4

FIRST FLOOR

DINING 12×12

FOYER

STUDY 8×9

BEDRM 12×12

PORCH

9'-0" CEILINGS (TYPICAL)

Units	Single
Price Code	B
Total Finished	1,554 sq. ft.
First Finished	806 sq. ft.
Second Finished	748 sq. ft.
Garage Unfinished	467 sq. ft.
Dimensions	50'x40'
Foundation	Basement
	Crawl space
	Slab
Bedrooms	3
Full Baths	2
Half Baths	1
First Ceiling	8'
Second Ceiling	8'
Primary Roof Pitch	8:12
Secondary Roof Pitch	12:12
Max Ridge Height	29'
Roof Framing	Stick
Exterior Walls	2x4

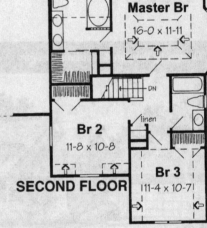

SECOND FLOOR

Master Br
16-0 x 11-11

DN

Br 2
11-8 x 10-8

linen

Br 3
11-4 x 10-71

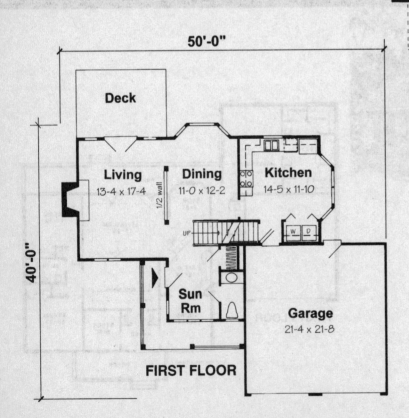

50'-0"

40'-0"

Deck

Living
13-4 x 17-4

1/2 wall

Dining
11-0 x 12-2

Kitchen
14-5 x 11-10

UP

W D

Sun
Rm

Garage
21-4 x 21-8

FIRST FLOOR

Units	Single
Price Code	F
Total Finished	2,715 sq. ft.
First Finished	1,400 sq. ft.
Second Finished	1,315 sq. ft.
Garage Unfinished	631 sq. ft.
Dimensions	75'1.5''x38'
Foundation	Basement
	Slab
Bedrooms	4
Full Baths	3
Half Baths	1
First Ceiling	9'
Second Ceiling	8'10''
Primary Roof Pitch	9:12
Secondary Roof Pitch	12:12
Max Ridge Height	30'4''
Roof Framing	Stick
Exterior Walls	2x4

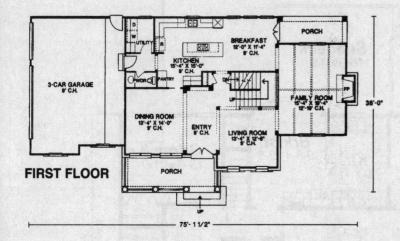

FIRST FLOOR

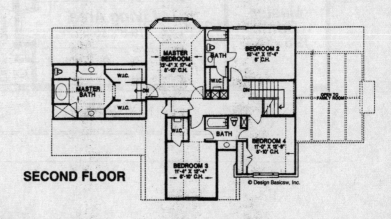

SECOND FLOOR

© Design Basicsw, Inc.

Units	Single
Price Code	C
Total Finished	1,778 sq. ft.
Main Finished	1,778 sq. ft.
Basement Unfinished	1,008 sq. ft.
Garage Unfinished	728 sq. ft.
Dimensions	62'x28'
Foundation	Basement
Bedrooms	3
Full Baths	2
Main Ceiling	8'
Vaulted Ceiling	10'4"
Primary Roof Pitch	6:12
Max Ridge Height	26'
Roof Framing	Stick/Truss
Exterior Walls	2x4

MAIN FLOOR

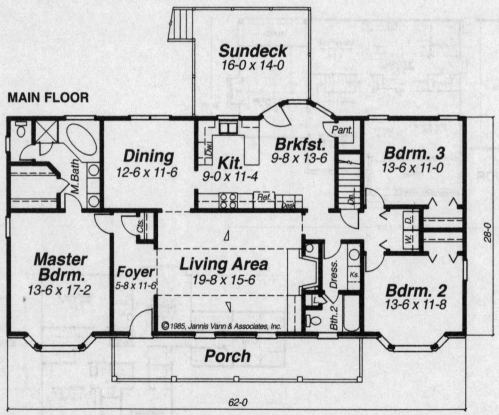

Sundeck
16-0 x 14-0

Dining
12-6 x 11-6

Kit.
9-0 x 11-4

Brkfst.
9-8 x 13-6

Pant.

Bdrm. 3
13-6 x 11-0

M. Bath

Master Bdrm.
13-6 x 17-2

Foyer
5-8 x 11-6

Living Area
19-8 x 15-6

Dress.

Bth.2

Bdrm. 2
13-6 x 11-8

Ref.

Desk

Cts.

W. D.

Ks.

28-0

© 1985, Jannis Vann & Associates, Inc.

Porch

62-0

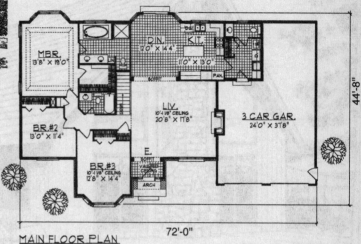

Units	Single
Price Code	C
Total Finished	1,906 sq. ft.
Main Finished	1,906 sq. ft.
Basement Unfinished	1,906 sq. ft.
Dimensions	72'x44'8"
Foundation	Basement
Bedrooms	3
Full Baths	2
Half Baths	1
Primary Roof Pitch	10:12
Secondary Roof Pitch	10:12
Max Ridge Height	12'4"
Roof Framing	Truss
Exterior Walls	2x6

MAIN FLOOR PLAN

Units	Single
Price Code	C
Total Finished	1,856 sq. ft.
First Finished	1,856 sq. ft.
Basement Unfinished	1,856 sq. ft.
Garage Unfinished	429 sq. ft.
Dimensions	59'x54'6"
Foundation	Basement
	Crawl space
	Slab
Bedrooms	3
Full Baths	2
First Ceiling	9'
Primary Roof Pitch	8:12
Max Ridge Height	25'6"
Roof Framing	Stick
Exterior Walls	2x4

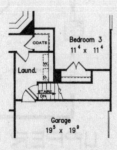

OPT. BASEMENT STAIR LOCATION

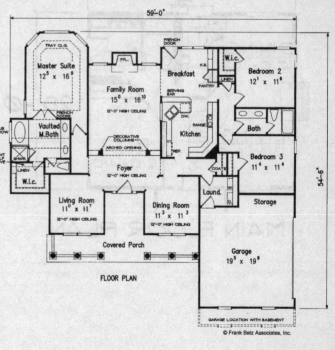

FLOOR PLAN

© Frank Betz Associates, Inc.

137

Units	Single
Price Code	A
Total Finished	1,249 sq. ft.
Main Finished	952 sq. ft.
Upper Finished	297 sq. ft.
Dimensions	34'x28'
Foundation	Basement
	Crawl space
Bedrooms	2
Full Baths	2
Main Ceiling	8'
Primary Roof Pitch	12:12
Max Ridge Height	24'
Roof Framing	Stick
Exterior Walls	2x6

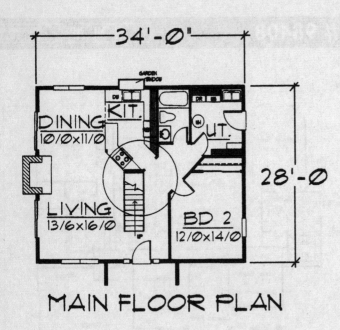

MAIN FLOOR PLAN

DINING 10/0x11/0
KIT.
UT.
LIVING 13/6x16/0
BD 2 12/0x14/0

34'-0"
28'-0

OPTIONAL BASEMENT PLAN

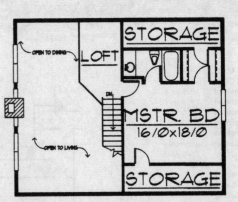

OPEN TO DINING
LOFT
STORAGE
MSTR. BD 16/0x18/0
STORAGE
OPEN TO LIVING

UPPER FLOOR PLAN

Weather Shield
Windows & Doors

www.weathershield.com

Weather Shield Windows and Doors offers project planning guides for your remodeling or new home project. FREE. Specify "Remodeling" or "New Home" Planning Guide by calling

1-800-477-6808

Units	Single
Price Code	B
Total Finished	1,654 sq. ft.
First Finished	1,654 sq. ft.
Garage Unfinished	480 sq. ft.
Dimensions	68'x46'
Foundation	Crawl space
	Slab
Bedrooms	3
Full Baths	2
Half Baths	1
First Ceiling	9'
Primary Roof Pitch	9:12
Max Ridge Height	21
Roof Framing	Stick
Exterior Walls	2x4

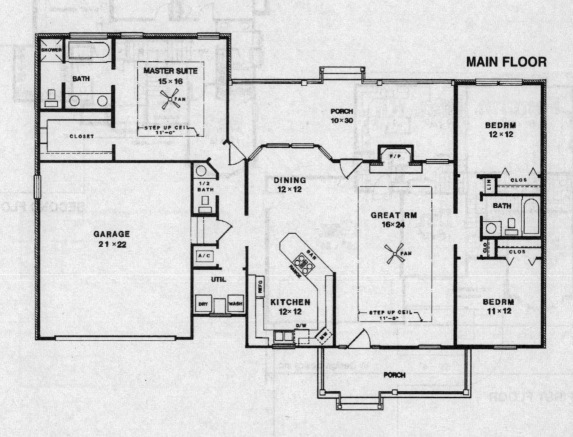

MAIN FLOOR

SHOWER

BATH

MASTER SUITE
15 × 16
FAN
STEP UP CEIL 11'-0"

CLOSET

PORCH
10 × 30

F/P

BEDRM
12 × 12

CLOS
LIN

DINING
12 × 12

1/2 BATH

BATH

CLO
CLOS

GARAGE
21 × 22

A/C

BAR
RANGE

GREAT RM
16 × 24
FAN

UTIL

MFG

DRY | WASH

KITCHEN
12 × 12

D/W

STEP UP CEIL 11'-0"

BEDRM
11 × 12

PORCH

© design basics inc.

Units	Single
Price Code	E
Total Finished	2,283 sq. ft.
First Finished	1,134 sq. ft.
Second Finished	1,149 sq. ft.
Garage Unfinished	560 sq. ft.
Dimensions	53'4"x42'
Foundation	Basement
Bedrooms	4
Full Baths	2
Half Baths	1
First Ceiling	8'
Primary Roof Pitch	8:12
Secondary Roof Pitch	8:12
Max Ridge Height	27'9"
Roof Framing	Stick
Exterior Walls	2x4

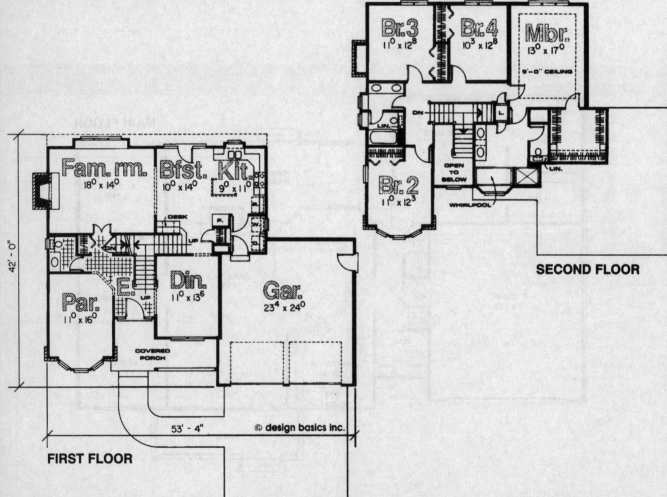

SECOND FLOOR

Br. 3 11⁰ x 12⁸
Br. 4 10³ x 12⁸
Mbr. 13⁰ x 17⁰ 9'-0" CEILING
Br. 2 11⁰ x 12³
LIN.
DN
OPEN TO BELOW
WHIRLPOOL
LIN.

Fam. rm. 18⁰ x 14⁰
Bfst. 10⁰ x 14⁰
Kit. 9⁰ x 11⁰
DESK
UP
Par. 11⁰ x 16⁰
Din. 11⁰ x 13⁶
Gar. 23⁴ x 24⁰
COVERED PORCH
DN

42' - 0"

53' - 4"

© design basics inc.

FIRST FLOOR

Design by Lifestyles Home Design

Plan # 99327

BL ML
See order pages
& index for info

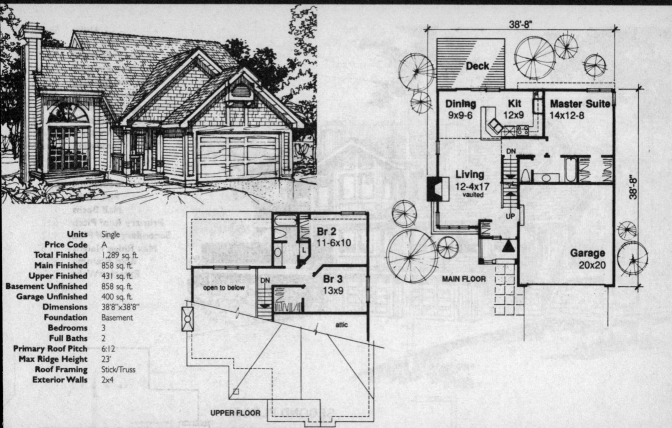

Units	Single
Price Code	A
Total Finished	1,289 sq. ft.
Main Finished	858 sq. ft.
Upper Finished	431 sq. ft.
Basement Unfinished	858 sq. ft.
Garage Unfinished	400 sq. ft.
Dimensions	38'8"x38'8"
Foundation	Basement
Bedrooms	3
Full Baths	2
Primary Roof Pitch	6:12
Max Ridge Height	23'
Roof Framing	Stick/Truss
Exterior Walls	2x4

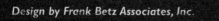

Design by Frank Betz Associates, Inc.

Plan # 98411

BL ML
See order pages
& index for info

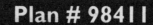

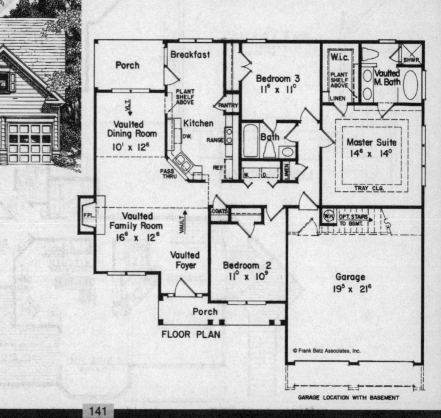

Units	Single
Price Code	A
Total Finished	1,373 sq. ft.
Main Finished	1,373 sq. ft.
Basement Unfinished	1,386 sq. ft.
Dimensions	50'4"x45'
Foundation	Basement, Crawl space
Bedrooms	3
Full Baths	2
Main Ceiling	9'
Primary Roof Pitch	8:12
Max Ridge Height	23'6"
Roof Framing	Stick
Exterior Walls	2x4, 2x6

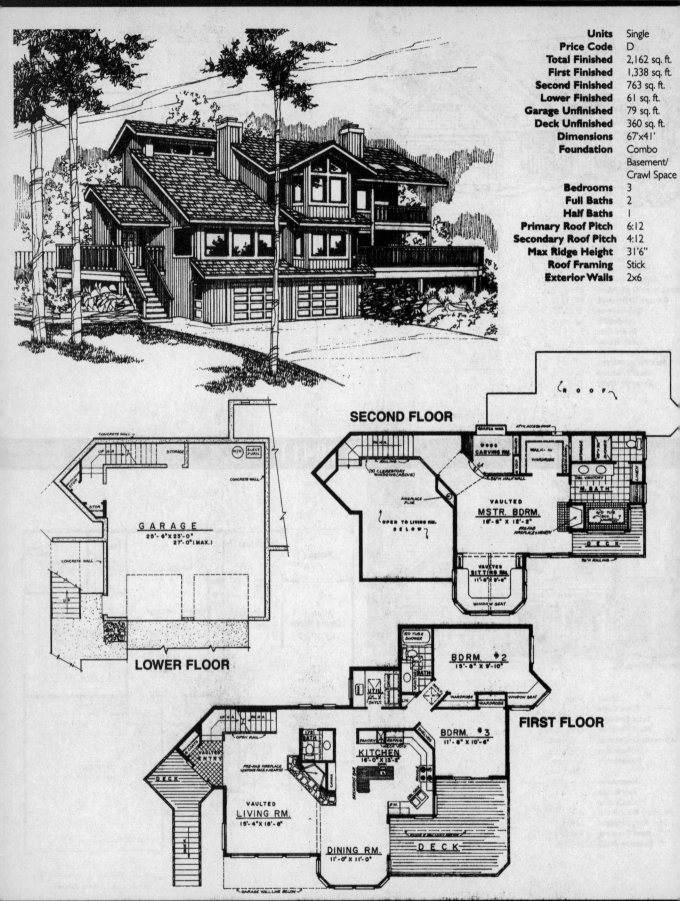

Units	Single
Price Code	D
Total Finished	2,162 sq. ft.
First Finished	1,338 sq. ft.
Second Finished	763 sq. ft.
Lower Finished	61 sq. ft.
Garage Unfinished	79 sq. ft.
Deck Unfinished	360 sq. ft.
Dimensions	67x41'
Foundation	Combo Basement/ Crawl Space
Bedrooms	3
Full Baths	2
Half Baths	1
Primary Roof Pitch	6:12
Secondary Roof Pitch	4:12
Max Ridge Height	31'6"
Roof Framing	Stick
Exterior Walls	2x6

SECOND FLOOR

LOWER FLOOR

FIRST FLOOR

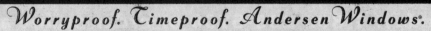

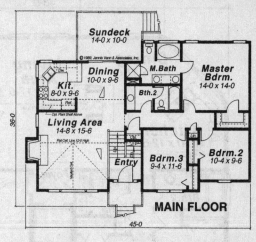

FIRST FLOOR

Units	Single
Price Code	C
Total Finished	1,947 sq. ft.
First Finished	1,947 sq. ft.
Basement Unfinished	1,947 sq. ft.
Dimensions	69'8''x46'
Foundation	Basement
Bedrooms	3
Full Baths	2
Half Baths	1
First Ceiling	8'
Primary Roof Pitch	8:12
Secondary Roof Pitch	8:12
Max Ridge Height	22'4''
Roof Framing	Truss
Exterior Walls	2x4

MAIN FLOOR

LOWER FLOOR

Units	Single
Price Code	A
Total Finished	1,325 sq. ft.
Main Finished	1,269 sq. ft.
Lower Finished	56 sq. ft.
Basement Unfinished	382 sq. ft.
Garage Unfinished	598 sq. ft.
Dimensions	45'x36'
Foundation	Basement
Bedrooms	3
Full Baths	2
Primary Roof Pitch	7:12
Secondary Roof Pitch	6.5:12
Max Ridge Height	16'
Roof Framing	Stick/Truss
Exterior Walls	2x4

ine at

Units	Single
Price Code	A
Total Finished	1,388 sq. ft.
Main Finished	1,388 sq. ft.
Garage Unfinished	400 sq. ft.
Dimensions	48'x46'
Foundation	Crawl space
	Slab
Bedrooms	3
Full Baths	2
Main Ceiling	8'
Primary Roof Pitch	7:12
Secondary Roof Pitch	8:12
Max Ridge Height	18'
Roof Framing	Truss
Exterior Walls	2x4

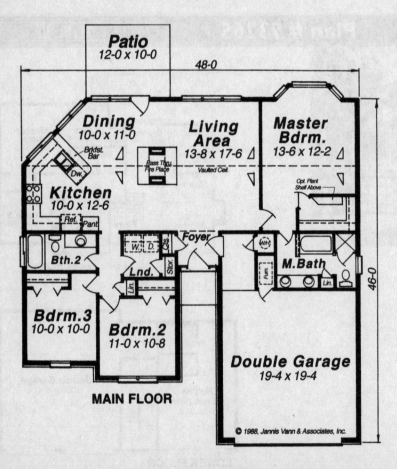

Patio
12-0 x 10-0

48-0

Dining
10-0 x 11-0

Brkfst. Bar

Living Area
13-8 x 17-6

Pass Thru Fire Place

Vaulted Ceil.

Master Bdrm.
13-6 x 12-2

Dw.

Opt. Plant Shelf Above

Kitchen
10-0 x 12-6

Ref.   Pant.

Foyer

W/H

Bth.2

W.   D.   Cls.

Lnd.   Stor.

Lin.

Furn.

M.Bath

Lin.

Bdrm.3
10-0 x 10-0

Bdrm.2
11-0 x 10-8

Double Garage
19-4 x 19-4

46-0

MAIN FLOOR

© 1988, Jannis Vann & Associates, Inc.

Plan # 99424

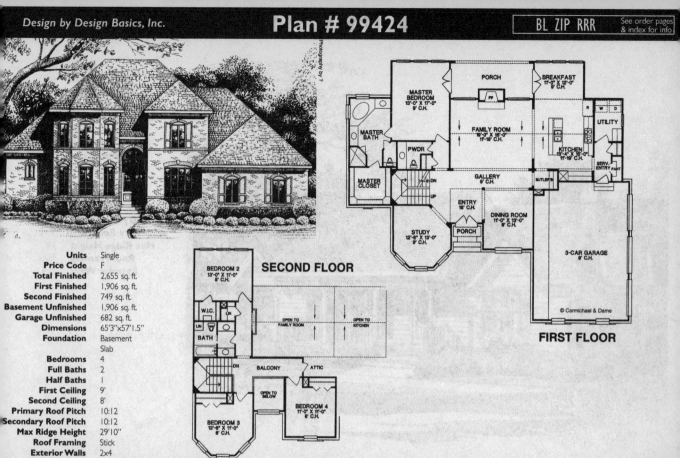

FIRST FLOOR

SECOND FLOOR

© Carmichael & Dame

Units	Single
Price Code	F
Total Finished	2,655 sq. ft.
First Finished	1,906 sq. ft.
Second Finished	749 sq. ft.
Basement Unfinished	1,906 sq. ft.
Garage Unfinished	682 sq. ft.
Dimensions	65'3"x57'1.5"
Foundation	Basement
	Slab
Bedrooms	4
Full Baths	2
Half Baths	1
First Ceiling	9'
Second Ceiling	8'
Primary Roof Pitch	10:12
Secondary Roof Pitch	10:12
Max Ridge Height	29'10"
Roof Framing	Stick
Exterior Walls	2x4

Plan # 91501

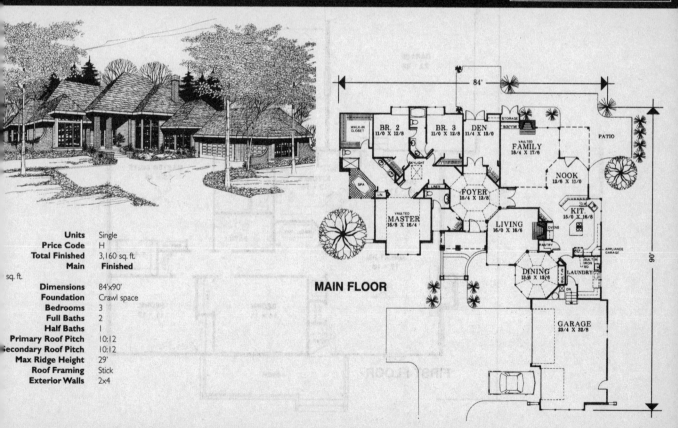

MAIN FLOOR

Units	Single
Price Code	H
Total Finished	3,160 sq. ft.
Main	Finished
sq. ft.	
Dimensions	84'x90'
Foundation	Crawl space
Bedrooms	3
Full Baths	2
Half Baths	1
Primary Roof Pitch	10:12
Secondary Roof Pitch	10:12
Max Ridge Height	29'
Roof Framing	Stick
Exterior Walls	2x4

Units	Single
Price Code	A
Total Finished	1,438 sq. ft.
First Finished	1,438 sq. ft.
Garage Unfinished	486 sq. ft.
Deck Unfinished	282 sq. ft.
Porch Unfinished	126 sq. ft.
Dimensions	54'x57'
Foundation	Crawl space
	Slab
Bedrooms	3
Full Baths	2
Primary Roof Pitch	7:12
Secondary Roof Pitch	3:12
Max Ridge Height	19'
Roof Framing	Stick
Exterior Walls	2x4

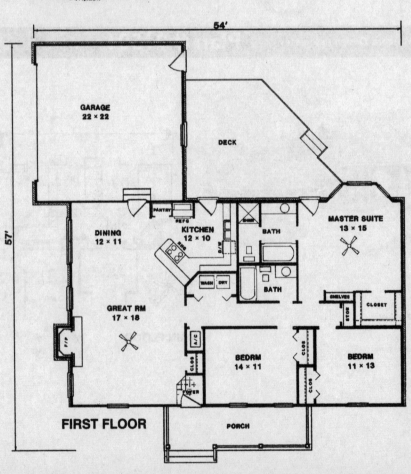

FIRST FLOOR

Units	Single
Price Code	F
Total Finished	2,543 sq. ft.
First Finished	1,406 sq. ft.
Second Finished	1,137 sq. ft.
Bonus Unfinished	96 sq. ft.
Garage Unfinished	792 sq. ft.
Dimensions	62'x51'4''
Foundation	Basement
Bedrooms	4
Full Baths	2
Half Baths	1
First Ceiling	9'
Primary Roof Pitch	8:12
Secondary Roof Pitch	12:12
Max Ridge Height	30'
Roof Framing	Stick
Exterior Walls	2x4

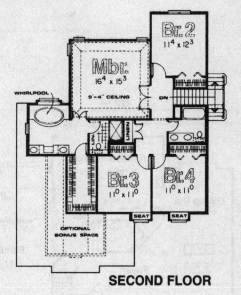

SECOND FLOOR

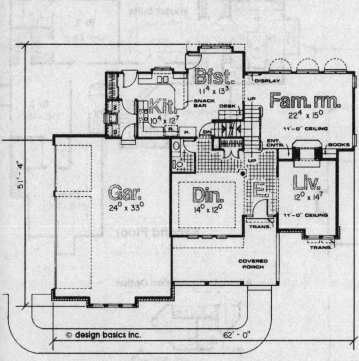

FIRST FLOOR

Worryproof. Timeproof. Andersen Windows.

Built, Backed and Serviced by the Exclusive Perma-Shield® System.

Units	Single
Price Code	H
Total Finished	3,022 sq. ft.
First Finished	1,623 sq. ft.
Second Finished	1,399 sq. ft.
Bonus Unfinished	264 sq. ft.
Basement Unfinished	1,584 sq. ft.
Garage Unfinished	492 sq. ft.
Porch Unfinished	209 sq. ft.
Dimensions	60'4"x57'4"
Foundation	Basement
	Crawl space
	Slab
Bedrooms	3
Full Baths	3
Half Baths	1
First Ceiling	9'
Second Ceiling	8'
Primary Roof Pitch	12:12
Secondary Roof Pitch	3.5:12
Max Ridge Height	35'
Roof Framing	Truss
Exterior Walls	2x4

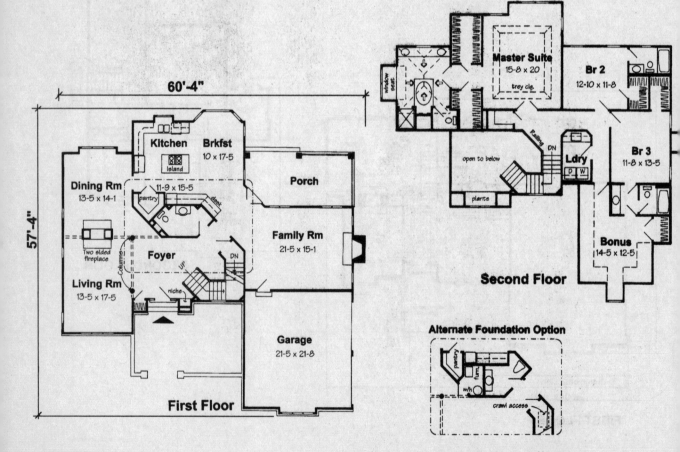

60'-4"

57'-4"

Kitchen

Brkfst
10 x 17-5

Porch

Dining Rm
13-5 x 14-1

11-9 x 15-5
pantry   desk

Two sided fireplace

Foyer

Family Rm
21-5 x 15-1

DN
UP

Living Rm
13-5 x 17-5

niche

Garage
21-5 x 21-8

First Floor

Master Suite
15-8 x 20
trey clg.

Br 2
12-10 x 11-8

window seat

open to below

Railing

DN

Ldry
D W

Br 3
11-8 x 13-5

plants

Bonus
14-5 x 12-5

Second Floor

Alternate Foundation Option

pantry
furn.
w/h
crawl access

Units	Single
Price Code	E
Total Finished	2,285 sq. ft.
First Finished	1,651 sq. ft.
Second Finished	634 sq. ft.
Garage Unfinished	530 sq. ft.
Dimensions	52'x50'
Foundation	Basement
Bedrooms	4
Full Baths	2
Half Baths	1
First Ceiling	8'
Second Ceiling	8'
Primary Roof Pitch	8:12
Secondary Roof Pitch	10:12
Max Ridge Height	27'6"
Roof Framing	Stick
Exterior Walls	2x4

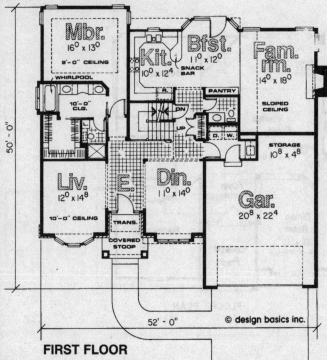

FIRST FLOOR

© design basics inc.

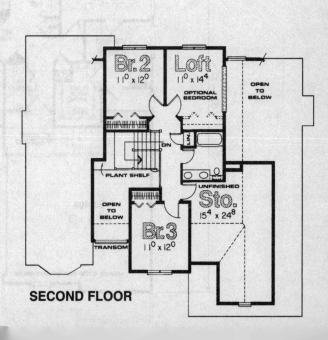

SECOND FLOOR

Units	Single
Price Code	A
Total Finished	1,429 sq. ft.
Main Finished	1,429 sq. ft.
Basement Unfinished	1,472 sq. ft.
Garage Unfinished	438 sq. ft.
Dimensions	49'x53'
Foundation	Basement
	Crawl space
	Slab
Bedrooms	3
Full Baths	2
Main Ceiling	8'
Primary Roof Pitch	10:12
Max Ridge Height	23'
Roof Framing	Stick
Exterior Walls	2x4

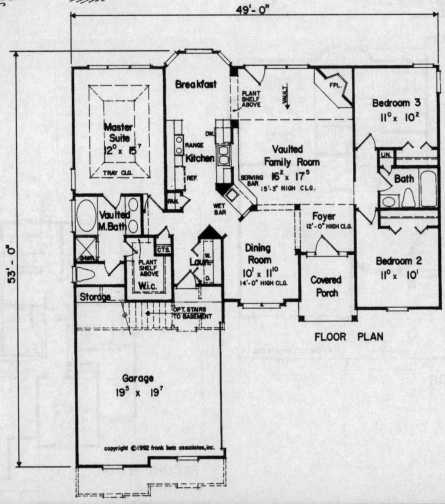

FLOOR PLAN

copyright ©1992 frank betz associates, inc.

Design by Jannis Vann & Associates, Inc.

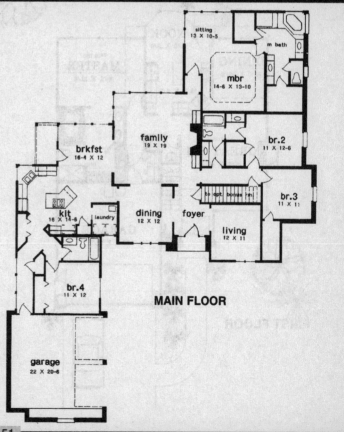

SECOND FLOOR

FIRST FLOOR

Units	Single
Price Code	D
Total Finished	2,038 sq. ft.
First Finished	1,062 sq. ft.
Second Finished	976 sq. ft.
Bonus Unfinished	410 sq. ft.
Basement Unfinished	1,012 sq. ft.
Garage Unfinished	536 sq. ft.
Dimensions	62'x38'
Foundation	Basement
	Crawl space
	Slab
Bedrooms	3
Full Baths	2
Half Baths	1
Primary Roof Pitch	10:12
Max Ridge Height	30'
Roof Framing	Stick
Exterior Walls	2x4

Design by Andy McDonald Design Group

MAIN FLOOR

Units	Single
Price Code	F
Total Finished	2,625 sq. ft.
Main Finished	2,625 sq. ft.
Bonus Unfinished	148 sq. ft.
Garage Unfinished	445 sq. ft.
Porch Unfinished	67 sq. ft.
Dimensions	67'6"x87'1"
Foundation	Slab
Bedrooms	4
Full Baths	3
Max Ridge Height	29'4"
Roof Framing	Stick
Exterior Walls	2x4

Units	Single
Price Code	B
Total Finished	1,707 sq. ft.
First Finished	1,230 sq. ft.
Second Finished	477 sq. ft.
Bonus Unfinished	195 sq. ft.
Dimensions	40'x53'
Foundation	Crawl space
Bedrooms	3
Full Baths	2
Half Baths	1
Primary Roof Pitch	8:12
Max Ridge Height	26'
Roof Framing	Stick
Exterior Walls	2x6

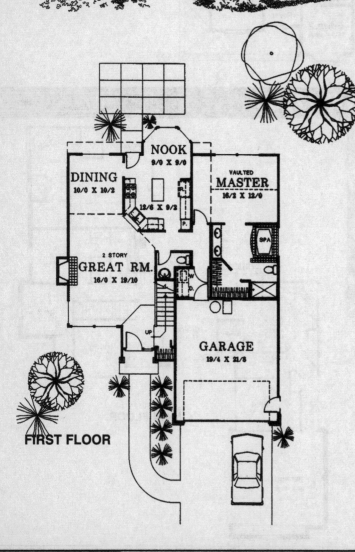

FIRST FLOOR

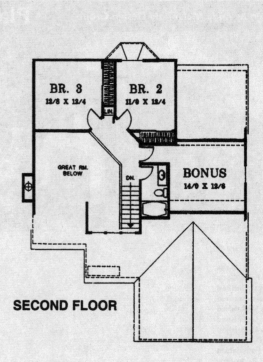

SECOND FLOOR

Units	Single
Price Code	H
Total Finished	3,020 sq. ft.
First Finished	3,020 sq. ft.
Garage Unfinished	469 sq. ft.
Porch Unfinished	95 sq. ft.
Dimensions	78'8''x79'9''
Foundation	Slab
Bedrooms	4
Full Baths	3
Max Ridge Height	30'7''
Roof Framing	Stick
Exterior Walls	2x4

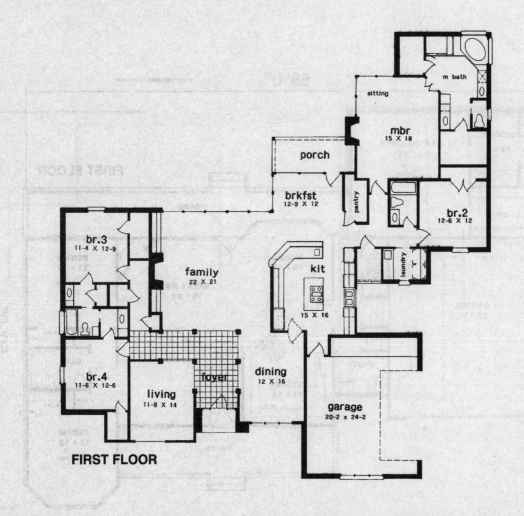

FIRST FLOOR

m bath

sitting

mbr
15 X 18

porch

brkfst
12-9 X 12

pantry

br.2
12-6 X 12

br.3
11-4 X 12-9

family
22 X 21

kit
15 X 16

laundry

br.4
11-6 X 12-6

living
11-8 X 14

foyer

dining
12 X 16

garage
20-2 x 24-2

Units	Single
Price Code	B
Total Finished	1,648 sq. ft
First Finished	1,648 sq. ft
Garage Unfinished	479 sq. ft.
Dimensions	68'x50'
Foundation	Crawl spac Slab
Bedrooms	3
Full Baths	2
Half Baths	I
First Ceiling	9'
Primary Roof Pitch	11:12
Secondary Roof Pitch	8:12
Max Ridge Height	20'
Roof Framing	Stick
Exterior Walls	2x4

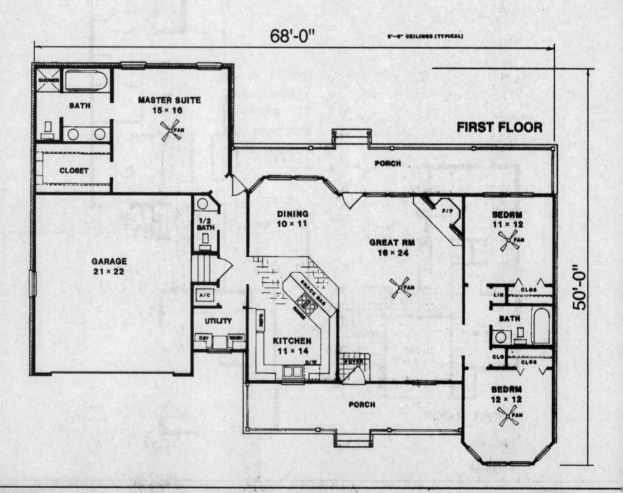

68'-0"   9'-0" CEILINGS (TYPICAL)

FIRST FLOOR

50'-0"

SHOWER
BATH
MASTER SUITE 15 × 16
FAN
CLOSET
PORCH
F/P
BEDRM 11 × 12
FAN
1/2 BATH
DINING 10 × 11
GREAT RM 16 × 24
FAN
LIN   CLOS
GARAGE 21 × 22
A/C
SNACK BAR
RANGE
FAN
BATH
UTILITY
REF
CLO   CLOS
DRY   WASH
KITCHEN 11 × 14
D/W
FOYER
BEDRM 12 × 12
FAN
PORCH

Units	Single
Price Code	B
Total Finished	1,619 sq. ft.
First Finished	1,133 sq. ft.
Second Finished	486 sq. ft.
Bonus Unfinished	134 sq. ft.
Basement Unfinished	1,133 sq. ft.
Garage Unfinished	406 sq. ft.
Dimensions	41'x46'4"
Foundation	Basement, Crawl space
Bedrooms	3
Full Baths	2
Half Baths	1
First Ceiling	8'
Primary Roof Pitch	12:12
Max Ridge Height	26'
Roof Framing	Stick
Exterior Walls	2x4

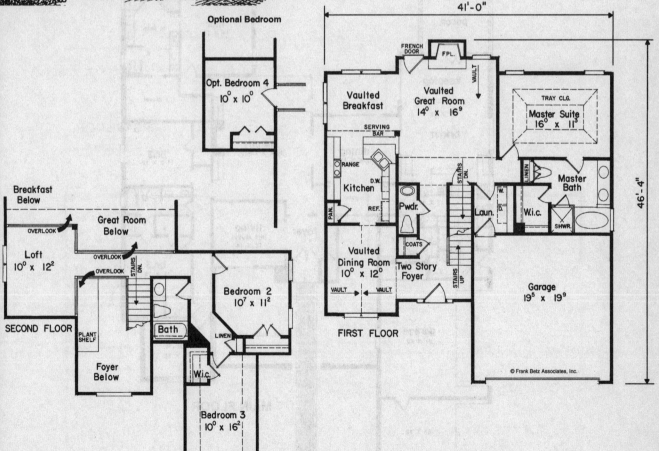

Optional Bedroom

Opt. Bedroom 4
10⁰ x 10⁰

SECOND FLOOR

Breakfast Below

Loft 10⁰ x 12²

Great Room Below

OVERLOOK

OVERLOOK

OVERLOOK

STAIRS DN.

PLANT SHELF

Bath

LINEN

Bedroom 2 10⁷ x 11²

Foyer Below

W.i.c.

Bedroom 3 10⁰ x 16²

41'-0"

FRENCH DOOR   FPL.

Vaulted Breakfast

Vaulted Great Room 14⁰ x 16⁹

VAULT

TRAY CLG.

Master Suite 16⁰ x 11⁵

SERVING BAR

RANGE

D.W.

Kitchen

REF.

PAN.

Pwdr.

COATS

LINEN

Master Bath

W. D.

Laun.

W.i.c.

SHWR.

STAIRS DN.

Vaulted Dining Room 10⁰ x 12⁰

VAULT   VAULT

Two Story Foyer

STAIRS UP

Garage 19⁵ x 19⁹

FIRST FLOOR

46'-4"

© Frank Betz Associates, Inc.

Units	Single
Price Code	I
Total Finished	3,327 sq. ft.
Main Finished	3,327 sq. ft.
Garage Unfinished	818 sq. ft.
Porch Unfinished	155 sq. ft.
Dimensions	72'8"x91'
Foundation	Slab
Bedrooms	4
Full Baths	2
Half Baths	1
Primary Roof Pitch	12:12
Secondary Roof Pitch	18:12
Max Ridge Height	27'1"
Roof Framing	Stick
Exterior Walls	2x4

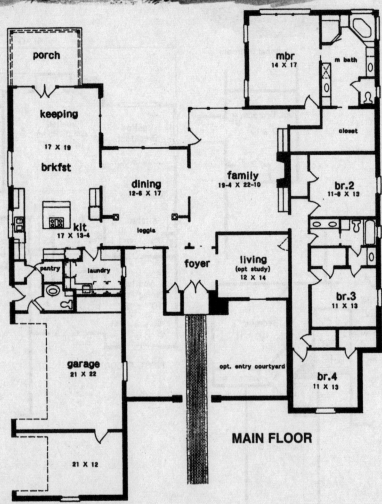

MAIN FLOOR

Units	Single
Price Code	A
Total Finished	1,312 sq. ft.
First Finished	1,312 sq. ft.
Basement Unfinished	1,293 sq. ft.
Garage Unfinished	459 sq. ft.
Deck Unfinished	185 sq. ft.
Porch Unfinished	84 sq. ft.
Dimensions	50'x40'
Foundation	Basement Crawl space Slab
Bedrooms	3
Full Baths	2
First Ceiling	8'
Primary Roof Pitch	6:12
Max Ridge Height	20'
Roof Framing	Stick
Exterior Walls	2x6

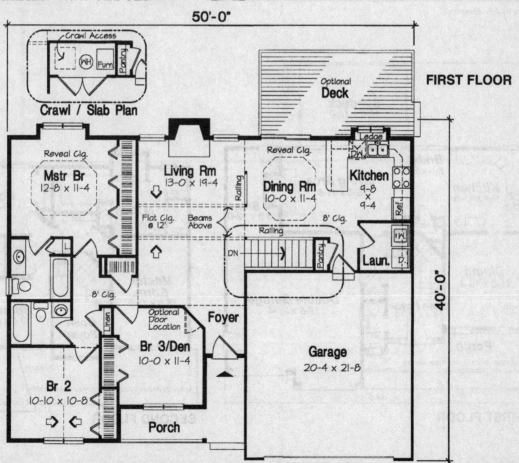

FIRST FLOOR

Crawl / Slab Plan

Crawl Access — WH — Furn — Pantry

50'-0"

40'-0"

Mstr Br 12-8 x 11-4 — Reveal Clg.

Living Rm 13-0 x 19-4

Dining Rm 10-0 x 11-4 — Reveal Clg.

Kitchen 9-8 x 9-4

Optional Deck

Flat Clg. @ 12' — Beams Above

Railing

8' Clg.

DN

Pantry

Laun.

Foyer

Br 3/Den 10-0 x 11-4

Optional Door Location

Linen

Garage 20-4 x 21-8

Br 2 10-10 x 10-8

Porch

157

Photography by John Ehrenclou

Units	Single
Price Code	B
Total Finished	1,683 sq. ft.
First Finished	797 sq. ft.
Second Finished	886 sq. ft.
Basement Unfinished	797 sq. ft.
Garage Unfinished	414 sq. ft.
Deck Unfinished	192 sq. ft.
Porch Unfinished	118 sq. ft.
Dimensions	44'x34'5"
Foundation	Basement
	Crawl space
	Slab
Bedrooms	3
Full Baths	2
Half Baths	1
Primary Roof Pitch	10:12
Secondary Roof Pitch	12:12
Max Ridge Height	29'
Roof Framing	Stick
Exterior Walls	2x4

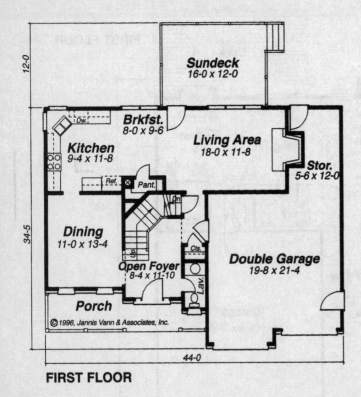

Sundeck 16-0 x 12-0

Brkfst. 8-0 x 9-6

Living Area 18-0 x 11-8

Kitchen 9-4 x 11-8

Stor. 5-6 x 12-0

Dw.

Ref.

Pant.

Dining 11-0 x 13-4

Open Foyer 8-4 x 11-10

Cts.

Lav.

Double Garage 19-8 x 21-4

Porch

© 1996, Jannis Vann & Associates, Inc.

44-0

12-0

34-5

FIRST FLOOR

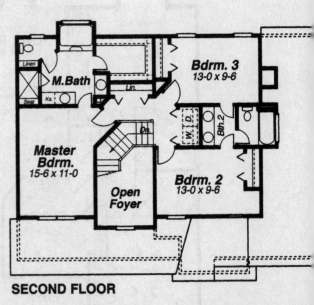

Linen

M. Bath

Lin.

Bdrm. 3 13-0 x 9-6

W.D.

Bth.2

Master Bdrm. 15-6 x 11-0

Open Foyer

Bdrm. 2 13-0 x 9-6

SECOND FLOOR

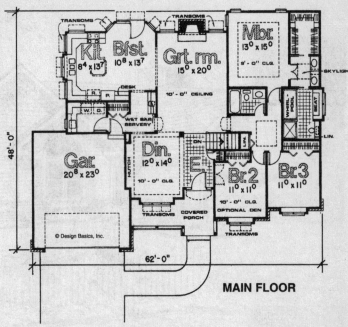

Units	Single
Price Code	C
Total Finished	1,850 sq. ft.
Main Finished	1,850 sq. ft.
Garage Unfinished	487 sq. ft.
Dimensions	62'x48'
Foundation	Basement
Bedrooms	3
Full Baths	2
Main Ceiling	8'
Primary Roof Pitch	6:12
Secondary Roof Pitch	8:12
Max Ridge Height	20'
Roof Framing	Stick
Exterior Walls	2x4

MAIN FLOOR

Mbr. 13⁰ x 15⁰
Kit. 8⁴ x 13⁷
Bfst. 10⁸ x 13⁷
Grt. rm. 15⁰ x 20⁰
Gar. 20⁸ x 23⁰
Din. 12⁰ x 14⁰
Br. 2 11⁰ x 11⁰
Br. 3 11⁰ x 11⁰

© Design Basics, Inc.

62'-0" 48'-0"

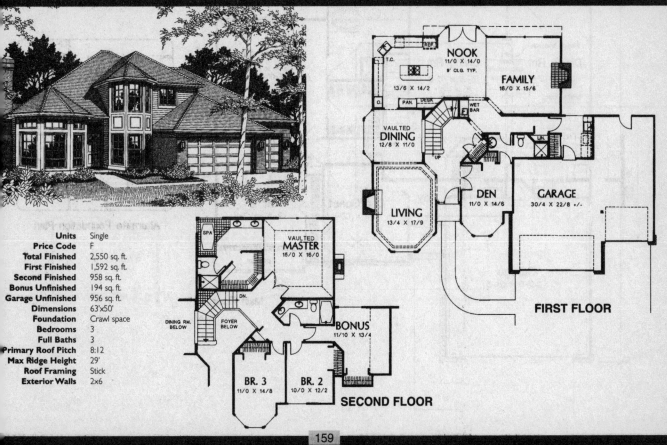

Units	Single
Price Code	F
Total Finished	2,550 sq. ft.
First Finished	1,592 sq. ft.
Second Finished	958 sq. ft.
Bonus Unfinished	194 sq. ft.
Garage Unfinished	956 sq. ft.
Dimensions	63'x50'
Foundation	Crawl space
Bedrooms	3
Full Baths	3
Primary Roof Pitch	8:12
Max Ridge Height	29'
Roof Framing	Stick
Exterior Walls	2x6

NOOK 11/0 X 14/0
FAMILY 16/0 X 15/6
VAULTED DINING 12/8 X 11/0
DEN 11/0 X 14/6
GARAGE 30/4 X 22/8 +/-
LIVING 13/4 X 17/9

FIRST FLOOR

VAULTED MASTER 15/0 X 16/0
BONUS 11/10 X 13/4
BR. 3 11/0 X 14/8
BR. 2 10/0 X 12/2

SECOND FLOOR

159

BL ML ZIP | See order p & index for

Units	Single
Price Code	B
Total Finished	1,625 sq. ft
Main Finished	1,625 sq. ft
Basement Unfinished	1,625 sq. ft
Garage Unfinished	455 sq. ft.
Dimensions	54'x48'4"
Foundation	Basement
	Crawl space
	Slab
Bedrooms	3
Full Baths	2
Main Ceiling	8'-9'
Primary Roof Pitch	8:12
Max Ridge Height	22'
Roof Framing	Stick
Exterior Walls	2x4, 2x6

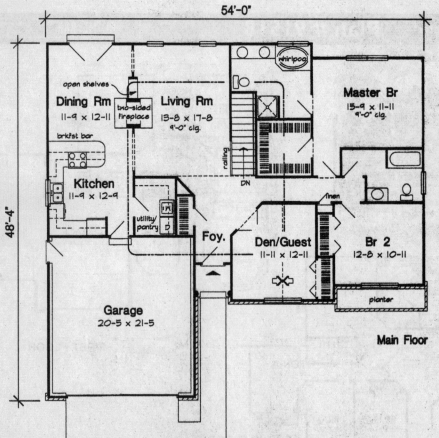

54'-0"

48'-4"

open shelves

Dining Rm
11-9 x 12-11

two-sided fireplace

Living Rm
13-8 x 17-8
9'-0" clg.

whirlpool

Master Br
15-9 x 11-11
9'-0" clg.

brkfst bar

Kitchen
11-9 x 12-9

railing

DN

utility/pantry

Foy.

Den/Guest
11-11 x 12-11

linen

Br 2
12-8 x 10-11

planter

Garage
20-5 x 21-5

Main Floor

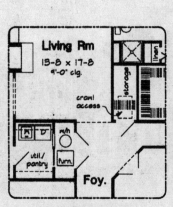

Living Rm
13-8 x 17-8
9'-0" clg.

storage

crawl access

linen

utility/pantry

furn.

Foy.

Alternate Foundation Plan

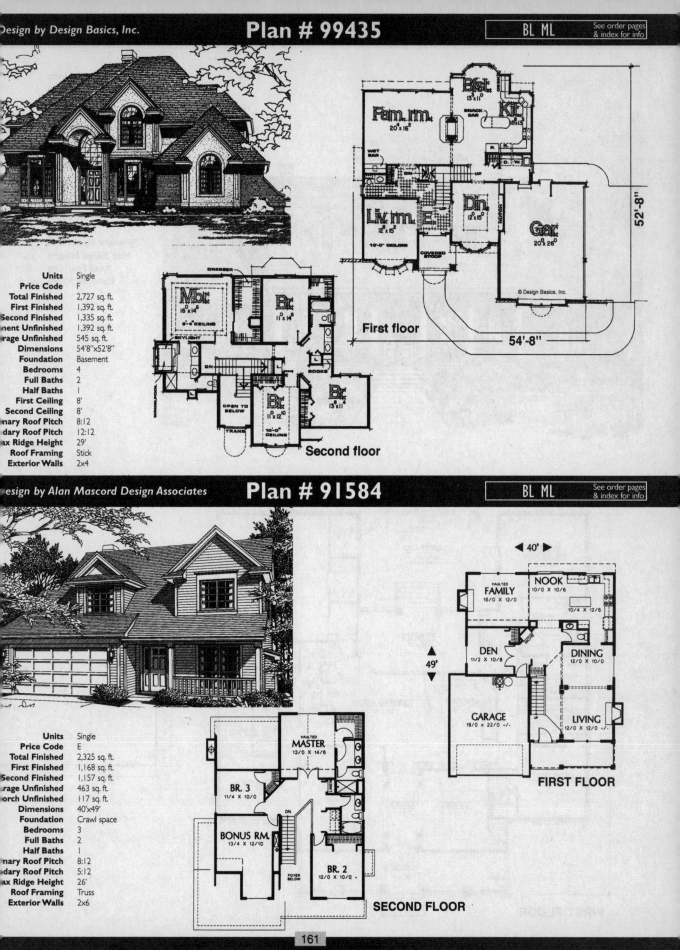

First floor

52'-8"

54'-8"

© Design Basics, Inc.

Second floor

Units	Single
Price Code	F
Total Finished	2,727 sq. ft.
First Finished	1,392 sq. ft.
Second Finished	1,335 sq. ft.
...ment Unfinished	1,392 sq. ft.
...rage Unfinished	545 sq. ft.
Dimensions	54'8"x52'8"
Foundation	Basement
Bedrooms	4
Full Baths	2
Half Baths	1
First Ceiling	8'
Second Ceiling	8'
...mary Roof Pitch	8:12
...dary Roof Pitch	12:12
...ax Ridge Height	29'
Roof Framing	Stick
Exterior Walls	2x4

Fam. rm. 20'x16'

Bfst. 13'x11'

Kit. 18'x13'

Liv. rm. 12'x15'

Dn. 12'x15'

Gar. 20'x26'

WET BAR

SNACK BAR

10'-0" CEILING

COVERED STOOP

Mbr. 16'x14'

Br. 11'x14'

Br. 11'x12'

Br. 13'x11'

DRESSER

SKYLIGHT

8'-4" CEILING

OPEN TO BELOW

TRANS.

BOOKS

10'-0" CEILING

FIRST FLOOR

40'

49'

VAULTED FAMILY 15'0 X 12'0

NOOK 10'0 X 10'6

10'4 X 12'6

DEN 11'2 X 10'8

DINING 12'0 X 10'0

GARAGE 19'0 X 22'0 +/-

LIVING 12'0 X 12'0 +/-

SECOND FLOOR

VAULTED MASTER 13'0 X 14'6

BR. 3 11'4 X 10'0

BONUS RM. 13'4 X 12'10

BR. 2 12'0 X 10'0 +/-

FOYER BELOW

Units	Single
Price Code	E
Total Finished	2,325 sq. ft.
First Finished	1,168 sq. ft.
Second Finished	1,157 sq. ft.
...rage Unfinished	463 sq. ft.
...orch Unfinished	117 sq. ft.
Dimensions	40'x49'
Foundation	Crawl space
Bedrooms	3
Full Baths	2
Half Baths	1
...mary Roof Pitch	8:12
...dary Roof Pitch	5:12
...ax Ridge Height	26'
Roof Framing	Truss
Exterior Walls	2x6

Units	Single
Price Code	H
Total Finished	3,084 s.
First Finished	3,084 s.
Bonus Unfinished	868 sq.
Garage Unfinished	672 sq.
Porch Unfinished	620 sq.
Dimensions	74'x72'
Foundation	Crawl s
	Slab
Bedrooms	4
Full Baths	3
Half Baths	1
Primary Roof Pitch	10:12
Max Ridge Height	30'
Roof Framing	Stick
Exterior Walls	2x6

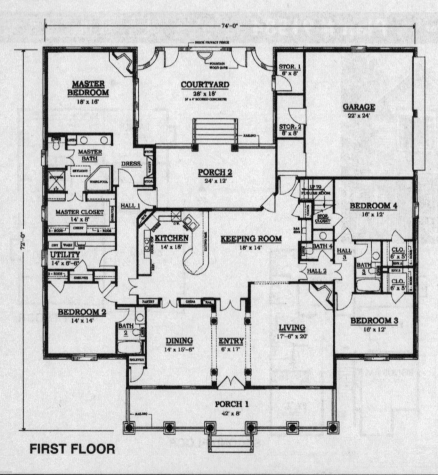

FIRST FLOOR

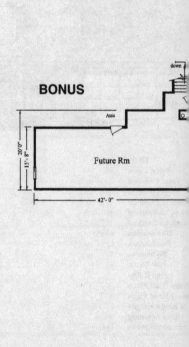

BONUS

Future Rm

Units	Single
Price Code	E
Total Finished	2,419 sq. ft.
First Finished	1,228 sq. ft.
Second Finished	1,191 sq. ft.
Basement Unfinished	1,228 sq. ft.
Garage Unfinished	528 sq. ft.
Dimensions	64'x35'
Foundation	Basement
Bedrooms	4
Full Baths	2
Half Baths	1
First Ceiling	8'6"
Second Ceiling	8'
Primary Roof Pitch	8:12
Secondary Roof Pitch	12:12
Max Ridge Height	30'
Roof Framing	Stick/Truss
Exterior Walls	2x6

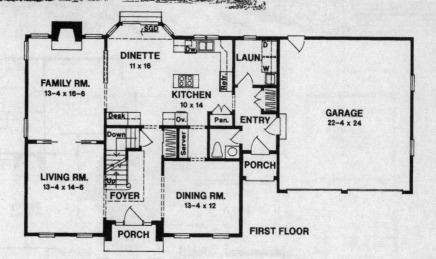

FIRST FLOOR

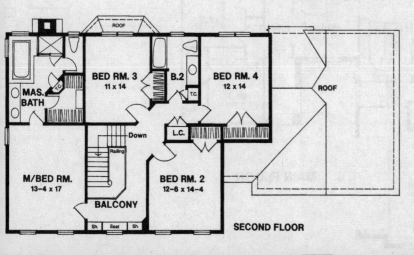

SECOND FLOOR

163

Units	Single
Price Code	E
Total Finished	2,364 sq.
Main Finished	2,364 sq.
Garage Unfinished	494 sq. ft
Dimensions	62'5"x87'
Foundation	Slab
Bedrooms	4
Full Baths	3
Primary Roof Pitch	14.5:12
Secondary Roof Pitch	9:12
Max Ridge Height	21'10"
Roof Framing	Stick
Exterior Walls	2x4

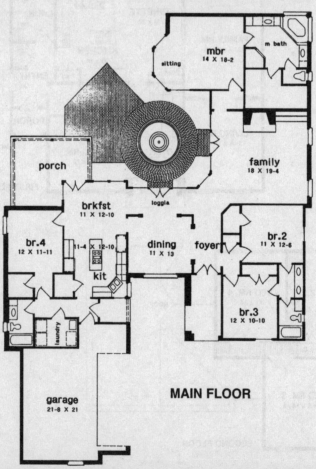

mbr
14 X 18-2

sitting

m bath

family
18 X 19-4

porch

brkfst
11 X 12-10

loggia

br.4
12 X 11-11

11-4 X 12-10

dining
11 X 13

foyer

br.2
11 X 12-6

kit

br.3
12 X 10-10

laundry

garage
21-8 X 21

MAIN FLOOR

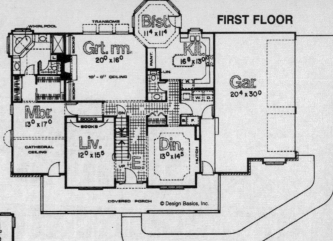

FIRST FLOOR

Grt. rm. 20⁰ x 16⁰   10'-0" CEILING   Bfst. 11⁴ x 11⁴   Kit. 16⁸ x 13⁰⁰

Gar 20⁴ x 30⁰

Mbr. 13⁰ x 17⁰   CATHEDRAL CEILING

Liv. 12⁰ x 15⁵

Din. 13⁰ x 14⁵

COVERED PORCH   © Design Basics, Inc.

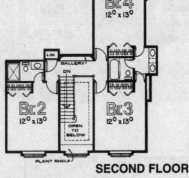

Br. 4 12⁰ x 13⁰

GALLERY DN

Br. 2 12⁰ x 13⁰

OPEN TO BELOW

Br. 3 12⁰ x 13⁰

PLANT SHELF

SECOND FLOOR

Units	Single
Price Code	F
Total Finished	2,695 sq. ft.
First Finished	1,881 sq. ft.
Second Finished	814 sq. ft.
Basement Unfinished	1,020 sq. ft.
Garage Unfinished	534 sq. ft.
Dimensions	72'x45'4"
Foundation	Basement
	Slab
Bedrooms	4
Full Baths	2
Half Baths	1
3/4 Baths	1
Primary Roof Pitch	8:12
Max Ridge Height	27'6"
Roof Framing	Stick
Exterior Walls	2x4

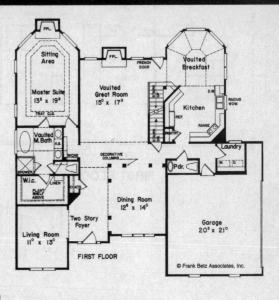

FPL.

Sitting Area

FPL.

FRENCH DOOR

Vaulted Breakfast

Master Suite 13⁵ x 19⁹

TRAY CLG.

Vaulted Great Room 15⁰ x 17³

Kitchen

D.W.

RADIUS WDW.

REF.

RANGE

Vaulted M. Bath

NICHE

DECORATIVE COLUMNS

Laundry

W.   D.

W.i.c.

PLANT SHELF ABOVE

LINEN

COATS

Pdr.

SHOWER

Living Room 11⁰ x 13⁰

Two Story Foyer

Dining Room 12⁶ x 14⁰

Garage 20⁰ x 21⁰

FIRST FLOOR   © Frank Betz Associates, Inc.

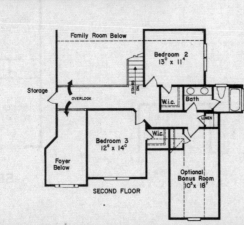

Family Room Below

Bedroom 2 13⁰ x 11⁴

Storage

OVERLOOK

STAIRS

W.i.c.   Bath

Bedroom 3 12⁶ x 14⁰

W.i.c.

LINEN

Foyer Below

Optional Bonus Room 10⁵ x 18⁷

SECOND FLOOR

Units	Single
Price Code	E
Total Finished	2,425 sq. ft.
First Finished	1,796 sq. ft.
Second Finished	629 sq. ft.
Bonus Unfinished	208 sq. ft.
Basement Unfinished	1,796 sq. ft.
Garage Unfinished	588 sq. ft.
Dimensions	54'x53'10"
Foundation	Basement
	Crawl space
	Slab
Bedrooms	3
Full Baths	2
Half Baths	1
First Ceiling	9'
Second Ceiling	8'
Primary Roof Pitch	12:12
Max Ridge Height	32'
Roof Framing	Stick
Exterior Walls	2x4

Units	Single
Price Code	F
Total Finished	2,750 sq.
First Finished	1,700 sq.
Second Finished	1,050 sq.
Basement Unfinished	1,700 sq.
Garage Unfinished	729 sq. ft
Porch Unfinished	384 sq. ft
Dimensions	71'10"x4
Foundation	Basemen Crawlspa Slab
Bedrooms	4
Full Baths	2
Half Baths	1
First Ceiling	9'
Second Ceiling	8'
Tray Ceiling	10'
Primary Roof Pitch	8:12
Secondary Roof Pitch	12:12
Max Ridge Height	29'6"
Roof Framing	Truss
Exterior Walls	2x4

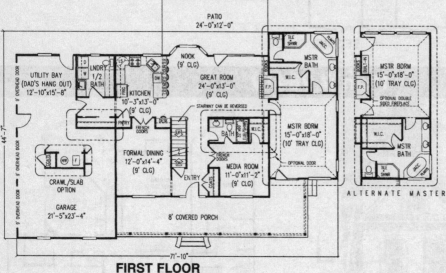

FIRST FLOOR

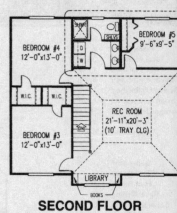

ALTERNATE MASTER

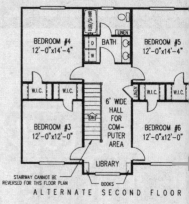

ALTERNATE SECOND FLOOR

ALTERNATE MEDIA ROOM BATH

SECOND FLOOR
ALTERNATE BATH, ETC.

SECOND FLOOR

Units	Single
Price Code	I
Total Finished	3,423 sq. ft.
Main Finished	2,787 sq. ft.
Upper Finished	636 sq. ft.
Garage Unfinished	832 sq. ft.
Deck Unfinished	152 sq. ft.
Porch Unfinished	212 sq. ft.
Dimensions	101'x58"8"
Foundation	Crawl space
	Slab
Bedrooms	4
Full Baths	2
Half Baths	1
Main Ceiling	9'
Upper Ceiling	7'-9'
Primary Roof Pitch	10:12
Secondary Roof Pitch	12:12
Max Ridge Height	28'6"
Roof Framing	Stick
Exterior Walls	2x4

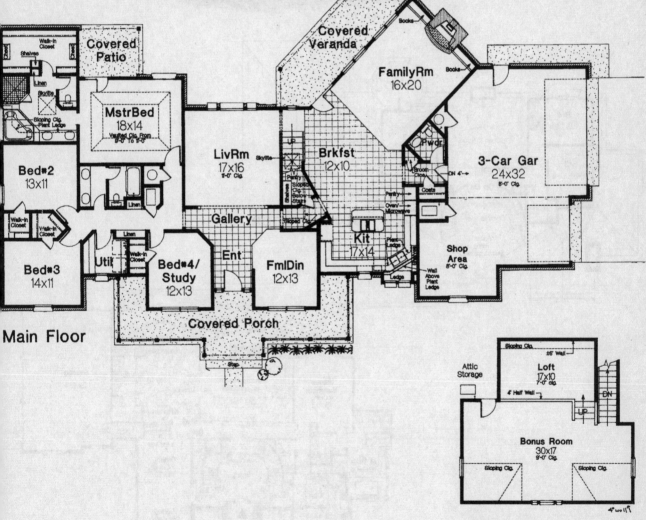

Main Floor

Upper Floor
Optional Bonus Room & Loft

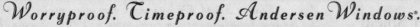

Units	Single
Price Code	1
Total Finished	3,500 sq. ft
First Finished	2,646 sq. ft
Second Finished	854 sq. ft.
Basement Unfinished	2,656 sq. ft
Dimensions	96'8"×57'8
Foundation	Basement
Bedrooms	4
Full Baths	3
Half Baths	1
First Ceiling	8'
Primary Roof Pitch	10:12
Secondary Roof Pitch	11:12
Max Ridge Height	29'8"
Roof Framing	Stick/Truss
Exterior Walls	2x4

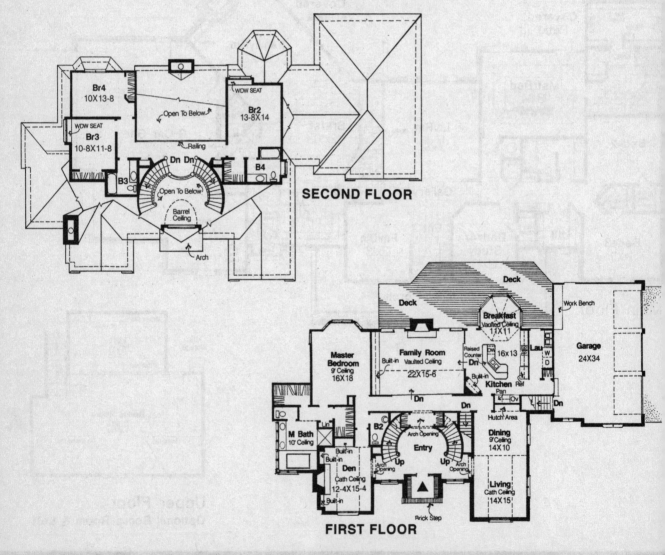

SECOND FLOOR

Br4 10X13-8
WDW SEAT
Open To Below
Br2 13-8X14
WDW SEAT
Br3 10-8X11-8
B3
Dn Dn
B4
Open To Below
Railing
Barrel Ceiling
Arch

FIRST FLOOR

Deck
Deck
Breakfast Vaulted Ceiling 11X11
Work Bench
Garage 24X34
Master Bedroom 9' Ceiling 16X18
Family Room Vaulted Ceiling 22X15-6
Built-in
Built-in
Raised Counter
16x13
Dn
Lau
W D
Ref
Kitchen
Pan
Dn
Ov
M Bath 10' Ceiling
Lin
B2
Built-in
Built-in
Den Cath Ceiling 12-4X15-4
Built-in
Arch Opening
Arch Opening
Entry
Up
Up
Arch Opening
Hutch Area
Dining 9'Ceiling 14X10
Living Cath Ceiling 14X15
Brick Step

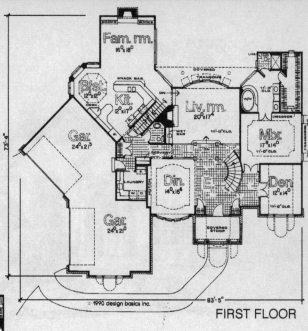

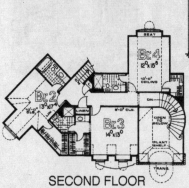

FIRST FLOOR

© 1990 design basics inc.

83'-5"

SECOND FLOOR

Units	Single
Price Code	J
Total Finished	3,689 sq. ft.
First Finished	2,617 sq. ft.
Second Finished	1,072 sq. ft.
Basement Unfinished	2,617 sq. ft.
Garage Unfinished	1,035 sq. ft.
Dimensions	83'5"x73'4"
Foundation	Basement
Bedrooms	4
Full Baths	2
Half Baths	1
3/4 Baths	2
Primary Roof Pitch	10:12
Secondary Roof Pitch	12:12
Max Ridge Height	30'5"
Roof Framing	Stick
Exterior Walls	2x4

Rear Elevation

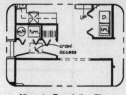
Alternate Foundation Plan

FIRST FLOOR

35'-0"

42'-0"

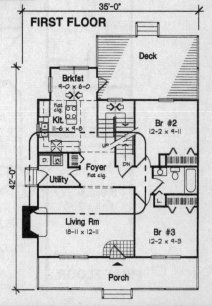

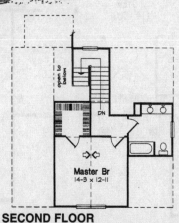

SECOND FLOOR

Units	Single
Price Code	A
Total Finished	1,470 sq. ft.
First Finished	1,035 sq. ft.
Second Finished	435 sq. ft.
Basement Unfinished	1,018 sq. ft.
Deck Unfinished	240 sq. ft.
Porch Unfinished	192 sq. ft.
Dimensions	35'x42'
Foundation	Basement, Crawl space Slab
Bedrooms	3
Full Baths	2
First Ceiling	8'
Second Ceiling	8'
Primary Roof Pitch	12:12
Secondary Roof Pitch	8:12
Max Ridge Height	27'
Roof Framing	Stick
Exterior Walls	2x4, 2x6

Units	Single
Price Code	E
Total Finished	2,437 sq. f
First Finished	2,437 sq. f
Bonus Unfinished	90 sq. ft.
Garage Unfinished	646 sq. ft.
Porch Unfinished	213 sq. ft.
Dimensions	64'9"x59'
Foundation	Basement
	Crawl spa
	Slab
Bedrooms	3
Full Baths	2
First Ceiling	9'
Primary Roof Pitch	9:12
Secondary Roof Pitch	12:12
Max Ridge Height	26'
Roof Framing	Stick
Exterior Walls	2x4

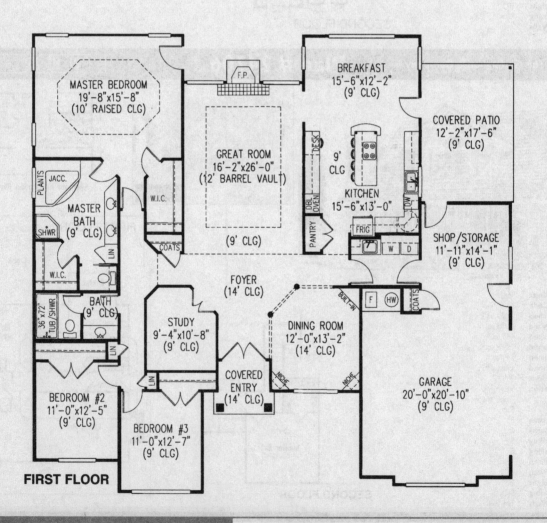

FIRST FLOOR

Units	Single
Price Code	A
Total Finished	1,361 sq. ft.
First Finished	1,361 sq. ft.
Basement Unfinished	1,359 sq. ft.
Garage Unfinished	530 sq. ft.
Dimensions	49'6"x45'4"
Foundation	Basement
	Crawl space
Bedrooms	3
Full Baths	2
First Ceiling	9'
Primary Roof Pitch	10:12
Max Ridge Height	24'8"
Roof Framing	Stick
Exterior Walls	2x4

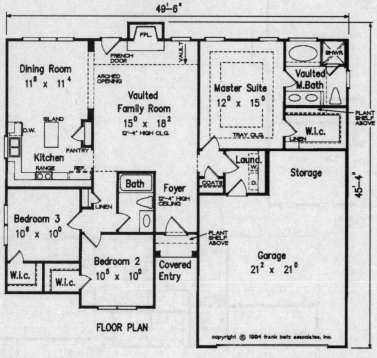

FLOOR PLAN

copyright © 1994 frank betz associates, inc.

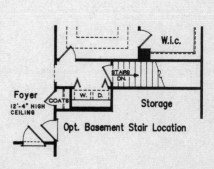

Opt. Basement Stair Location

171

Units	Single
Price Code	E
Total Finished	2,361 sq.
First Finished	1,294 sq.
Second Finished	1,067 sq.
Bonus Unfinished	168 sq. ft
Basement Unfinished	1,294 sq.
Garage Unfinished	252 sq. ft
Dimensions	54'4"×37
Foundation	Basement Crawl spa
Bedrooms	3
Full Baths	3
Primary Roof Pitch	9:12
Max Ridge Height	31'
Roof Framing	Stick
Exterior Walls	2x4

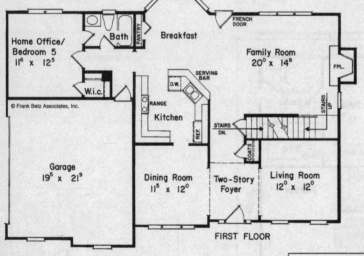

Home Office/ Bedroom 5 11^6 x 12^5

Bath

PANTRY

Breakfast

FRENCH DOOR

Family Room 20^0 x 14^8

FPL.

W.i.c.

© Frank Betz Associates, Inc.

SERVING BAR

D.W.

RANGE

Kitchen

REF.

STAIRS UP

STAIRS DN.

COATS

Garage 19^5 x 21^9

Dining Room 11^5 x 12^0

Two-Story Foyer

Living Room 12^0 x 12^0

FIRST FLOOR

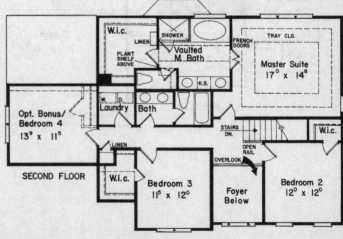

W.i.c.

LINEN

SHOWER

Vaulted M. Bath

FRENCH DOORS

TRAY CLG.

PLANT SHELF ABOVE

K.S.

Master Suite 17^0 x 14^8

Laundry

W. D.

Bath

Opt. Bonus/ Bedroom 4 13^9 x 11^5

STAIRS DN.

W.i.c.

OPEN RAIL

LINEN

OVERLOOK

W.i.c.

Bedroom 3 11^5 x 12^0

Foyer Below

Bedroom 2 12^0 x 12^0

SECOND FLOOR

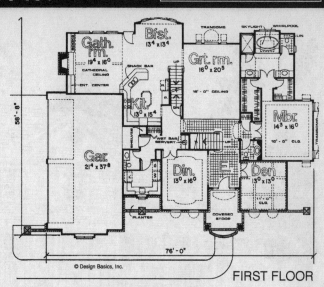

FIRST FLOOR

© Design Basics, Inc.

Units	Single
Price Code	J
Total Finished	3,556 sq. ft.
First Finished	2,555 sq. ft.
Second Finished	1,001 sq. ft.
Garage Unfinished	819 sq. ft.
Dimensions	76'x58'8''
Foundation	Basement
Bedrooms	4
Full Baths	2
Half Baths	2
3/4 Baths	1
Primary Roof Pitch	8:12
Secondary Roof Pitch	12:12
Max Ridge Height	31'7''
Roof Framing	Stick
Exterior Walls	2x4

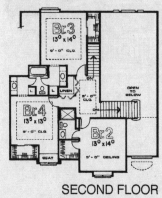

SECOND FLOOR

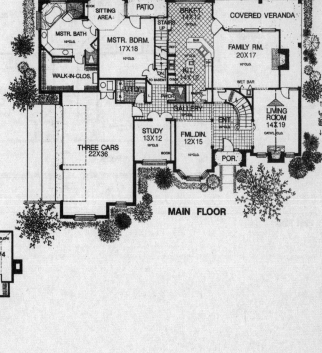

MAIN FLOOR

Units	Single
Price Code	K
Total Finished	3,936 sq. ft.
Main Finished	2,751 sq. ft.
Upper Finished	1,185 sq. ft.
Bonus Unfinished	343 sq. ft.
Garage Unfinished	790 sq. ft.
Deck Unfinished	242 sq. ft.
Porch Unfinished	36 sq. ft.
Dimensions	79'x66'4''
Foundation	Basement
	Slab
Bedrooms	4
Full Baths	3
Half Baths	1
Main Ceiling	10'
Primary Roof Pitch	12:12
Max Ridge Height	35'
Roof Framing	Stick
Exterior Walls	2x4

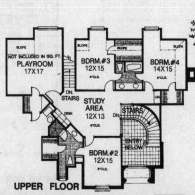

UPPER FLOOR

Units	Single
Price Code	E
Total Finished	2,269 sq. ft.
First Finished	1,279 sq. ft.
Second Finished	990 sq. ft.
Basement Unfinished	1,122 sq. ft.
Garage Unfinished	572 sq. ft.
Porch Unfinished	408 sq. ft.
Dimensions	68'x41'6"
Foundation	Basement
Bedrooms	3
Full Baths	3
First Ceiling	8'
Second Ceiling	8'
Vaulted Ceiling	9'
Tray Ceiling	10'
Primary Roof Pitch	8:12
Secondary Roof Pitch	5:12
Max Ridge Height	28'9"
Roof Framing	Stick
Exterior Walls	2x4

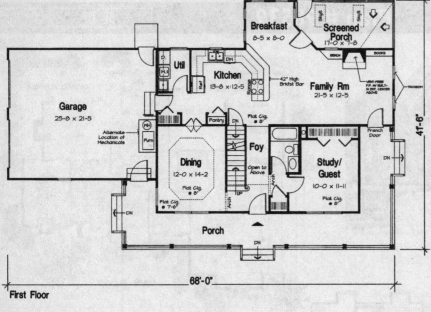

First Floor

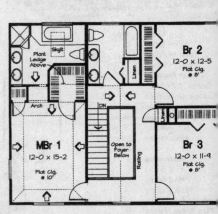

Second Floor

Units	Single
Price Code	B
Total Finished	1,671 sq. ft.
Main Finished	1,671 sq. ft.
Basement Unfinished	1,685 sq. ft.
Garage Unfinished	400 sq. ft.
Dimensions	50'x51'
Foundation	Basement
	Crawl space
	Slab
Bedrooms	3
Full Baths	2
Main Ceiling	9'
Primary Roof Pitch	9:12
Max Ridge Height	22'6"
Roof Framing	Stick
Exterior Walls	2x4

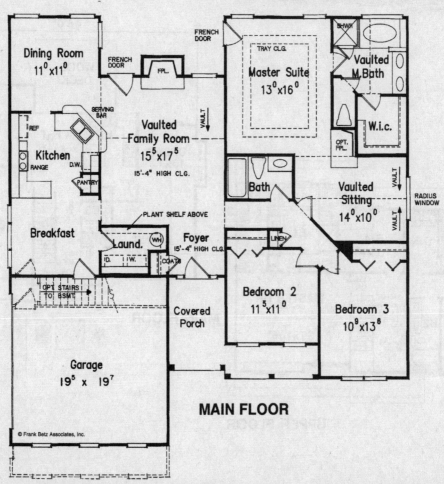

MAIN FLOOR

© Frank Betz Associates, Inc.

Units	Single
Price Code	E
Total Finished	2,314 sq. ft
Main Finished	1,064 sq. ft
Upper Finished	1,250 sq. ft
Basement Unfinished	1,064 sq. ft
Dimensions	48'x36'
Foundation	Basement
Bedrooms	4
Full Baths	2
Half Baths	1
Primary Roof Pitch	12:12
Max Ridge Height	32'
Roof Framing	Truss
Exterior Walls	2x4

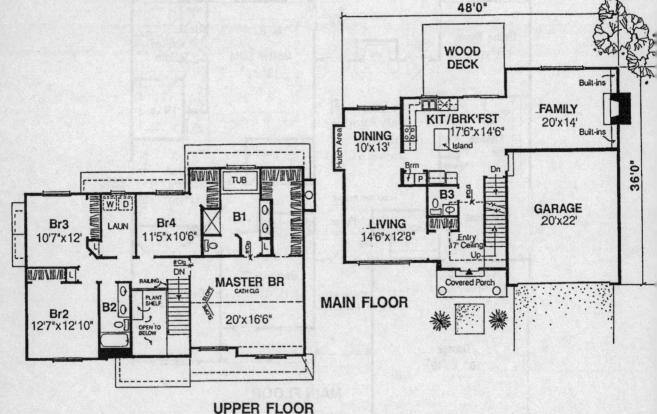

UPPER FLOOR

Br3 10'7"x12'
LAUN
W/D
Br4 11'5"x10'6"
B1
TUB
Br2 12'7"x12'10"
B2
MASTER BR CATH CLG 20'x16'6"
RAILING
PLANT SHELF
OPEN TO BELOW
DN
SLOPE

MAIN FLOOR

48'0"
WOOD DECK
Built-ins
FAMILY 20'x14'
Built-ins
DINING 10'x13'
Hutch Area
KIT/BRK'FST 17'6"x14'6"
Island
Brm
P
B3
Dn
36'0"
LIVING 14'6"x12'8"
Entry 17' Ceiling Up
GARAGE 20'x22'
Covered Porch

Plan # 93437

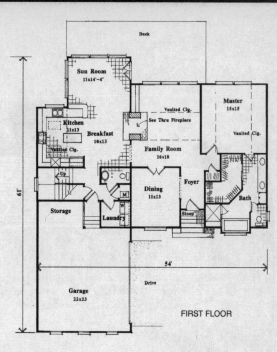

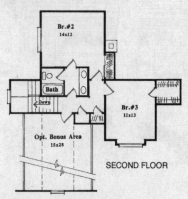

Units	Single
Price Code	D
Total Finished	2,210 sq. ft.
First Finished	1,670 sq. ft.
Second Finished	540 sq. ft.
Bonus Unfinished	455 sq. ft.
Basement Unfinished	1,677 sq. ft.
Garage Unfinished	594 sq. ft.
Dimensions	54'x61'
Foundation	Basement
Bedrooms	3
Full Baths	2
3/4 Baths	1
Primary Roof Pitch	12:12
Secondary Roof Pitch	4:12
Max Ridge Height	31'
Roof Framing	Stick
Exterior Walls	2x4

FIRST FLOOR

SECOND FLOOR

Plan # 97626

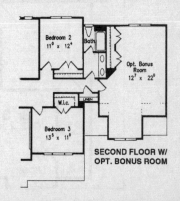

Units	Single
Price Code	E
Total Finished	2,420 sq. ft.
First Finished	1,420 sq. ft.
Second Finished	1,000 sq. ft.
Bonus Unfinished	509 sq. ft.
Basement Unfinished	1,379 sq. ft.
Garage Unfinished	498 sq. ft.
Dimensions	61'x41'
Foundation	Basement, Crawl space
Bedrooms	4
Full Baths	3
First Ceiling	9'
Second Ceiling	8'
Primary Roof Pitch	10:12
Max Ridge Height	33'8"
Roof Framing	Stick
Exterior Walls	2x4

FIRST FLOOR

SECOND FLOOR

SECOND FLOOR W/ OPT. BONUS ROOM

Units	Single
Price Code	A
Total Finished	1,452 sq. ft
Main Finished	1,452 sq. ft
Garage Unfinished	584 sq. ft.
Deck Unfinished	158 sq. ft.
Porch Unfinished	89 sq. ft.
Dimensions	67'x47'
Foundation	Crawl space Slab
Bedrooms	3
Full Baths	2
Main Ceiling	8'
Primary Roof Pitch	8:12
Secondary Roof Pitch	10:12
Max Ridge Height	21'
Roof Framing	Stick
Exterior Walls	2x4

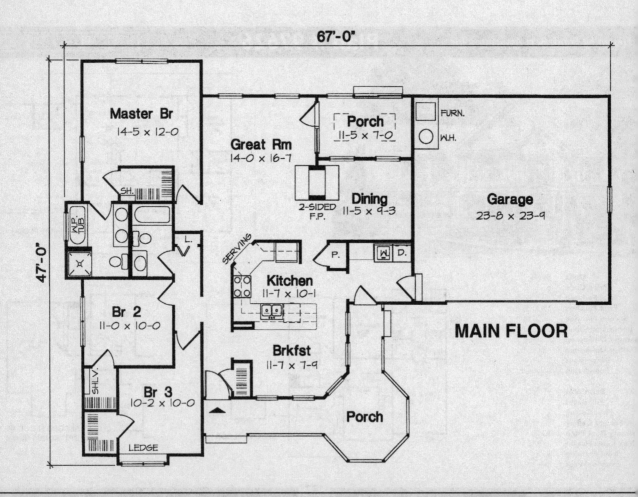

MAIN FLOOR

67'-0"

47'-0"

Master Br 14-5 x 12-0

Great Rm 14-0 x 16-7

Porch 11-5 x 7-0

FURN.

W.H.

Garage 23-8 x 23-9

2-SIDED F.P.

Dining 11-5 x 9-3

Br 2 11-0 x 10-0

SERVING

Kitchen 11-7 x 10-1

Br 3 10-2 x 10-0

Brkfst 11-7 x 7-9

LEDGE

Porch

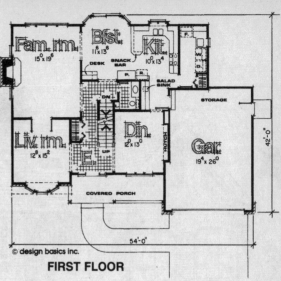

© design basics inc.

FIRST FLOOR

Fam. rm. 15⁰ x 19⁸
Bfst. 11⁸ x 13⁰
Kit. 10⁰ x 13⁴
SNACK BAR
DESK
SALAD SINK
STORAGE
Liv. rm. 12⁰ x 15²
Din. 12⁰ x 13⁰
HUTCH
UP
Gar. 19⁴ x 26⁰
COVERED PORCH
DN
42'-0"
54'-0"

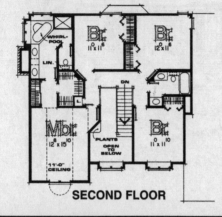

WHIRL-POOL
LIN.
Br. 11⁰ x 11⁸
Br. 12⁸ x 11⁸
DN
Mbr. 12⁸ x 15¹⁰
PLANTS OPEN TO BELOW
Br. 11⁰ x 11⁰
11'-0" CEILING

SECOND FLOOR

Units	Single
Price Code	E
Total Finished	2,387 sq. ft.
First Finished	1,303 sq. ft.
Second Finished	1,084 sq. ft.
Garage Unfinished	505 sq. ft.
Deck Unfinished	124 sq. ft.
Dimensions	42'x54'
Foundation	Basement
Bedrooms	4
Full Baths	2
Half Baths	1
First Ceiling	8'
Second Ceiling	8'
Primary Roof Pitch	6:12
Secondary Roof Pitch	10:12
Max Ridge Height	25'9"
Roof Framing	Stick
Exterior Walls	2x4

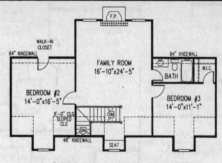

F.P.
WALK-IN CLOSET
84" KNEEWALL
84" KNEEWALL
FAMILY ROOM 16'-10"x24'-5"
BATH
W.I.C.
BEDROOM #2 14'-0"x16'-5"
8'-0" CLG SLOPED CLG
DN
BEDROOM #3 14'-0"x11'-1"
48" KNEEWALL
SEAT

SECOND FLOOR PLAN

COVERED PORCH 46'-0"x8'-0"
BREAKFAST 9'-11"x9'-0"
F.P.
SHWR
DRY WASH
LNDRY
FRZR
DW
KITCHEN 14'-0"x13'-7"
W.I.C.
MASTER BATH
MUD ROOM
FRIG
PNTRY
FAMILY ROOM 16'-10"x18'-1"
GARAGE 23'-5"x23'-5"
FORMAL DINING 14'-0"x11'-0" (TRAY CLG)
UP
FOYER
PWDR
COATS
MASTER BEDROOM 14'-0"x18'-0"
COVERED PORCH 46'-0"x8'-0"

FIRST FLOOR PLAN

Units	Single
Price Code	F
Total Finished	2,544 sq. ft.
First Finished	1,593 sq. ft.
Second Finished	951 sq. ft.
Basement Unfinished	1,421 sq. ft.
Garage Unfinished	572 sq. ft.
Porch Unfinished	693 sq. ft.
Dimensions	82'x46'
Foundation	Basement
	Crawl space
	Slab
Bedrooms	3
Full Baths	2
Half Baths	1
First Ceiling	9'
Second Ceiling	8'
Primary Roof Pitch	12:12
Secondary Roof Pitch	4:12
Max Ridge Height	24'3"
Roof Framing	Truss

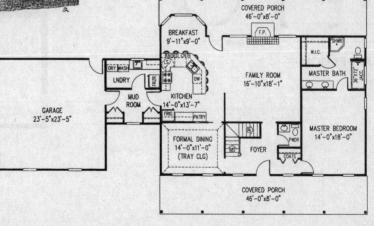

Units	Single
Price Code	C
Total Finished	1,963 sq. ft.
Main Finished	1,963 sq. ft.
Basement Unfinished	1,963 sq. ft.
Dimensions	58'10''x48'8
Foundation	Basement
Bedrooms	3
Full Baths	2
Main Ceiling	9'
Vaulted Ceiling	11'
Max Ridge Height	25'5''
Roof Framing	Truss
Exterior Walls	2x4

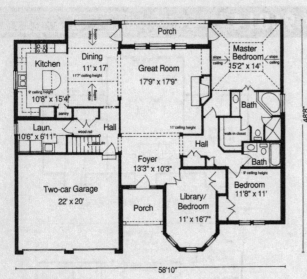

MAIN FLOOR

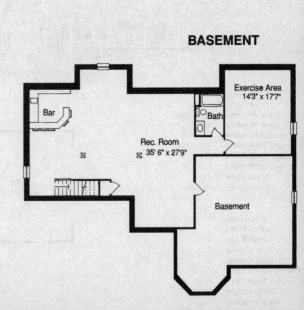

BASEMENT

Units	Single
Price Code	D
Total Finished	2,203 sq. ft.
First Finished	1,169 sq. ft.
Second Finished	1,034 sq. ft.
Bonus Unfinished	347 sq. ft.
Garage Unfinished	561 sq. ft.
Deck Unfinished	217 sq. ft.
Porch Unfinished	312 sq. ft.
Dimensions	55'4"x52'
Foundation	Crawl space
Bedrooms	3
Full Baths	2
Half Baths	1
First Ceiling	9'
Second Ceiling	8'
Primary Roof Pitch	8:12
Secondary Roof Pitch	11:12
Max Ridge Height	32'6"
Roof Framing	Stick
Exterior Walls	2x4

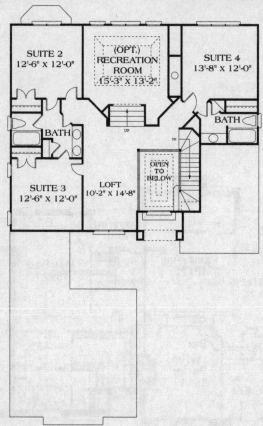

SUITE 2
12'-6" x 12'-0"

(OPT.) RECREATION ROOM
15'-3" x 13'-2"

SUITE 4
13'-8" x 12'-0"

BATH

BATH

UP
DN

SUITE 3
12'-6" x 12'-0"

LOFT
10'-2" x 14'-8"

OPEN TO BELOW

SECOND FLOOR

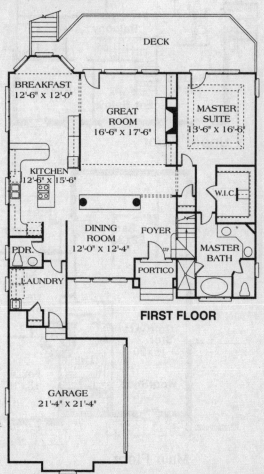

DECK

BREAKFAST
12'-6" x 12'-0"

GREAT ROOM
16'-6" x 17'-6"

MASTER SUITE
13'-6" x 16'-6"

KITCHEN
12'-6" x 15'-6"

W.I.C.

DINING ROOM
12'-0" x 12'-4"

FOYER

PDR.

MASTER BATH

PORTICO

UP

LAUNDRY

FIRST FLOOR

GARAGE
21'-4" x 21'-4"

BL ZIP
See order pa
& index for in

Units	Single
Price Code	I
Total Finished	3,335 sq. ft.
Main Finished	2,432 sq. ft.
Upper Finished	903 sq. ft.
Basement Unfinished	2,432 sq. ft.
Garage Unfinished	742 sq. ft.
Deck Unfinished	222 sq. ft.
Porch Unfinished	91 sq. ft.
Dimensions	90'x45'4''
Foundation	Basement
	Crawl space
	Slab
Bedrooms	4
Full Baths	2
Half Baths	I
3/4 Baths	I
Main Ceiling	10'
Upper Ceiling	9'
Primary Roof Pitch	12:9
Max Ridge Height	33'
Roof Framing	Stick
Exterior Walls	2x4

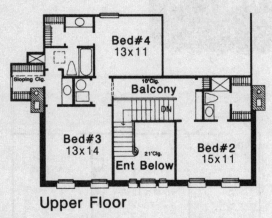

Upper Floor

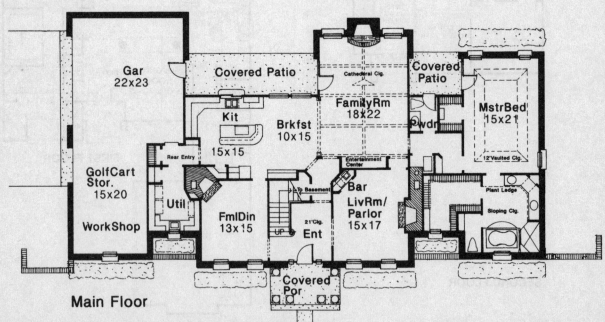

Main Floor

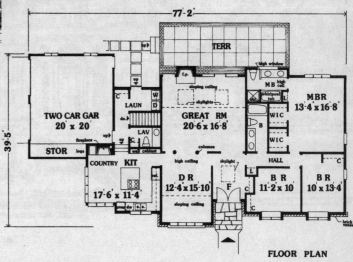

Units	Single
Price Code	C
Total Finished	1,926 sq. ft.
Main Finished	1,926 sq. ft.
Garage Unfinished	453 sq. ft.
Dimensions	77'2"x39'5"
Foundation	Basement
	Crawl space
	Slab
Bedrooms	3
Full Baths	2
Half Baths	1
Primary Roof Pitch	7:12
Max Ridge Height	19'
Roof Framing	Stick
Exterior Walls	2x6

FLOOR PLAN

77'-2'

39'-5'

TERR

TWO CAR GAR 20' x 20'

LAUN

GREAT RM 20-6 x 16-8

MB

MBR 13-4 x 16-8

WIC

WIC

STOR

LAV

HALL

COUNTRY KIT 17'-6 x 11'-4

DR 12-4 x 15-10

BR 11-2 x 10

BR 10 x 13-4

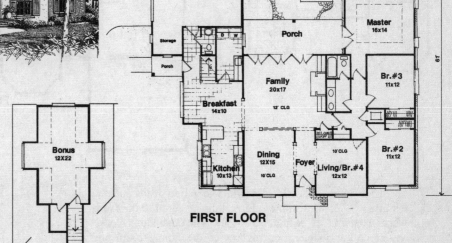

Units	Single
Price Code	D
Total Finished	2,215 sq. ft.
First Finished	2,215 sq. ft.
Bonus Unfinished	253 sq. ft.
Garage Unfinished	491 sq. ft.
Deck Unfinished	33 sq. ft.
Porch Unfinished	195 sq. ft.
Dimensions	63'x61'
Foundation	Slab
Bedrooms	3
Full Baths	2
Half Baths	1
Primary Roof Pitch	10:12
Secondary Roof Pitch	12:12
Max Ridge Height	25'8"
Roof Framing	Stick
Exterior Walls	2x4

Bonus 12X22

BONUS

63'

61'

Drive

Garage 22x22

Porch

Master 16x14

Storage

Porch

Family 20x17 12' CLG

Br.#3 11x12

Breakfast 14x10

Kitchen 10x13

Dining 12X15 10'CLG

Foyer

Living/Br.#4 12x12

Br.#2 11x12

FIRST FLOOR

Units	Single
Price Code	L
Total Finished	4,106 sq. ft.
First Finished	3,027 sq. ft.
Second Finished	1,079 sq. ft.
Basement Unfinished	3,027 sq. ft.
Garage Unfinished	802 sq. ft.
Deck Unfinished	245 sq. ft.
Porch Unfinished	884 sq. ft.
Dimensions	87'4''x80'4''
Foundation	Basement Slab
Bedrooms	4
Full Baths	1
Half Baths	1
3/4 Baths	2
Primary Roof Pitch	10:12
Max Ridge Height	38'
Roof Framing	Truss
Exterior Walls	2x6

SECOND FLOOR

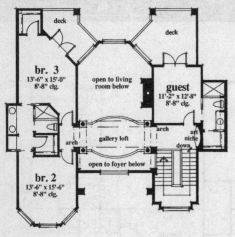

FIRST FLOOR

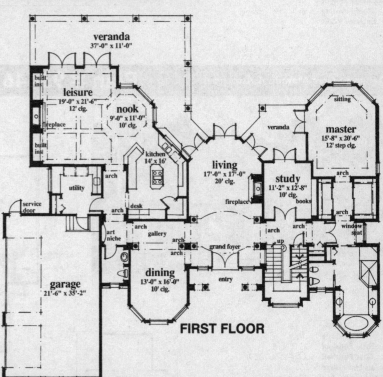

This traditional elevation features stucco and stone for a warm, elegant feel. Round columns grace the double door covered entryway. The living room features a warming fireplace, a two-story ceiling and bayed glass doors to the rear yard. The gallery leads past the formal dining room to the family areas. The open kitchen easily serves the dining room and family nook. A gallery catwalk overlooks the two-story living room and foyer.

Photography by John Ehrenclou

Units	Single
Price Code	D
Total Finished	2,083 sq. ft.
First Finished	1,113 sq. ft.
Second Finished	970 sq. ft.
Basement Unfinished	1,113 sq. ft.
Garage Unfinished	480 sq. ft.
Deck Unfinished	330 sq. ft.
Porch Unfinished	581 sq. ft.
Dimensions	74'x41'6"
Foundation	Basement
	Crawl space
	Slab
Bedrooms	3
Full Baths	2
Half Baths	1
First Ceiling	8'
Second Ceiling	8'
Primary Roof Pitch	8:12
Secondary Roof Pitch	12:12
Max Ridge Height	28'6"
Roof Framing	Stick
Exterior Walls	2x4, 2x6

Rear Elevation

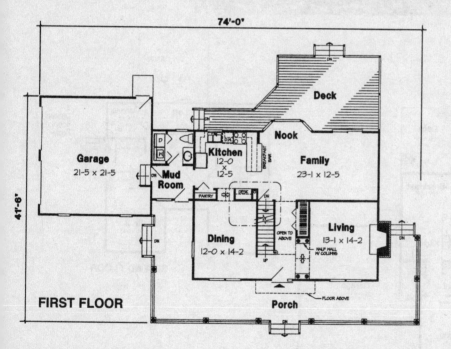

FIRST FLOOR

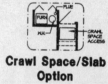
Crawl Space/Slab Option

SECOND FLOOR

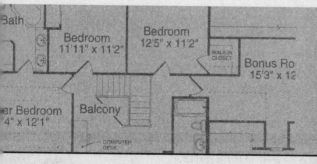

Picture a porch swing, cozy rocking chairs and a pitcher of lemonade on this country porch. The living room includes a fireplace and the dining room has direct access to the kitchen. The U-shaped kitchen includes a breakfast bar, built-in pantry and a double sink. A mudroom entry will help keep the dirt from muddy shoes away from the rest of the house. A convenient laundry area is close at hand in the half-bath off the mudroom. The sunny breakfast nook is a cheerful place to start your day, and the expansive family room has direct access to the rear wood deck.

HOME PLAN OF THE YEAR

Units	Single
Price Code	D
Total Finished	2,226 sq. ft.
First Finished	1,368 sq. ft.
Second Finished	858 sq. ft.
Bonus Unfinished	550 sq. ft.
Basement Unfinished	1,243 sq. ft.
Garage Unfinished	523 sq. ft.
Deck Unfinished	120 sq. ft.
Porch Unfinished	282 sq. ft.
Dimensions	62'x50'
Foundation	Basement
	Crawl space
	Slab
Bedrooms	4
Full Baths	2
Half Baths	1
First Ceiling	8'
Second Ceiling	8'
Primary Roof Pitch	10:12
Secondary Roof Pitch	12:12
Max Ridge Height	27'6"
Roof Framing	Truss
Exterior Walls	2x4

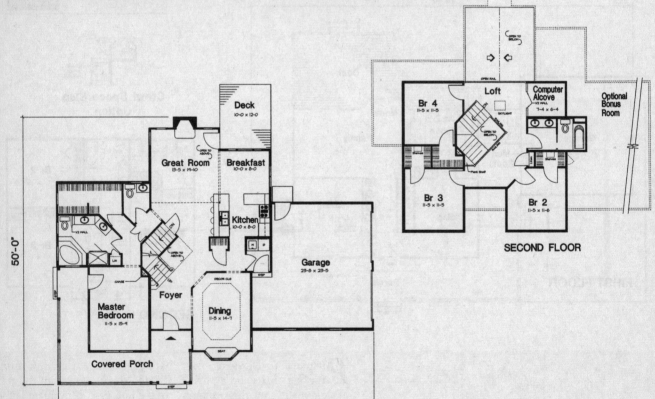

FIRST FLOOR

SECOND FLOOR

Units	Single
Price Code	E
Total Finished	2,453 sq. ft.
First Finished	1,411 sq. ft.
Second Finished	1,042 sq. ft.
Bonus Unfinished	331 sq. ft.
Basement Unfinished	1,411 sq. ft.
Garage Unfinished	473 sq. ft.
Porch Unfinished	42 sq. ft.
Dimensions	53'x42'
Foundation	Basement
Bedrooms	3
Full Baths	2
Half Baths	1
First Ceiling	8'
Second Ceiling	8'
Vaulted Ceiling	17'
Primary Roof Pitch	12:8
Max Ridge Height	29'6"
Roof Framing	Truss
Exterior Walls	2x4

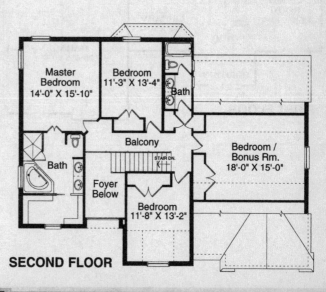

FIRST FLOOR

53'-0"

42'-0"

Deck

Breakfast
13'-6" X 10'-2"

Great Room
16'-2" X 19'-3"

Kitchen
16'-2" X 11'-6"

Bath

Laun.

Hall

STAIR UP   STAIR DN.

Library
11'-0" X 12'-8"

Foyer

Dining Room
11'-8" X 15'-6"

Garage
20'-8" X 28'-4"

Porch

SECOND FLOOR

Master Bedroom
14'-0" X 15'-10"

Bedroom
11'-3" X 13'-4"

Bath

Balcony

STAIR DN.

Bath

Foyer Below

Bedroom
11'-8" X 13'-2"

Bedroom / Bonus Rm.
18'-0" X 15'-0"

187

Units	Single
Price Code	F
Total Finished	2,741 sq. ft.
First Finished	1,426 sq. ft.
Second Finished	1,315 sq. ft.
Bonus Unfinished	200 sq. ft.
Garage Unfinished	508 sq. ft.
Deck Unfinished	223 sq. ft.
Porch Unfinished	44 sq. ft.
Dimensions	57'8"x44'10"
Foundation	Crawl space
Bedrooms	4
Full Baths	2
Half Baths	1
Primary Roof Pitch	10:12
Secondary Roof Pitch	12:12
Max Ridge Height	35'
Roof Framing	Stick
Exterior Walls	2x4

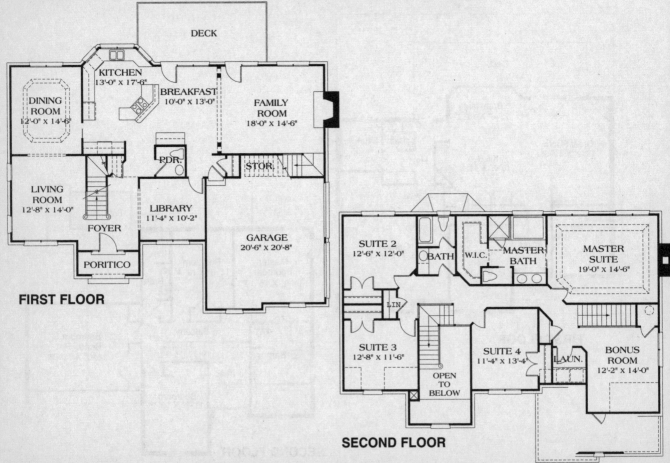

FIRST FLOOR

DECK

KITCHEN 13'-0" x 17'-6"

BREAKFAST 10'-0" x 13'-0"

FAMILY ROOM 18'-0" x 14'-6"

DINING ROOM 12'-0" x 14'-6"

PDR.

STOR.

LIVING ROOM 12'-8" x 14'-0"

FOYER

LIBRARY 11'-4" x 10'-2"

GARAGE 20'-6" x 20'-8"

PORITICO

SECOND FLOOR

SUITE 2 12'-6" x 12'-0"

BATH

W.I.C.

MASTER BATH

MASTER SUITE 19'-0" x 14'-6"

LIN.

SUITE 3 12'-8" x 11'-6"

OPEN TO BELOW

SUITE 4 11'-4" x 13'-4"

LAUN.

BONUS ROOM 12'-2" x 14'-0"

Units	Single
Price Code	C
Total Finished	1,845 sq. ft.
Main Finished	1,845 sq. ft.
Bonus Unfinished	409 sq. ft.
Basement Unfinished	1,845 sq. ft.
Garage Unfinished	529 sq. ft.
Dimensions	56'x60'
Foundation	Basement, Crawl space
Bedrooms	3
Full Baths	2
Half Baths	1
Main Ceiling	9'
Primary Roof Pitch	10:12
Max Ridge Height	26'6''
Roof Framing	Stick
Exterior Walls	2x4

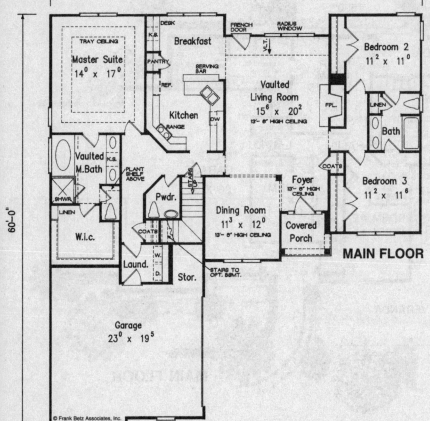

56'-0"

60'-0"

TRAY CEILING
Master Suite 14⁰ x 17⁰

DESK
K.S.
Breakfast
PANTRY
REF.
SERVING BAR
Kitchen
RANGE
DW

FRENCH DOOR
RADIUS WINDOW
V.L.T.

Bedroom 2 11² x 11⁰

Vaulted Living Room 15⁶ x 20²
13'- 6" HIGH CEILING

FPL.

LINEN
Bath

Vaulted M.Bath
K.S.
PLANT SHELF ABOVE
SHWR.
LINEN
W.i.c.

STAIRS

Pwdr.

Dining Room 11³ x 12⁰
13'- 6" HIGH CEILING

Foyer
13'- 6" HIGH CEILING

COATS

Bedroom 3 11² x 11⁶

COATS

Covered Porch

MAIN FLOOR

Laund.
W. D.
Stor.

STAIRS TO OPT. BSMT.

Garage 23⁰ x 19⁵

© Frank Betz Associates, Inc.

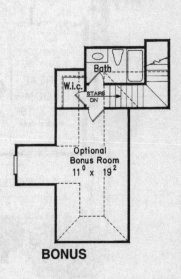

Bath
W.i.c.
STAIRS DN

Optional Bonus Room 11⁰ x 19²

BONUS

Units	Single
Price Code	C
Total Finished	1,830 sq. ft.
Main Finished	1,830 sq. ft.
Garage Unfinished	759 sq. ft.
Deck Unfinished	315 sq. ft.
Porch Unfinished	390 sq. ft.
Dimensions	75'x52'3''
Foundation	Basement
	Crawl space
	Slab
Bedrooms	3
Full Baths	2
Primary Roof Pitch	9:12
Max Ridge Height	27'3''
Roof Framing	Stick
Exterior Walls	2x4

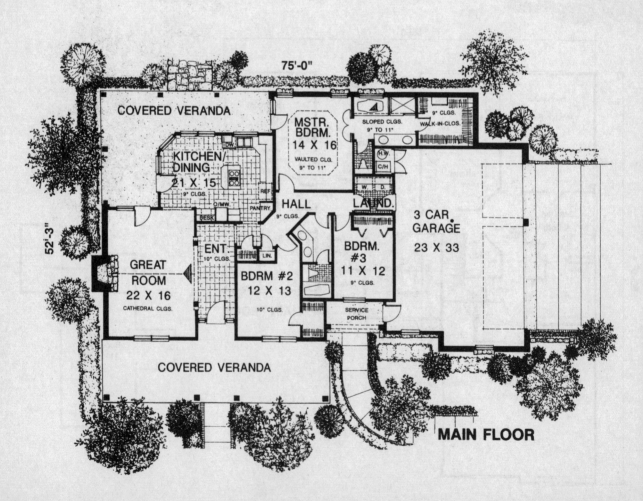

75'-0"

52'-3"

COVERED VERANDA

KITCHEN/
DINING
21 X 15
9" CLGS.

MSTR.
BDRM.
14 X 16
VAULTED CLG.
9" TO 11"

SLOPED CLGS.
9" TO 11"

9" CLGS.

WALK-IN-CLOS.

H.W.
C/H

W. D.

HALL
9" CLGS.

LAUND.

3 CAR
GARAGE
23 X 33

REF
O/MW.
PANTRY
DESK

ENT
10" CLGS.

LIN.

BDRM.
#3
11 X 12
9" CLGS.

GREAT
ROOM
22 X 16
CATHEDRAL CLGS.

BDRM #2
12 X 13
10" CLGS.

SERVICE
PORCH

COVERED VERANDA

MAIN FLOOR

Units	Single
Price Code	D
Total Finished	2,081 sq. ft.
Main Finished	2,081 sq. ft.
Garage Unfinished	422 sq. ft.
Porch Unfinished	240 sq. ft.
Dimensions	55'x57'10"
Foundation	Slab
Bedrooms	3
Full Baths	3
Primary Roof Pitch	9:12
Max Ridge Height	24'6"
Roof Framing	Stick
Exterior Walls	2x4

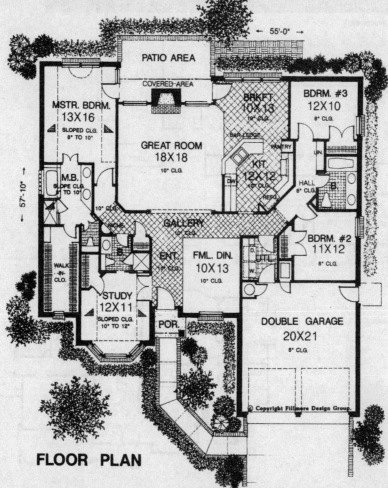

FLOOR PLAN

← 55'-0" →

57'-10"

PATIO AREA

COVERED AREA

MSTR. BDRM.
13X16
SLOPED CLG.
8' TO 10'

M.B.
SLOPE CLG.
8' TO 10'

WALK-IN-CLO.

STUDY
12X11
SLOPED CLG.
10' TO 12'

GREAT ROOM
18X18
10' CLG.

GALLERY
10' CLG.

ENT
10' CLG.

FML. DIN.
10X13
10' CLG.

POR.

BRKFT.
10X13
10' CLG.

KIT
12X12
10' CLG.

BAR LEDGE

PANTRY

DW

REFG.

BDRM. #3
12X10
8' CLG.

LIN.

HALL
8' CLG.

B

BDRM. #2
11X12
8' CLG.

UTL.

D.

W.

DOUBLE GARAGE
20X21
8' CLG.

© Copyright Fillmore Design Group

Photography supplied by The Meredith Corporation

Units	Single
Price Code	L
Total Finished	5,288 sq. ft.
Main Finished	3,322 sq. ft.
Upper Finished	1,966 sq. ft.
Basement Unfinished	3,275 sq. ft.
Garage Unfinished	774 sq. ft.
Deck Unfinished	1,476 sq. ft.
Porch Unfinished	338 sq. ft.
Dimensions	111'2"x66'2"
Foundation	Basement
Bedrooms	4
Full Baths	4
Half Baths	1
Main Ceiling	8'-10'
Upper Ceiling	8'
Primary Roof Pitch	12:12
Secondary Roof Pitch	6:12
Max Ridge Height	35'
Roof Framing	Stick
Exterior Walls	2x6

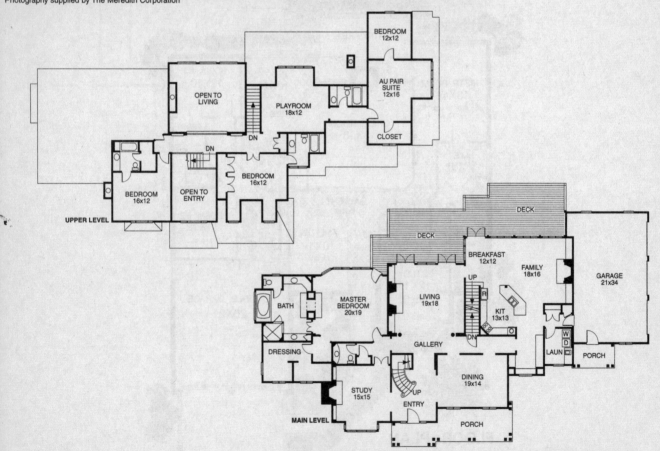

Units	Single
Price Code	G
Total Finished	2,780 sq. ft.
First Finished	2,145 sq. ft.
Second Finished	635 sq. ft.
Garage Unfinished	470 sq. ft.
Dimensions	60'x44'
Foundation	Crawl space
Bedrooms	3
Full Baths	2
Half Baths	1
First Ceiling	8'
Second Ceiling	8'
Primary Roof Pitch	12:12
Secondary Roof Pitch	3.5:12
Max Ridge Height	26'6''
Roof Framing	Stick
Exterior Walls	2x6

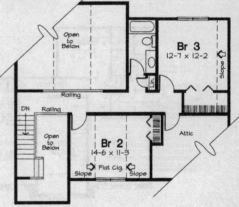

SECOND FLOOR PLAN

Br 3
12-7 x 12-2

Br 2
14-6 x 11-3

Open to Below

Railing

Slope

Flat Clg.

Attic

DN

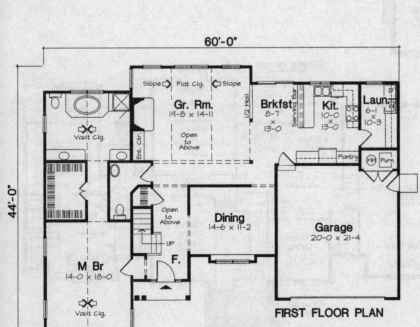

60'-0"

44'-0"

Gr. Rm.
19-8 x 14-11

Brkfst
8-7 x 13-0

Kit.
10-0 x 13-0

Laun.
6-1 x 10-3

M Br
14-0 x 18-0

Dining
14-6 x 11-2

Garage
20-0 x 21-4

Vault Clg.

Open to Above

Pantry

Furn

UP

FIRST FLOOR PLAN

Units	Single
Price Code	K
Total Finished	3,783 sq. ft.
Lower Finished	2,804 sq. ft.
Upper Finished	979 sq. ft.
Basement Unfinished	2,804 sq. ft.
Garage Unfinished	802 sq. ft.
Dimensions	98'x45'10''
Foundation	Basement
	Slab
Bedrooms	4
Full Baths	3
Half Baths	1
Primary Roof Pitch	10:12
Max Ridge Height	32'
Roof Framing	Stick
Exterior Walls	2x4

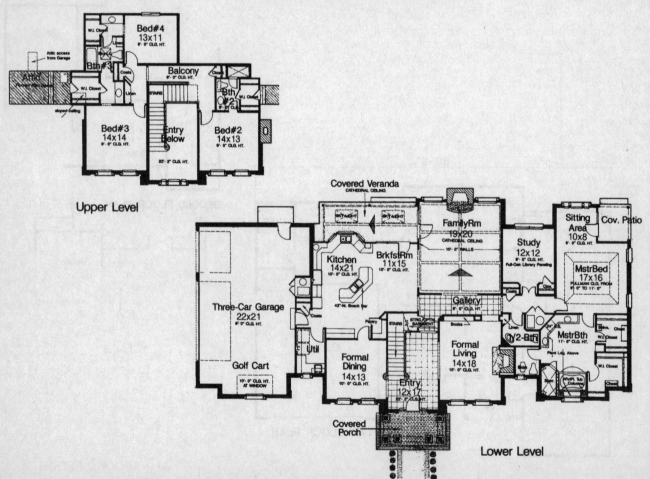

Upper Level

Lower Level

Units	Single
Price Code	F
Total Finished	2,561 sq. ft.
First Finished	1,331 sq. ft.
Second Finished	1,230 sq. ft.
Garage Unfinished	514 sq. ft.
Porch Unfinished	321 sq. ft.
Dimensions	36'x67'6''
Foundation	Crawl space
Bedrooms	4
Full Baths	2
Half Baths	1
First Ceiling	10'
Second Ceiling	9'
Primary Roof Pitch	8:12
Secondary Roof Pitch	14:12
Max Ridge Height	34'6''
Roof Framing	Truss
Exterior Walls	2x4

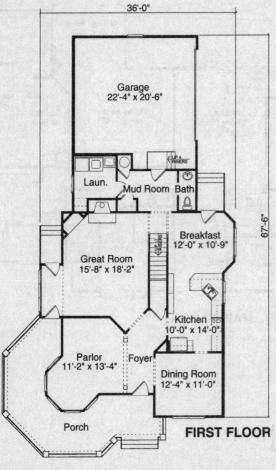

FIRST FLOOR

36'-0"

67'-6"

Garage
22'-4" x 20'-6"

Laun.

Mud Room   Bath

UP 4 RISERS

Breakfast
12'-0" x 10'-9"

Great Room
15'-8" x 18'-2"

Kitchen
10'-0" x 14'-0"

Parlor
11'-2" x 13'-4"

Foyer

Dining Room
12'-4" x 11'-0"

Porch

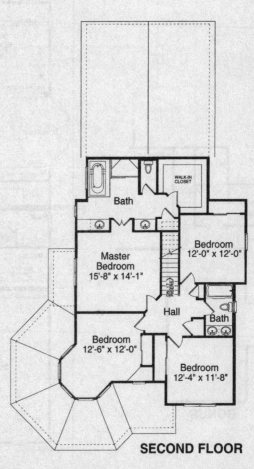

SECOND FLOOR

WALK-IN CLOSET

Bath

Master Bedroom
15'-8" x 14'-1"

Bedroom
12'-0" x 12'-0"

Hall

Bath

Bedroom
12'-6" x 12'-0"

Bedroom
12'-4" x 11'-8"

Units	Single
Price Code	F
Total Finished	2,622 sq. ft.
Main Finished	2,622 sq. ft.
Bonus Unfinished	478 sq. ft.
Basement Unfinished	2,622 sq. ft.
Garage Unfinished	506 sq. ft.
Dimensions	69'x71'4"
Foundation	Basement, Crawl space
Bedrooms	3
Full Baths	2
Half Baths	1
Main Ceiling	9'
Primary Roof Pitch	12:12
Max Ridge Height	29'4"
Roof Framing	Stick
Exterior Walls	2x4

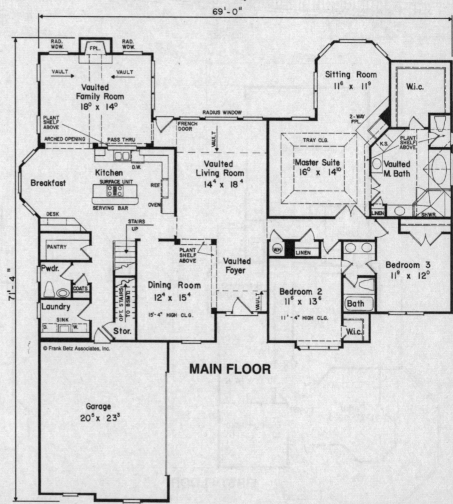

MAIN FLOOR

BONUS

© Frank Betz Associates, Inc.

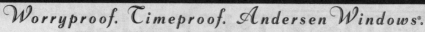

Units	Single
Price Code	E
Total Finished	2,500 sq. ft.
Main Finished	2,500 sq. ft.
Garage Unfinished	659 sq. ft.
Porch Unfinished	33 sq. ft.
Dimensions	73'x65'10''
Foundation	Crawl space
Bedrooms	3
Full Baths	2
Half Baths	1
First Ceiling	9'
Vaulted Ceiling	13'
Primary Roof Pitch	10:12
Secondary Roof Pitch	13:12
Max Ridge Height	30'
Roof Framing	Stick
Exterior Walls	2x4

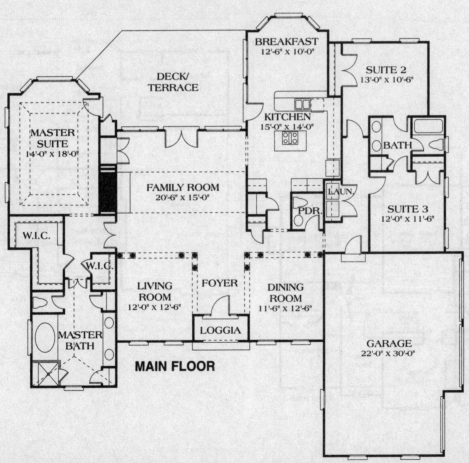

BREAKFAST 12'-6" x 10'-0"

DECK/TERRACE

SUITE 2 13'-0" x 10'-6"

KITCHEN 15'-0" x 14'-0"

MASTER SUITE 14'-0" x 18'-0"

BATH

FAMILY ROOM 20'-6" x 15'-0"

LAUN.

PDR.

SUITE 3 12'-0" x 11'-6"

W.I.C.

W.I.C.

LIVING ROOM 12'-0" x 12'-6"

FOYER

DINING ROOM 11'-6" x 12'-6"

LOGGIA

MASTER BATH

GARAGE 22'-0" x 30'-0"

MAIN FLOOR

Units	Single
Price Code	I
Total Finished	3,378 sq. ft.
First Finished	1,615 sq. ft.
Second Finished	1,763 sq. ft.
Basement Unfinished	1,615 sq. ft.
Garage Unfinished	747 sq. ft.
Dimensions	61'3"x49'
Foundation	Basement, Crawl space
Bedrooms	5
Full Baths	4
Half Baths	I
Primary Roof Pitch	9:12
Max Ridge Height	36'8"
Roof Framing	Stick
Exterior Walls	2x4

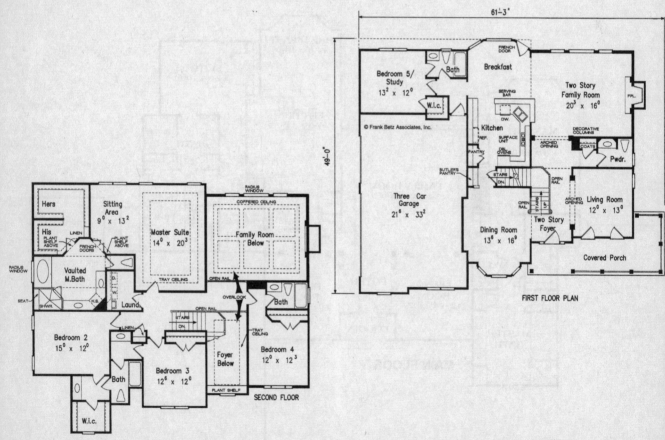

FIRST FLOOR PLAN

SECOND FLOOR

otography supplied by The Meredith Corporation

Units	Single
Price Code	L
Total Finished	4,292 sq. ft.
Main Finished	1,928 sq. ft.
Upper Finished	2,364 sq. ft.
Garage Unfinished	578 sq. ft.
Deck Unfinished	532 sq. ft.
Porch Unfinished	329 sq. ft.
Dimensions	64'x65'
Foundation	Crawl space
Bedrooms	5
Full Baths	4
Half Baths	1
Main Ceiling	9'
Upper Ceiling	8'
Primary Roof Pitch	6:12
Secondary Roof Pitch	4:12
Max Ridge Height	33'
Roof Framing	Stick
Exterior Walls	2x4

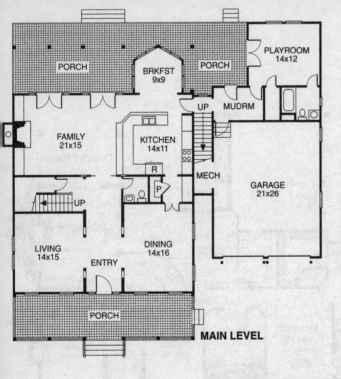

MAIN LEVEL

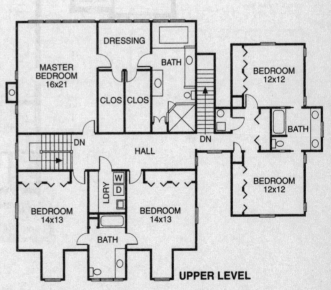

UPPER LEVEL

Units	Single
Price Code	H
Total Finished	3,110 sq. ft.
Main Finished	2,190 sq. ft.
Upper Finished	920 sq. ft.
Garage Unfinished	624 sq. ft.
Dimensions	69'x53'10''
Foundation	Basement
	Slab
Bedrooms	4
Full Baths	3
Half Baths	1
Main Ceiling	10'
Upper Ceiling	8'
Primary Roof Pitch	12:12
Max Ridge Height	29'
Roof Framing	Stick
Exterior Walls	2x4

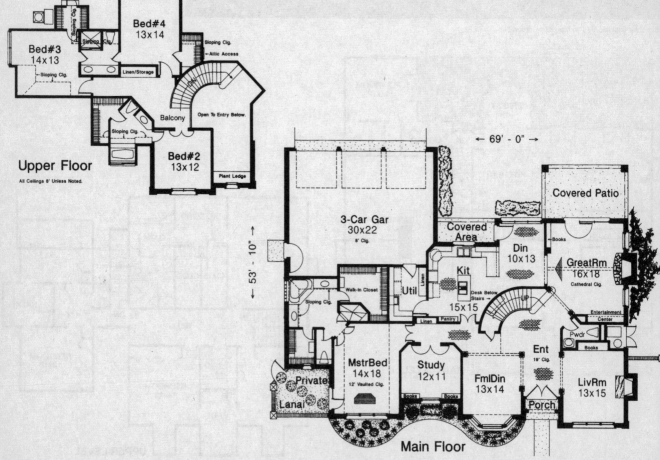

Upper Floor

Main Floor

Units	Single
Price Code	J
Total Finished	3,525 sq. ft.
First Finished	1,786 sq. ft.
Second Finished	1,739 sq. ft.
Basement Unfinished	1,786 sq. ft.
Garage Unfinished	704 sq. ft.
Dimensions	59'x53'
Foundation	Basement, Crawl space
Bedrooms	5
Full Baths	4
Half Baths	1
First Ceiling	9'
Second Ceiling	9'
Primary Roof Pitch	10:12
Max Ridge Height	35'
Roof Framing	Stick
Exterior Walls	2x4

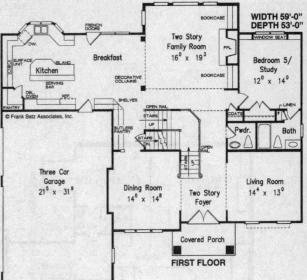

WIDTH 59'-0"
DEPTH 53'-0"

FIRST FLOOR

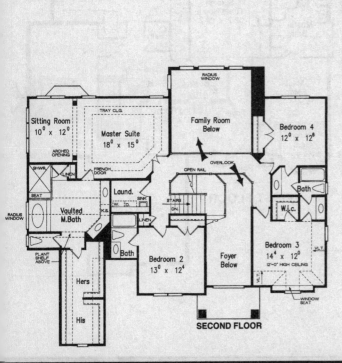

SECOND FLOOR

Units	Single
Price Code	1
Total Finished	3,378 sq. ft.
First Finished	2,323 sq. ft.
Second Finished	1,055 sq. ft.
Basement Unfinished	2,323 sq. ft.
Garage Unfinished	840 sq. ft.
Deck Unfinished	134 sq. ft.
Porch Unfinished	55 sq. ft.
Dimensions	63'8"x78'
Foundation	Basement
Bedrooms	4
Full Baths	3
Half Baths	1
First Ceiling	9'
Second Ceiling	8'
Vaulted Ceiling	18'7"
Primary Roof Pitch	8:12
Secondary Roof Pitch	12:12
Max Ridge Height	32'3"
Roof Framing	Stick
Exterior Walls	2x4

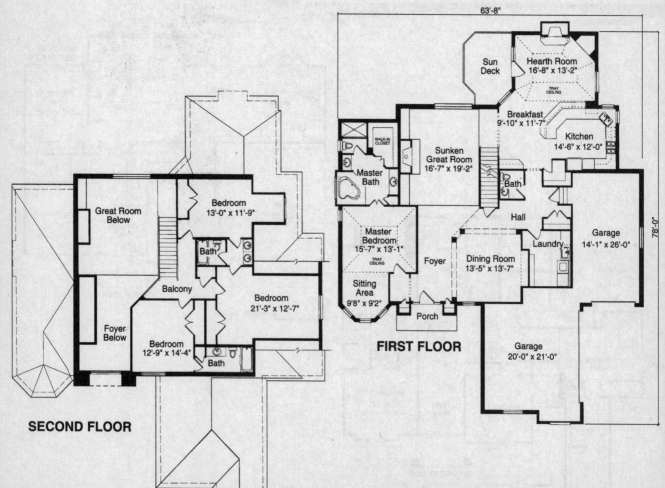

SECOND FLOOR

FIRST FLOOR

Units	Single
Price Code	D
Total Finished	2,051 sq. ft.
Main Finished	2,051 sq. ft.
Basement Unfinished	2,051 sq. ft.
Garage Unfinished	441 sq. ft.
Dimensions	56'x60'6''
Foundation	Basement
	Crawl space
	Slab
Bedrooms	3
Full Baths	2
Main Ceiling	9'
Primary Roof Pitch	10:12
Max Ridge Height	27'5''
Roof Framing	Stick
Exterior Walls	2x4

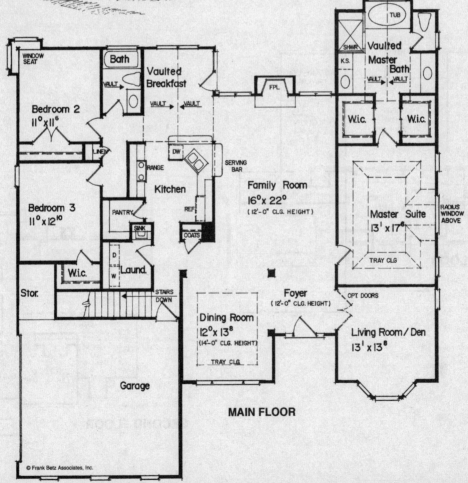

MAIN FLOOR

© Frank Betz Associates, Inc.

Units	Single
Price Code	E
Total Finished	2,464 sq. ft.
First Finished	1,737 sq. ft.
Second Finished	727 sq. ft.
Bonus Unfinished	376 sq. ft.
Basement Unfinished	1,737 sq. ft.
Garage Unfinished	534 sq. ft.
Deck Unfinished	210 sq. ft.
Porch Unfinished	33 sq. ft.
Dimensions	65'6"x53'
Foundation	Basement
	Crawl space
Bedrooms	4
Full Baths	2
Half Baths	1
First Ceiling	9'
Second Ceiling	8'
Vaulted Ceiling	18'6"
Tray Ceiling	10'6"
Primary Roof Pitch	10:12
Secondary Roof Pitch	12:12
Max Ridge Height	31'6"
Exterior Walls	2x4

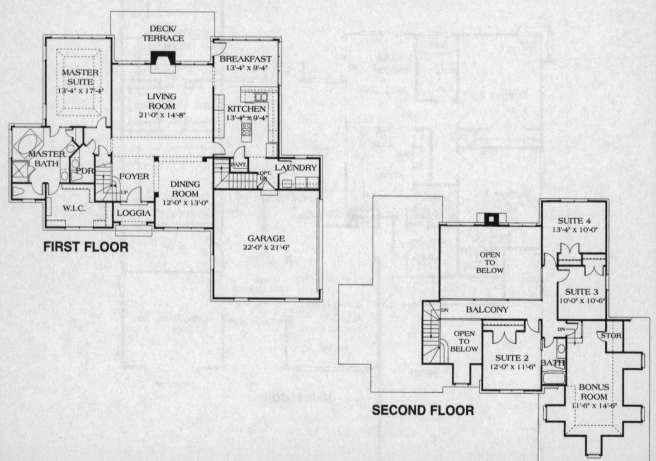

FIRST FLOOR

MASTER SUITE 13'-4" x 17'-4"

DECK/ TERRACE

BREAKFAST 13'-4" x 9'-4"

LIVING ROOM 21'-0" x 14'-8"

KITCHEN 13'-4" x 9'-4"

MASTER BATH

PDR

W.I.C.

FOYER

LOGGIA

DINING ROOM 12'-0" x 13'-0"

PANT.

OPT. DN

LAUNDRY

GARAGE 22'-0" x 21'-6"

SECOND FLOOR

OPEN TO BELOW

SUITE 4 13'-4" x 10'-0"

SUITE 3 10'-0" x 10'-6"

BALCONY

OPEN TO BELOW

SUITE 2 12'-0" x 11'-6"

BATH

STOR

BONUS ROOM 11'-6" x 14'-6"

Units	Single
Price Code	F
Total Finished	2,620 sq. ft.
Main Finished	2,620 sq. ft.
Garage Unfinished	567 sq. ft.
Deck Unfinished	201 sq. ft.
Porch Unfinished	25 sq. ft.
Dimensions	73'x64'
Foundation	Crawl space
	Slab
Bedrooms	4
Full Baths	3
Primary Roof Pitch	12:10
Max Ridge Height	26'6''
Roof Framing	Stick
Exterior Walls	2x4

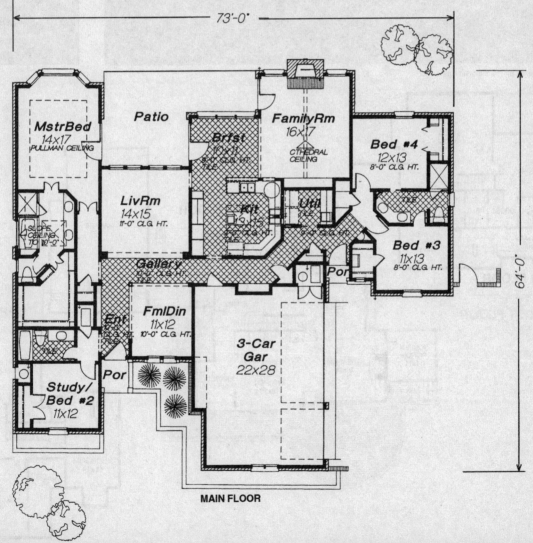

MAIN FLOOR

Photography supplied by The Meredith Corporation

Units	Single
Price Code	L
Total Finished	4,283 sq. ft.
Main Finished	1,642 sq. ft.
Upper Finished	1,411 sq. ft.
Lower Finished	1,230 sq. ft.
Basement Unfinished	412 sq. ft.
Deck Unfinished	207 sq. ft.
Porch Unfinished	1,000 sq. ft.
Dimensions	92'x61'
Foundation	Basement
Bedrooms	4
Full Baths	4
Half Baths	1
Main Ceiling	9'
Upper Ceiling	8'
Primary Roof Pitch	14:12
Max Ridge Height	35'
Roof Framing	Stick
Exterior Walls	2x6

Rear Elevatio

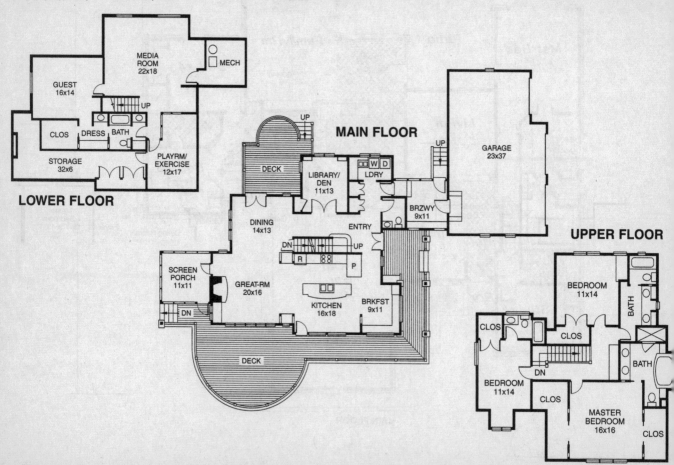

LOWER FLOOR

GUEST 16x14
MEDIA ROOM 22x18
MECH
CLOS
DRESS
BATH
STORAGE 32x6
PLAYRM/ EXERCISE 12x17
UP

MAIN FLOOR

DECK
LIBRARY/ DEN 11x13
W D
LDRY
GARAGE 23x37
UP
BRZWY 9x11
DINING 14x13
ENTRY
SCREEN PORCH 11x11
GREAT-RM 20x16
KITCHEN 16x18
BRKFST 9x11
DN
R
UP
P
DN
DECK

UPPER FLOOR

BEDROOM 11x14
BATH
CLOS
CLOS
BATH
BEDROOM 11x14
DN
CLOS
MASTER BEDROOM 16x16
CLOS

Units	Single
Price Code	1
Total Finished	3,431 sq. ft.
First Finished	2,341 sq. ft.
Second Finished	1,090 sq. ft.
Basement Unfinished	2,341 sq. ft.
Garage Unfinished	850 sq. ft.
Deck Unfinished	134 sq. ft.
Porch Unfinished	118 sq. ft.
Dimensions	65'8"×76'
Foundation	Basement
Bedrooms	4
Full Baths	3
Half Baths	1
First Ceiling	9'
Second Ceiling	8'
Vaulted Ceiling	18'
Tray Ceiling	11'
Primary Roof Pitch	8:12
Secondary Roof Pitch	12:12
Max Ridge Height	32'
Roof Framing	Stick
Exterior Walls	2x4

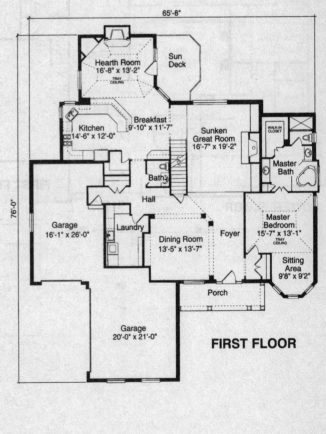

FIRST FLOOR

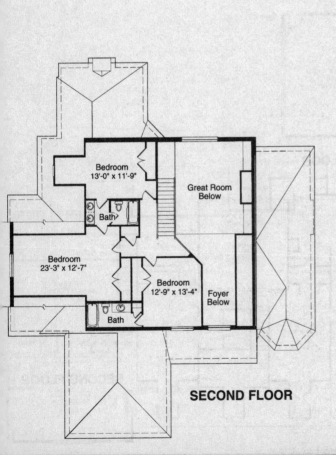

SECOND FLOOR

Units	Single
Price Code	E
Total Finished	2,375 sq. ft.
First Finished	1,669 sq. ft.
Second Finished	706 sq. ft.
Bonus Unfinished	342 sq. ft.
Garage Unfinished	549 sq. ft.
Porch Unfinished	264 sq. ft.
Dimensions	70'8"x48'
Foundation	Crawl space
Bedrooms	3
Full Baths	2
Half Baths	1
First Ceiling	9'
Second Ceiling	9'
Primary Roof Pitch	9:12
Max Ridge Height	29'6"
Roof Framing	Stick
Exterior Walls	2x4

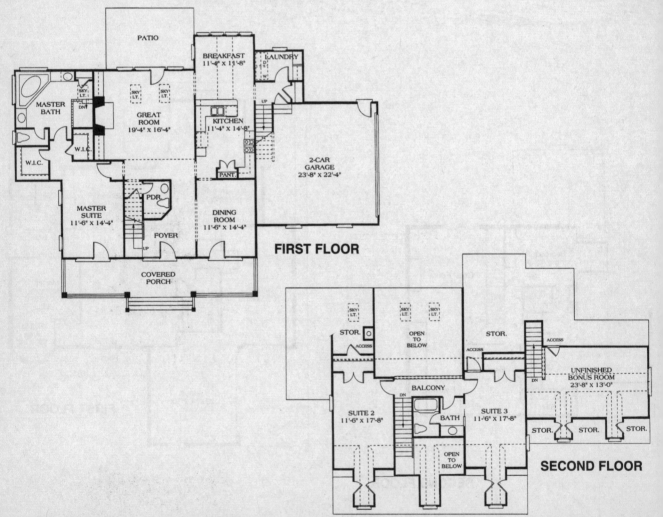

FIRST FLOOR

PATIO

BREAKFAST 11'-4" x 11'-8"

LAUNDRY

MASTER BATH

SKY LT.

SKY LT.

GREAT ROOM 19'-4" x 16'-4"

KITCHEN 11'-4" x 14'-8"

UP

W.I.C.

W.I.C.

2-CAR GARAGE 23'-8" x 22'-4"

PANT.

MASTER SUITE 11'-6" x 14'-4"

PDR.

DINING ROOM 11'-6" x 14'-4"

FOYER

UP

COVERED PORCH

SECOND FLOOR

STOR.

ACCESS

SKY LT.

OPEN TO BELOW

STOR.

ACCESS

SKY LT.

SKY LT.

ACCESS

DN

UNFINISHED BONUS ROOM 23'-8" x 13'-0"

BALCONY

DN

STOR.

STOR.

STOR.

SUITE 2 11'-6" x 17'-8"

BATH

SUITE 3 11'-6" x 17'-8"

OPEN TO BELOW

Units	Single
Price Code	E
Total Finished	2,396 sq. ft.
First Finished	1,244 sq. ft.
Second Finished	1,152 sq. ft.
Basement Unfinished	1,244 sq. ft.
Garage Unfinished	484 sq. ft.
Porch Unfinished	89 sq. ft.
Dimensions	53'4"x37'8"
Foundation	Basement
Bedrooms	4
Full Baths	2
Half Baths	1
First Ceiling	8'
Second Ceiling	8'
Primary Roof Pitch	12:8
Secondary Roof Pitch	12:8
Max Ridge Height	30'
Roof Framing	Truss
Exterior Walls	2x4

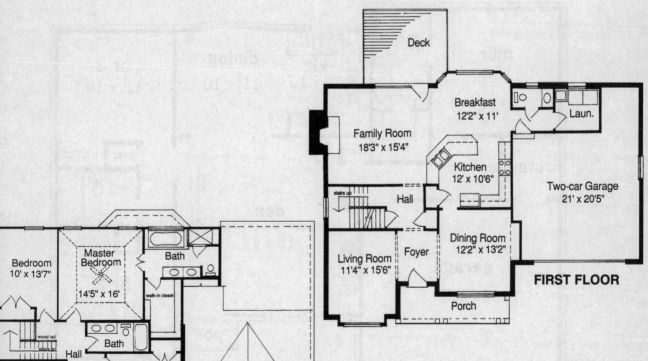

FIRST FLOOR

Deck

Breakfast 12'2" x 11'

Laun.

Family Room 18'3" x 15'4"

Kitchen 12' x 10'6"

Two-car Garage 21' x 20'5"

stairs up

Hall

Dining Room 12'2" x 13'2"

Living Room 11'4" x 15'6"

Foyer

Porch

SECOND FLOOR

Bedroom 10' x 13'7"

Master Bedroom 14'5" x 16'

Bath

walk-in closet

Bath

wood rail

Hall

Bedroom 12'8" x 11'3"

Bedroom 11'8" x 11'1"

Units	Single
Price Code	A
Total Finished	1,237 sq. ft
Main Finished	1,237 sq. ft
Garage Unfinished	436 sq. ft.
Dimensions	50'x38'
Foundation	Crawl spac
	Slab
Bedrooms	3
Full Baths	2
Main Ceiling	8'
Primary Roof Pitch	8:12
Max Ridge Height	18'6''
Roof Framing	Stick
Exterior Walls	2x4

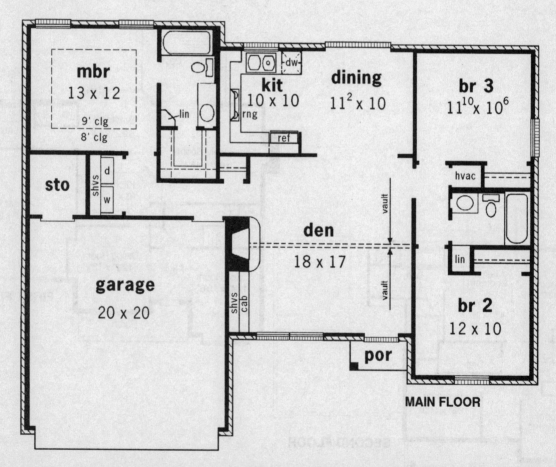

MAIN FLOOR

Units	Single
Price Code	C
Total Finished	1,884 sq. ft.
Main Finished	1,884 sq. ft.
Basement Unfinished	1,908 sq. ft.
Garage Unfinished	495 sq. ft.
Dimensions	50'x55'4"
Foundation	Basement, Crawl space Slab
Bedrooms	3
Full Baths	2
Half Baths	1
Main Ceiling	9'
Primary Roof Pitch	10:12
Max Ridge Height	25'
Roof Framing	Stick
Exterior Walls	2x4

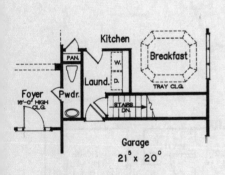

OPT. BASEMENT STAIRS LOCATION

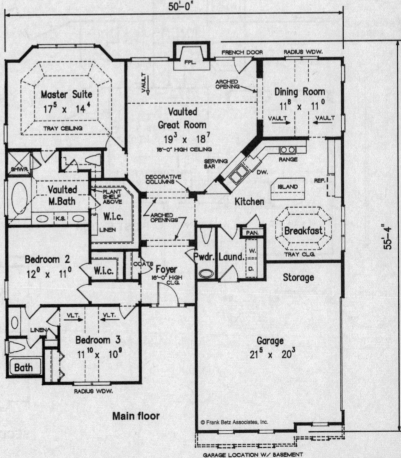

Main floor

© Frank Betz Associates, Inc.

GARAGE LOCATION W/ BASEMENT

Units	Single
Price Code	L
Total Finished	4,070 sq. ft.
First Finished	2,696 sq. ft.
Second Finished	1,374 sq. ft.
Garage Unfinished	943 sq. ft.
Porch Unfinished	902 sq. ft.
Dimensions	108'4"x71'6"
Foundation	Crawl space
Bedrooms	4
Full Baths	3
Half Baths	1
First Ceiling	10'
Second Ceiling	9'
Primary Roof Pitch	12:12
Secondary Roof Pitch	11.5:12
Max Ridge Height	38'
Roof Framing	Stick
Exterior Walls	2x4

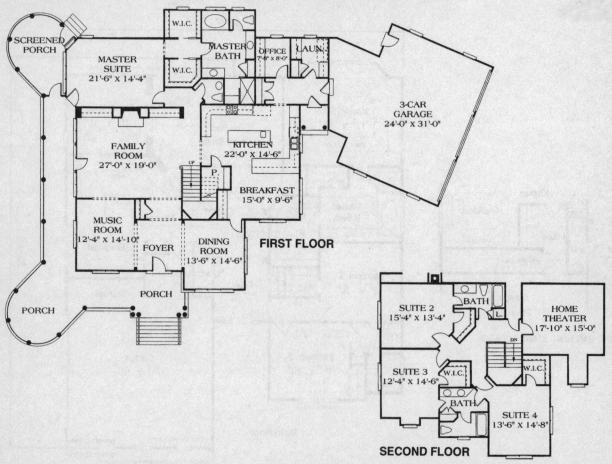

Photography supplied by The Meredith Corporation

Units	Single
Price Code	D
Total Finished	2,038 sq. ft.
Main Finished	1,213 sq. ft.
Upper Finished	825 sq. ft.
Basement Unfinished	1,213 sq. ft.
Deck Unfinished	535 sq. ft.
Porch Unfinished	144 sq. ft.
Dimensions	46'4"x37'8"
Foundation	Basement
Bedrooms	3
Full Baths	2
Half Baths	1
Main Ceiling	9'
Upper Ceiling	8'
Primary Roof Pitch	4:12
Max Ridge Height	24'8"
Roof Framing	Stick/Truss
Exterior Walls	2x6

Rear Elevation

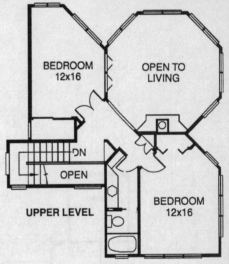

UPPER LEVEL

BEDROOM 12x16

OPEN TO LIVING

DN

OPEN

BEDROOM 12x16

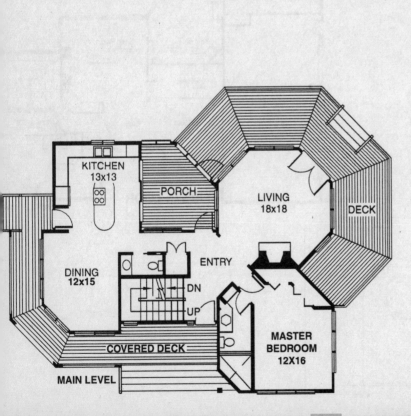

MAIN LEVEL

KITCHEN 13x13

PORCH

LIVING 18x18

DECK

DINING 12x15

ENTRY

DN

UP

COVERED DECK

MASTER BEDROOM 12X16

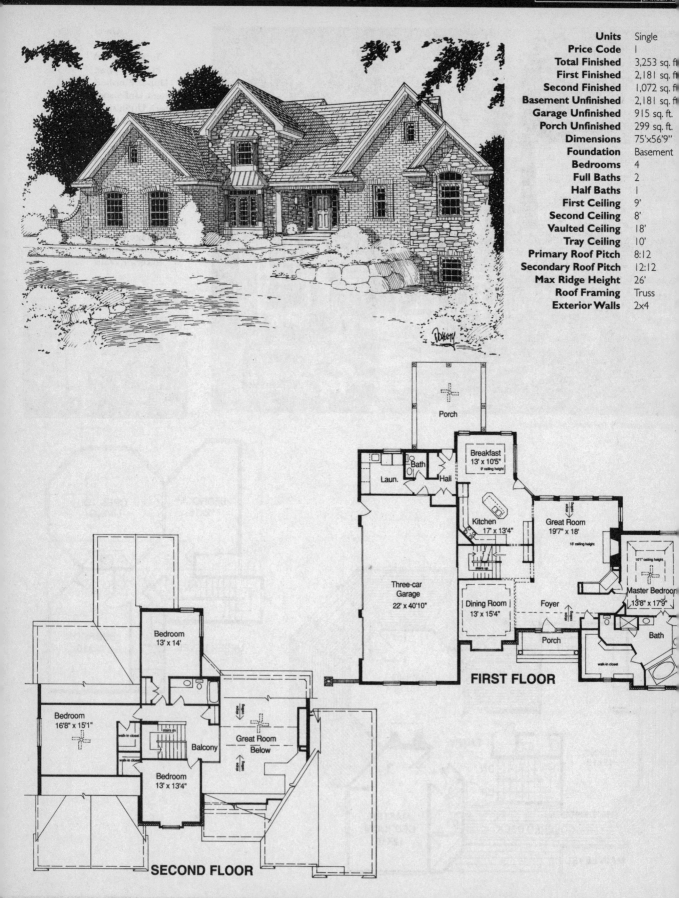

Units	Single
Price Code	I
Total Finished	3,253 sq. ft
First Finished	2,181 sq. ft
Second Finished	1,072 sq. ft
Basement Unfinished	2,181 sq. ft
Garage Unfinished	915 sq. ft.
Porch Unfinished	299 sq. ft.
Dimensions	75'x56'9"
Foundation	Basement
Bedrooms	4
Full Baths	2
Half Baths	1
First Ceiling	9'
Second Ceiling	8'
Vaulted Ceiling	18'
Tray Ceiling	10'
Primary Roof Pitch	8:12
Secondary Roof Pitch	12:12
Max Ridge Height	26'
Roof Framing	Truss
Exterior Walls	2x4

FIRST FLOOR

Porch

Breakfast 13' x 10'5"

Bath

Laun.

Hall

Kitchen 17' x 13'4"

Great Room 19'7" x 18'

Three-car Garage 22' x 40'10"

Dining Room 13' x 15'4"

Foyer

Master Bedroom 13'8" x 17'9"

Bath

walk-in closet

Porch

SECOND FLOOR

Bedroom 13' x 14'

Bedroom 16'8" x 15'1"

walk-in closet

Balcony

Great Room Below

Bedroom 13' x 13'4"

Units	Single
Price Code	B
Total Finished	1,675 sq. ft.
First Finished	882 sq. ft.
Second Finished	793 sq. ft.
Bonus Unfinished	416 sq. ft.
Basement Unfinished	882 sq. ft.
Garage Unfinished	510 sq. ft.
Dimensions	49'6"x35'4"
Foundation	Basement, Crawl space Slab
Bedrooms	3
Full Baths	2
Half Baths	1
First Ceiling	8'
Second Ceiling	8'
Primary Roof Pitch	10:12
Max Ridge Height	29'6"
Roof Framing	Stick
Exterior Walls	2x4

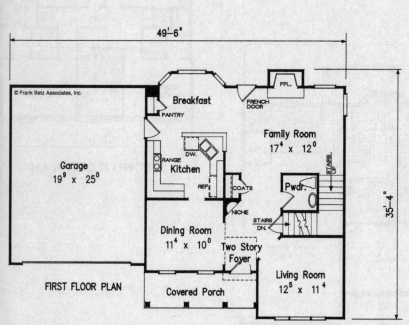

FIRST FLOOR PLAN

© Frank Betz Associates, Inc.

49'-6"

35'-4"

Garage 19⁹ x 25⁰

Breakfast
PANTRY
Kitchen
RANGE
DW.
REF.
COATS
NICHE

Family Room 17⁴ x 12⁰
FPL.
FRENCH DOOR
STAIRS UP
Pwdr.
STAIRS DN.

Dining Room 11⁴ x 10⁰
Two Story Foyer
Living Room 12⁵ x 11⁴
Covered Porch

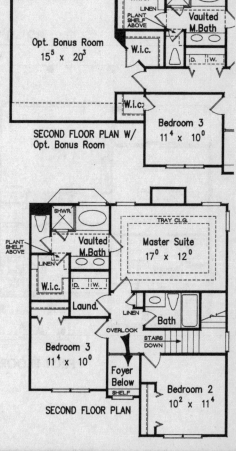

SECOND FLOOR PLAN W/ Opt. Bonus Room

Opt. Bonus Room 15⁵ x 20³
SHWR.
W.i.c.
LINEN
PLANT SHELF ABOVE
W.i.c.
Vaulted M.Bath
D. W.
W.i.c.
Bedroom 3 11⁴ x 10⁰

SECOND FLOOR PLAN

SHWR.
TRAY CLG.
Master Suite 17⁰ x 12⁰
PLANT SHELF ABOVE
LINEN
Vaulted M.Bath
W.i.c.
D. W.
Laund.
LINEN
Bath
OVERLOOK
STAIRS DOWN
Bedroom 3 11⁴ x 10⁰
Foyer Below
SHELF
Bedroom 2 10² x 11⁴

Units	Single
Price Code	K
Total Finished	3,813 sq. ft.
First Finished	2,553 sq. ft.
Second Finished	1,260 sq. ft.
Garage Unfinished	714 sq. ft.
Dimensions	82'×52'
Foundation	Crawl space
	Slab
Bedrooms	4
Full Baths	3
Half Baths	1
First Ceiling	9'
Second Ceiling	9'
Primary Roof Pitch	10:12
Max Ridge Height	36'
Roof Framing	Stick
Exterior Walls	2x4

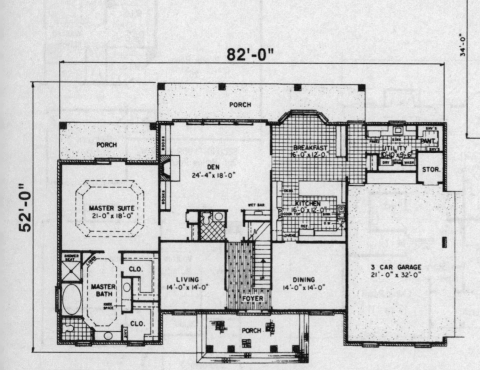

SECOND FLOOR PLAN

FIRST FLOOR PLAN

Units	Single
Price Code	J
Total Finished	3,709 sq. ft.
First Finished	2,538 sq. ft.
Second Finished	1,171 sq. ft.
Basement Unfinished	2,621 sq. ft.
Garage Unfinished	779 sq. ft.
Dimensions	67'7"x85'1"
Foundation	Basement
Bedrooms	4
Full Baths	3
Half Baths	1
First Ceiling	10'
Second Ceiling	9'
Tray Ceiling	11'
Primary Roof Pitch	8:12
Max Ridge Height	34'6"
Roof Framing	Stick
Exterior Walls	2x4

Rear Elevation

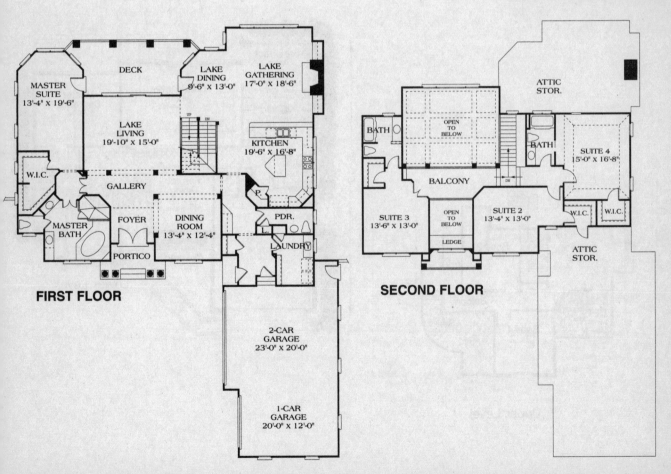

FIRST FLOOR

MASTER SUITE 13'-4" x 19'-6"

DECK

LAKE DINING 9'-6" x 13'-0"

LAKE GATHERING 17'-0" x 18'-6"

LAKE LIVING 19'-10" x 15'-0"

KITCHEN 19'-6" x 16'-8"

W.I.C.

GALLERY

MASTER BATH

FOYER

DINING ROOM 13'-4" x 12'-4"

P.

PDR.

L.

LAUNDRY

PORTICO

2-CAR GARAGE 23'-0" x 20'-0"

1-CAR GARAGE 20'-0" x 12'-0"

SECOND FLOOR

ATTIC STOR.

BATH

OPEN TO BELOW

BATH

SUITE 4 15'-0" x 16'-8"

BALCONY

SUITE 3 13'-6" x 13'-0"

OPEN TO BELOW

SUITE 2 13'-4" x 13'-0"

W.I.C.

W.I.C.

LEDGE

ATTIC STOR.

217

Units	Single
Price Code	F
Total Finished	2,538 sq. ft.
Lower Finished	1,719 sq. ft.
Upper Finished	819 sq. ft.
Garage Unfinished	470 sq. ft.
Deck Unfinished	272 sq. ft.
Porch Unfinished	48 sq. ft.
Dimensions	56'x51'8''
Foundation	Slab
Bedrooms	4
Full Baths	2
Half Baths	1
3/4 Baths	1
Lower Ceiling	9'
Upper Ceiling	8'
Primary Roof Pitch	12:12
Max Ridge Height	29'
Roof Framing	Stick
Exterior Walls	2x4

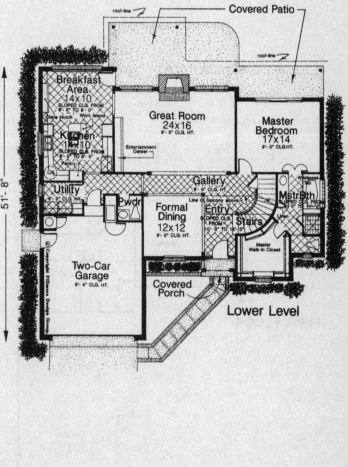

Lower Level

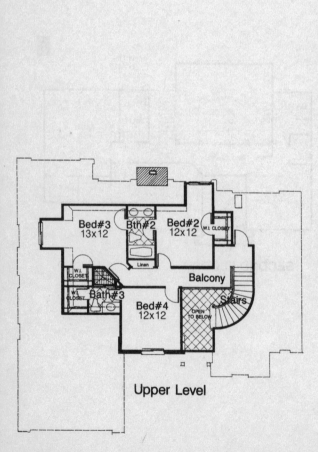

Upper Level

Units	Single
Price Code	A
Total Finished	1,346 sq. ft.
Main Finished	1,346 sq. ft.
Basement Unfinished	1,358 sq. ft.
Garage Unfinished	395 sq. ft.
Dimensions	39'x51'
Foundation	Basement, Crawl space Slab
Bedrooms	3
Full Baths	2
Primary Roof Pitch	8:12
Max Ridge Height	21'6"
Roof Framing	Stick
Exterior Walls	2x4

39'-0"

51'-0"

Dining Room

FPL.

Vaulted Living Room
14⁸ x 17⁶

VAULT

W.i.c.

Vaulted M. Bath

SHWR.

TRAY CLG.

Master Suite
14⁰ x 12²

VAULT

SERVING BAR

RANGE

D.W.

Kitchen

REF.

W. D.

PANTRY

Laundry

Storage

OPT. STAIRS TO BASEMENT

© Frank Betz Associates, Inc.

Bath

Bedroom 2
10⁰ x 11⁰

Foyer

Vaulted Bedroom 3
10² x 13³

PLANT SHELF ABOVE

Garage

MAIN FLOOR

Photography supplied by The Meredith Corporation

Units	Single
Price Code	K
Total Finished	3,895 sq. ft.
Main Finished	2,727 sq. ft.
Upper Finished	1,168 sq. ft.
Bonus Unfinished	213 sq. ft.
Basement Unfinished	2,250 sq. ft.
Garage Unfinished	984 sq. ft.
Deck Unfinished	230 sq. ft.
Porch Unfinished	402 sq. ft.
Dimensions	73'8"x72'2"
Foundation	Basement
Bedrooms	4
Full Baths	4
Half Baths	1
Main Ceiling	9'
Upper Ceiling	8'
Vaulted Ceiling	22'
Primary Roof Pitch	12:12
Secondary Roof Pitch	8:12
Max Ridge Height	43'
Roof Framing	Stick
Exterior Walls	2x6

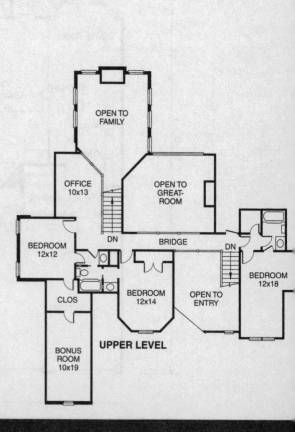

MAIN LEVEL

- PATIO
- FAMILY 15x19
- DECK
- BRKFST 12x10
- MASTER BEDROOM 15x18
- PORCH
- CLOS
- UP
- GREATROOM 18x16
- KIT 18x14
- DN
- CLOS
- BATH
- W D P
- LDRY
- DINING 12x17
- ENTRY
- GUEST/ STUDY 14x11
- UP
- GARAGE 20x14
- PORCH

UPPER LEVEL

- OPEN TO FAMILY
- OFFICE 10x13
- OPEN TO GREATROOM
- DN
- BRIDGE
- DN
- BEDROOM 12x12
- BEDROOM 12x18
- CLOS
- BEDROOM 12x14
- OPEN TO ENTRY
- BONUS ROOM 10x19

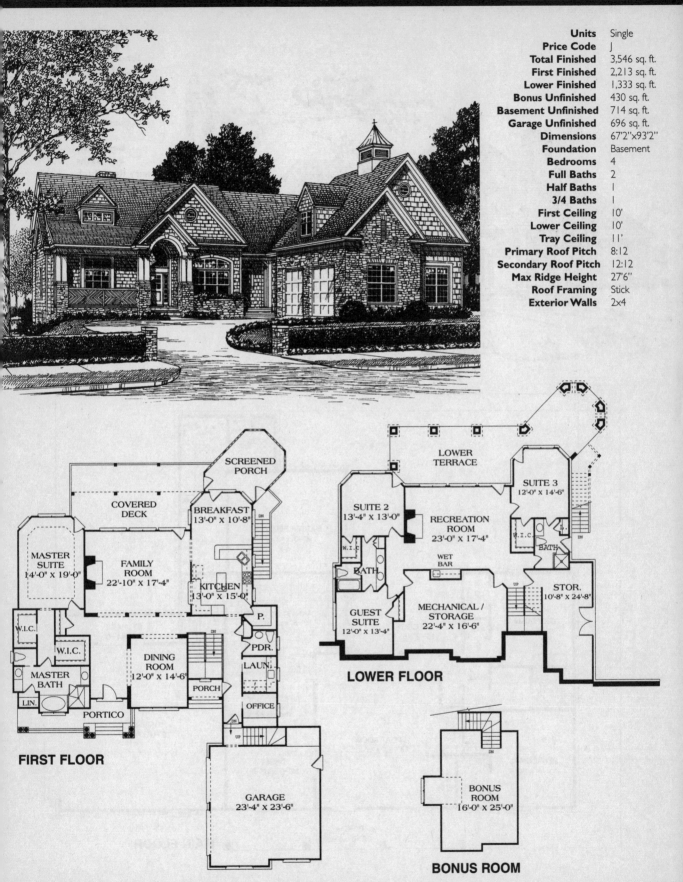

Units	Single
Price Code	J
Total Finished	3,546 sq. ft.
First Finished	2,213 sq. ft.
Lower Finished	1,333 sq. ft.
Bonus Unfinished	430 sq. ft.
Basement Unfinished	714 sq. ft.
Garage Unfinished	696 sq. ft.
Dimensions	67'2"x93'2"
Foundation	Basement
Bedrooms	4
Full Baths	2
Half Baths	1
3/4 Baths	1
First Ceiling	10'
Lower Ceiling	10'
Tray Ceiling	11'
Primary Roof Pitch	8:12
Secondary Roof Pitch	12:12
Max Ridge Height	27'6"
Roof Framing	Stick
Exterior Walls	2x4

FIRST FLOOR

SCREENED PORCH

COVERED DECK

BREAKFAST 13'-0" X 10'-8"

MASTER SUITE 14'-0" X 19'-0"

FAMILY ROOM 22'-10" X 17'-4"

KITCHEN 13'-0" X 15'-0"

W.I.C.

W.I.C.

MASTER BATH

DINING ROOM 12'-0" X 14'-6"

P.

PDR.

LAUN.

PORCH

LIN.

PORTICO

OFFICE

UP

GARAGE 23'-4" X 23'-6"

LOWER FLOOR

LOWER TERRACE

SUITE 2 13'-4" X 13'-0"

RECREATION ROOM 23'-0" X 17'-4"

SUITE 3 12'-0" X 14'-6"

W.I.C.

BATH

W.I.C.

WET BAR

BATH

GUEST SUITE 12'-0" X 13'-4"

MECHANICAL / STORAGE 22'-4" X 16'-6"

UP

STOR. 10'-8" X 24'-8"

BONUS ROOM

BONUS ROOM 16'-0" X 25'-0"

DN

221

Units	Single
Price Code	C
Total Finished	1,754 sq. ft.
Main Finished	1,754 sq. ft.
Garage Unfinished	552 sq. ft.
Porch Unfinished	236 sq. ft.
Dimensions	69'10"x53'5"
Foundation	Crawl space
	Slab
Bedrooms	3
Full Baths	2
Primary Roof Pitch	10:12
Max Ridge Height	22'
Roof Framing	Stick
Exterior Walls	2x4

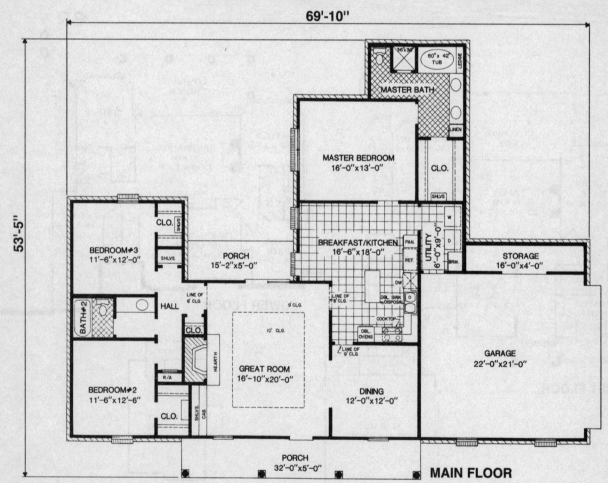

69'-10"

53'-5"

MASTER BATH

36"x36" 60"x 42" TUB LEDGE

MASTER BEDROOM
16'-0"x13'-0"

CLO.

SHLVS

LINEN

W
D

UTILITY
6'-0"x9'-0"

BRM.

STORAGE
16'-0"x4'-0"

CLO.
SHLVS

BEDROOM #3
11'-6"x12'-0"

CLO.
SHLVS

PORCH
15'-2"x5'-0"

BREAKFAST/KITCHEN
16'-6"x18'-0"

PAN.

REF.

LINE OF 8' CLG.

LINE OF 8' CLG.

DBL. SINK/DISPOSAL

COOKTOP

DBL. OVENS

LINE OF 9' CLG.

9' CLG.

10' CLG.

BATH #2

HALL

CLO.

HEARTH

R/A

SHLVS CAB

GREAT ROOM
16'-10"x20'-0"

BEDROOM #2
11'-6"x12'-6"

CLO.

DINING
12'-0"x12'-0"

GARAGE
22'-0"x21'-0"

PORCH
32'-0"x5'-0"

MAIN FLOOR

photography supplied by The Meredith Corporation

Units	Single
Price Code	K
Total Finished	3,878 sq. ft.
Main Finished	2,770 sq. ft.
Upper Finished	1,108 sq. ft.
Dimensions	81'8"x62'
Foundation	Basement
Bedrooms	4
Full Baths	3
Half Baths	1
Primary Roof Pitch	12:12
Max Ridge Height	40'
Roof Framing	Truss
Exterior Walls	2x4

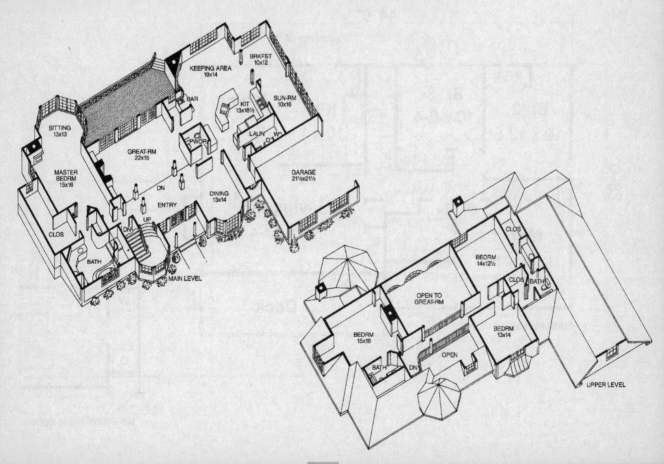

Units	Single
Price Code	A
Total Finished	1,146 sq. ft.
Main Finished	1,146 sq. ft.
Dimensions	44'x28'
Foundation	Basement
	Crawl space
	Slab
Bedrooms	3
Full Baths	2
Main Ceiling	8'
Primary Roof Pitch	5:12
Max Ridge Height	16'
Roof Framing	Stick
Exterior Walls	2x4, 2x6

Rear Elevation

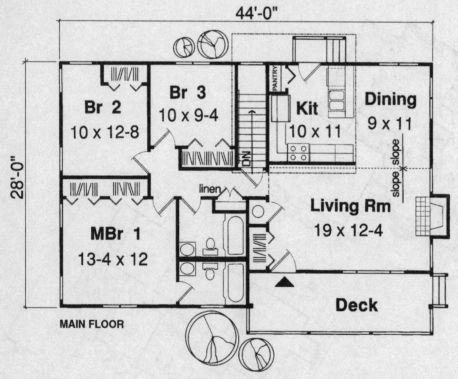

44'-0"

28'-0"

Br 2
10 x 12-8

Br 3
10 x 9-4

PANTRY

Kit
10 x 11

Dining
9 x 11

DN

UP

linen

MBr 1
13-4 x 12

slope slope

Living Rm
19 x 12-4

Deck

MAIN FLOOR

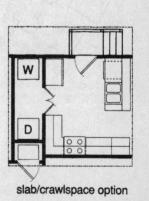

W

D

slab/crawlspace option

Units	Single
Price Code	E
Total Finished	2,387 sq. ft.
Main Finished	2,387 sq. ft.
Garage Unfinished	505 sq. ft.
Porch Unfinished	194 sq. ft.
Dimensions	64'10''x54'10''
Foundation	Crawl space
	Slab
Bedrooms	4
Full Baths	2
Half Baths	1
Main Ceiling	9'
Primary Roof Pitch	8:12
Secondary Roof Pitch	12:12
Max Ridge Height	28'
Roof Framing	Truss
Exterior Walls	2x4

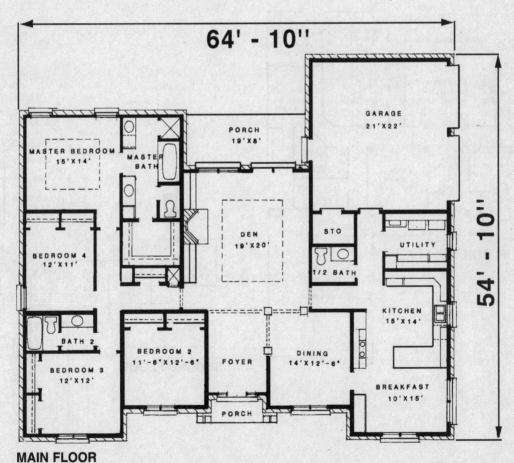

MAIN FLOOR

Units	Single
Price Code	H
Total Finished	3,058 sq. ft.
First Finished	2,167 sq. ft.
Second Finished	891 sq. ft.
Bonus Unfinished	252 sq. ft.
Garage Unfinished	725 sq. ft.
Deck Unfinished	234 sq. ft.
Porch Unfinished	159 sq. ft.
Dimensions	64'x73'7"
Foundation	Crawl space
Bedrooms	4
Full Baths	3
Primary Roof Pitch	10:12
Secondary Roof Pitch	12:12
Max Ridge Height	33'6"
Roof Framing	Stick
Exterior Walls	2x4

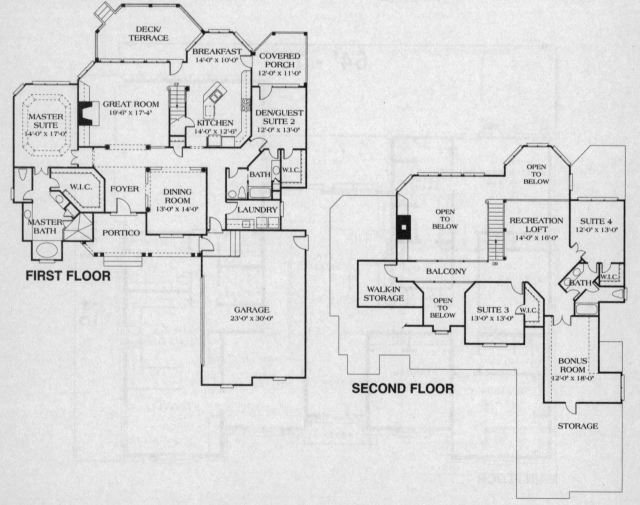

FIRST FLOOR

DECK/TERRACE
BREAKFAST 14'-0" x 10'-0"
COVERED PORCH 12'-0" x 11'-0"
GREAT ROOM 19'-6" x 17'-4"
KITCHEN 14'-0" x 12'-6"
DEN/GUEST SUITE 2 12'-0" x 13'-0"
MASTER SUITE 14'-0" x 17'-0"
W.I.C.
BATH
W.I.C.
FOYER
DINING ROOM 13'-0" x 14'-0"
LAUNDRY
MASTER BATH
PORTICO
GARAGE 23'-0" x 30'-0"

SECOND FLOOR

OPEN TO BELOW
OPEN TO BELOW
RECREATION LOFT 14'-0" x 16'-0"
SUITE 4 12'-0" x 13'-0"
BALCONY
BATH
W.I.C.
WALK-IN STORAGE
OPEN TO BELOW
SUITE 3 13'-0" x 13'-0"
W.I.C.
BONUS ROOM 12'-0" x 18'-0"
STORAGE

Units	Single
Price Code	D
Total Finished	2,229 sq. ft.
Main Finished	2,229 sq. ft.
Basement Unfinished	2,229 sq. ft.
Garage Unfinished	551 sq. ft.
Dimensions	65'x56'
Foundation	Basement
Bedrooms	3
Full Baths	2
Primary Roof Pitch	8:12
Secondary Roof Pitch	10:12
Max Ridge Height	26'
Roof Framing	Truss
Exterior Walls	2x6

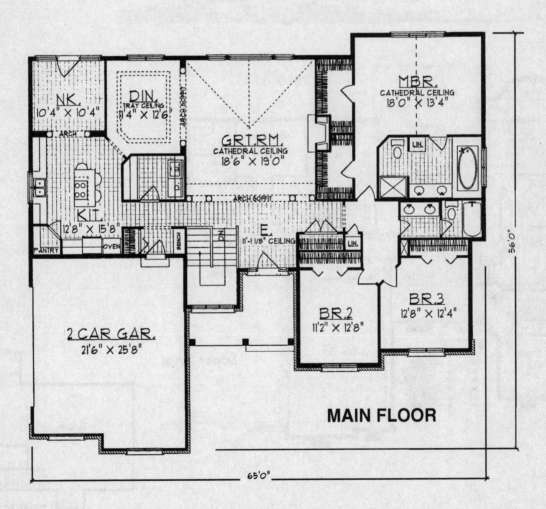

MAIN FLOOR

NK. 10'4" X 10'4"

DIN. TRAY CEILING 11'4" X 12'6"

GRT. RM. CATHEDRAL CEILING 18'6" X 19'0"

MBR. CATHEDRAL CEILING 18'0" X 13'4"

KIT. 12'8" X 15'8"

PANTRY

OVEN

BENCH

DN

FOYER 11'-1 1/8" CEILING

BR.2 11'2" X 12'8"

BR.3 12'8" X 12'4"

2 CAR GAR. 21'6" X 25'8"

65'0"

56'0"

Units	Single
Price Code	G
Total Finished	2,789 sq. ft.
Lower Finished	2,789 sq. ft.
Bonus Unfinished	637 sq. ft.
Garage Unfinished	632 sq. ft.
Deck Unfinished	252 sq. ft.
Porch Unfinished	60 sq. ft.
Dimensions	75'x68'4''
Foundation	Slab
Bedrooms	3
Full Baths	3
Lower Ceiling	9'-10'
Primary Roof Pitch	12:12
Max Ridge Height	29'
Roof Framing	Stick
Exterior Walls	2x4

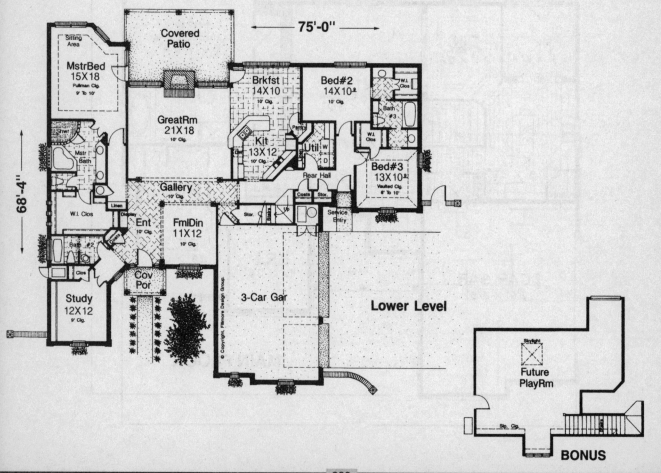

Photography by Charles Brooks

Units	Single
Price Code	B
Total Finished	1,686 sq. ft.
Main Finished	1,686 sq. ft.
Basement Unfinished	1,676 sq. ft.
Garage Unfinished	484 sq. ft.
Dimensions	61'x54'
Foundation	Basement Crawl space Slab
Bedrooms	3
Full Baths	1
3/4 Baths	1
Main Ceiling	8'
Primary Roof Pitch	8:12
Secondary Roof Pitch	16:12
Max Ridge Height	23'
Roof Framing	Stick
Exterior Walls	2x4, 2x6

Rear Elevation

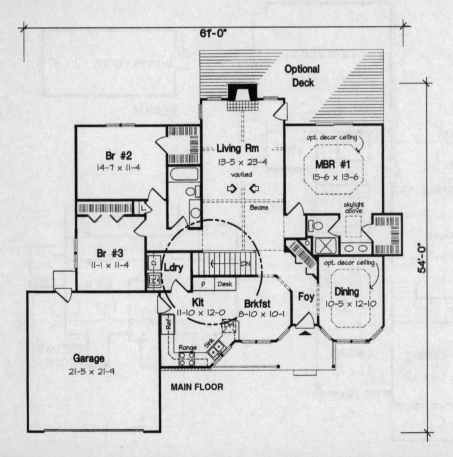

61'-0"

Optional Deck

Living Rm
13-5 x 23-4
vaulted

opt. decor ceiling

MBR #1
15-6 x 13-6

skylight above

Beams

Br #2
14-7 x 11-4

Br #3
11-1 x 11-4

Ldry

DN

P Desk

Kit
11-10 x 12-0

Brkfst
8-10 x 10-1

Foy

opt. decor ceiling

Dining
10-5 x 12-10

54'-0"

Garage
21-5 x 21-9

Ref.

Range Sink

MAIN FLOOR

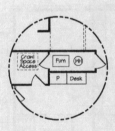

Crawl Space Access   Furn   WH

P   Desk

Slab/Crawl Space Option

229

Units	Single
Price Code	G
Total Finished	2,858 sq. ft.
First Finished	2,256 sq. ft.
Second Finished	602 sq. ft.
Bonus Unfinished	264 sq. ft.
Garage Unfinished	484 sq. ft.
Dimensions	65'6"x74'5"
Foundation	Crawl space
	Slab
Bedrooms	5
Full Baths	3
Half Baths	1
First Ceiling	9'
Second Ceiling	8'
Primary Roof Pitch	10:12
Secondary Roof Pitch	12:12

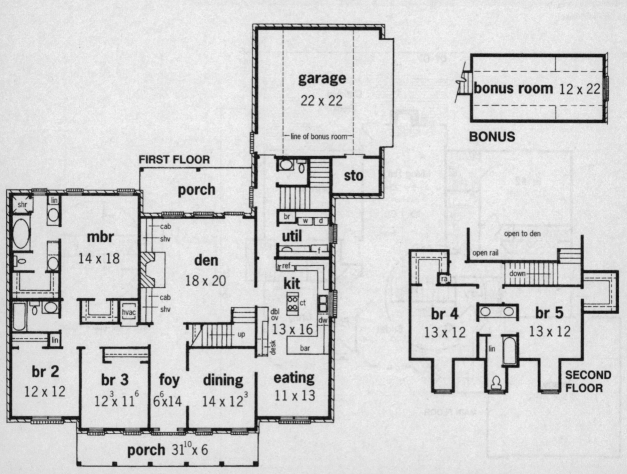

Order Today! 1-800-235-5700 or order online at www.familyhomeplans.com

Units	Single
Price Code	B
Total Finished	1,502 sq. ft.
Main Finished	1,502 sq. ft.
Basement Unfinished	1,555 sq. ft.
Garage Unfinished	448 sq. ft.
Dimensions	51'x50'6''
Foundation	Basement, Crawl space
Bedrooms	3
Full Baths	2
Primary Roof Pitch	10:12
Max Ridge Height	24'9''
Roof Framing	Stick
Exterior Walls	2x4

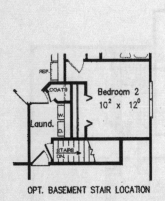

OPT. BASEMENT STAIR LOCATION

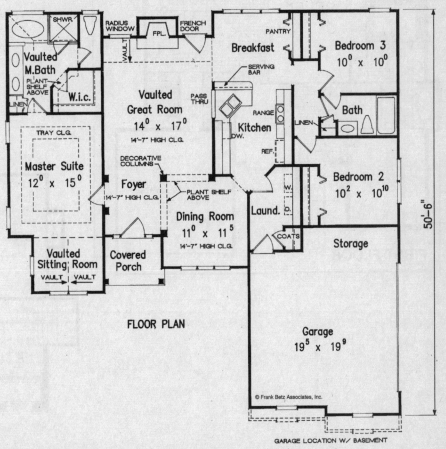

FLOOR PLAN

© Frank Betz Associates, Inc.

Units	Single
Price Code	D
Total Finished	2,249 sq. ft.
First Finished	1,554 sq. ft.
Second Finished	695 sq. ft.
Basement Unfinished	1,554 sq. ft.
Garage Unfinished	389 sq. ft.
Dimensions	56'x49'
Foundation	Basement
Bedrooms	4
Full Baths	2
Half Baths	1
Primary Roof Pitch	8:12
Secondary Roof Pitch	10:12
Max Ridge Height	30'
Roof Framing	Truss
Exterior Walls	2x6

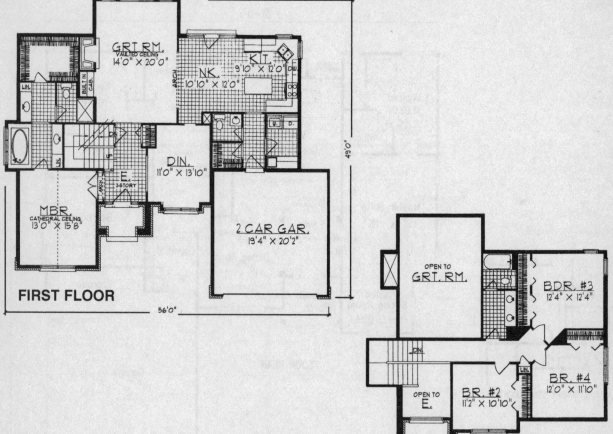

FIRST FLOOR

GRT. RM.
VAULTED CEILING
14'0" X 20'0"

KIT.
9'10" X 12'0"

NK.
10'10" X 12'0"

DIN.
11'0" X 13'10"

MBR.
CATHEDRAL CEILING
13'0" X 15'8"

2 CAR GAR.
19'4" X 20'2"

49'0"

56'0"

SECOND FLOOR

OPEN TO GRT. RM.

BDR. #3
12'4" X 12'4"

BR. #2
11'2" X 10'10"

BR. #4
12'0" X 11'10"

OPEN TO E.

BRICK ARCH.

Photography by Donna & Ron Kolb, Exposures Unlimited

Units	Single
Price Code	C
Total Finished	1,768 sq. ft.
First Finished	960 sq. ft.
Second Finished	808 sq. ft.
Basement Unfinished	922 sq. ft.
Garage Unfinished	413 sq. ft.
Dimensions	55'4"x40'4"
Foundation	Basement
Bedrooms	3
Full Baths	2
Half Baths	1
Vaulted Ceiling	12'
Primary Roof Pitch	8:12
Secondary Roof Pitch	12:12
Max Ridge Height	25'8"
Roof Framing	Truss
Exterior Walls	2x4

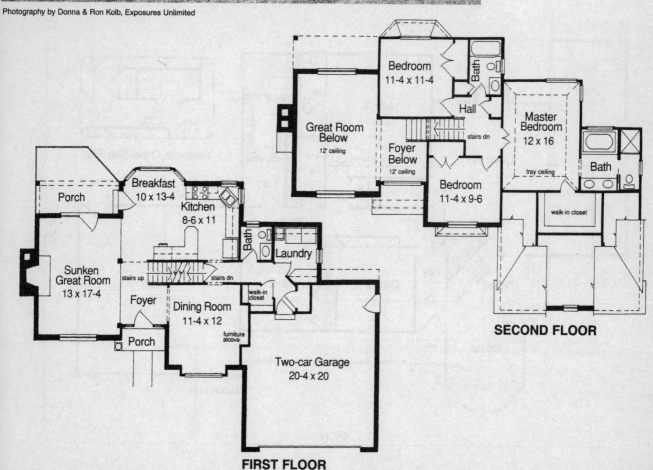

SECOND FLOOR

FIRST FLOOR

Units	Single
Price Code	B
Total Finished	1,583 sq. ft.
Main Finished	1,583 sq. ft.
Basement Unfinished	1,573 sq. ft.
Garage Unfinished	484 sq. ft.
Dimensions	70'x46'
Foundation	Basement
	Crawl space
	Slab
Bedrooms	3
Full Baths	2
Main Ceiling	8'
Primary Roof Pitch	6:12
Secondary Roof Pitch	8:12
Max Ridge Height	20'
Roof Framing	Stick
Exterior Walls	2x4,2x6

Rear Elevation

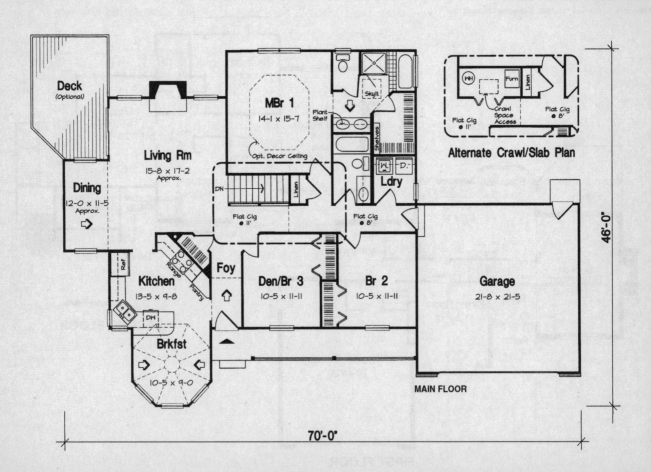

Deck (Optional)

Living Rm
15-8 x 17-2
Approx.

Dining
12-0 x 11-5
Approx.

MBr 1
14-1 x 15-7

Plant Shelf

Skylt

Opt. Decor Ceiling

DN

Linen

Flat Clg
● 11"

Ldry

Flat Clg
● 8'

Ref

Kitchen
13-5 x 9-8

Foy

Den/Br 3
10-5 x 11-11

Br 2
10-5 x 11-11

Garage
21-8 x 21-5

Pantry

DW

Brkfst
10-5 x 9-0

MAIN FLOOR

46'-0"

70'-0"

Alternate Crawl/Slab Plan

Fum

Linen

Crawl Space Access

Flat Clg
● 11"

Flat Clg
● 8'

Units	Single
Price Code	H
Total Finished	3,194 sq. ft.
Lower Finished	2,118 sq. ft.
Upper Finished	1,076 sq. ft.
Garage Unfinished	524 sq. ft.
Deck Unfinished	216 sq. ft.
Porch Unfinished	120 sq. ft.
Dimensions	79'4"x37'10"
Foundation	Slab
Bedrooms	4
Full Baths	2
Half Baths	1
Primary Roof Pitch	8:12
Max Ridge Height	29'
Roof Framing	Stick
Exterior Walls	2x4

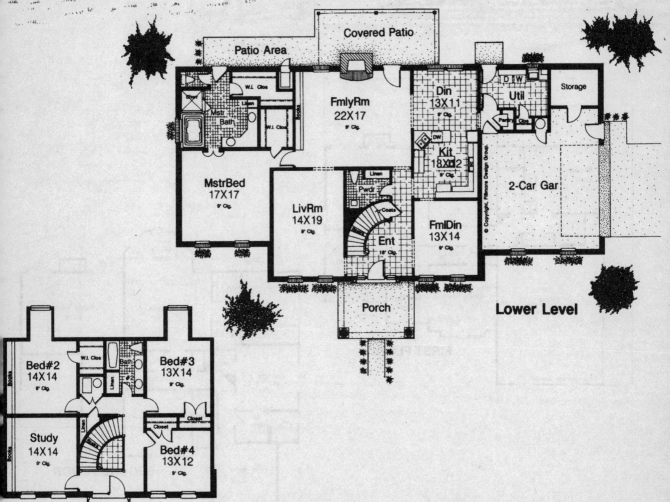

Covered Patio

Patio Area

FmlyRm 22X17 9' Clg.

Din 13X11 9' Clg.

Util

Storage

Kit 18X12 9' Clg.

2-Car Gar

MstrBed 17X17 9' Clg.

Mstr. Bath

W.I. Clos

LivRm 14X19 9' Clg.

Linen

Pwdr

Coats

Ent 18' Clg.

FmlDin 13X14 9' Clg.

© Copyright, Fillmore Design Group.

Lower Level

Porch

Bed#2 14X14 9' Clg.

W.I. Clos

Bath

Bed#3 13X14 9' Clg.

Study 14X14 9' Clg.

Linen

Closet

Closet

Bed#4 13X12 9' Clg.

Balcony

Upper Level

Units	Single
Price Code	F
Total Finished	2,712 sq. ft.
First Finished	1,548 sq. ft.
Second Finished	1,164 sq. ft.
Bonus Unfinished	198 sq. ft.
Basement Unfinished	1,548 sq. ft.
Garage Unfinished	542 sq. ft.
Dimensions	54'6"x52'
Foundation	Basement
	Crawl space
	Slab
Bedrooms	4
Full Baths	3
First Ceiling	9'
Second Ceiling	8'
Primary Roof Pitch	10:12
Max Ridge Height	34'
Roof Framing	Stick
Exterior Walls	2x4

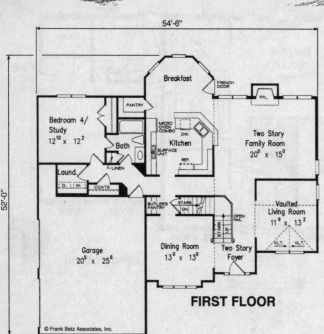

FIRST FLOOR

© Frank Betz Associates, Inc.

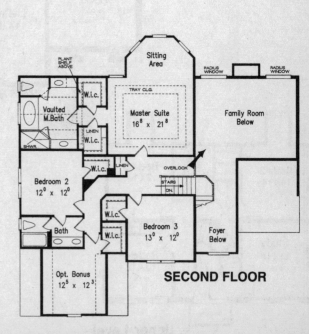

SECOND FLOOR

Photography by Donna & Ron Kolb, Exposures Unlimited

Units	Single
Price Code	D
Total Finished	2,101 sq. ft.
First Finished	1,626 sq. ft.
Second Finished	475 sq. ft.
Basement Unfinished	1,512 sq. ft.
Garage Unfinished	438 sq. ft.
Dimensions	59'x60'8''
Foundation	Basement
Bedrooms	3
Full Baths	2
Half Baths	1
First Ceiling	8'
Second Ceiling	8'
Primary Roof Pitch	10:12
Secondary Roof Pitch	12:12
Max Ridge Height	31'
Framing	Truss
Exterior Walls	2x4

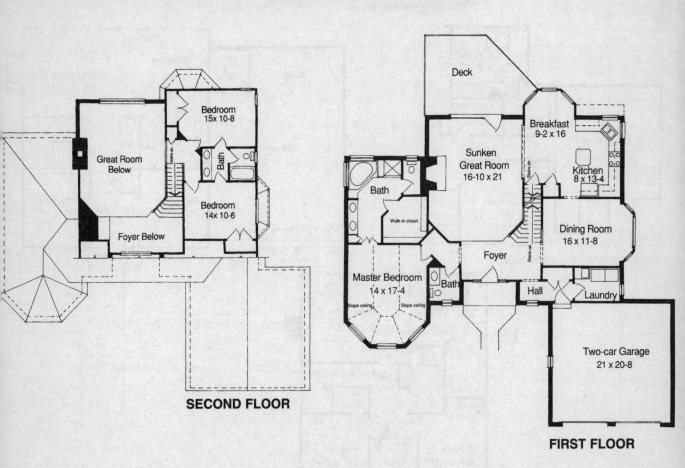

SECOND FLOOR

- Bedroom 15x 10-8
- Great Room Below
- Bath
- Foyer Below
- Bedroom 14x 10-6

FIRST FLOOR

- Deck
- Breakfast 9-2 x 16
- Sunken Great Room 16-10 x 21
- Kitchen 8 x 13-4
- Bath
- Walk-in closet
- Dining Room 16 x 11-8
- Foyer
- Master Bedroom 14 x 17-4
- Slope ceiling   Slope ceiling
- Bath
- Hall
- Laundry
- Two-car Garage 21 x 20-8

Units	Single
Price Code	B
Total Finished	1,700 sq. ft.
First Finished	922 sq. ft.
Second Finished	778 sq. ft.
Bonus Unfinished	369 sq. ft.
Basement Unfinished	922 sq. ft.
Garage Unfinished	530 sq. ft.
Dimensions	50'4"x34'8"
Foundation	Basement, Crawl space
Bedrooms	3
Full Baths	2
Half Baths	1
First Ceiling	9'
Second Ceiling	8'
Primary Roof Pitch	8:12
Max Ridge Height	30'
Roof Framing	Stick
Exterior Walls	2x4

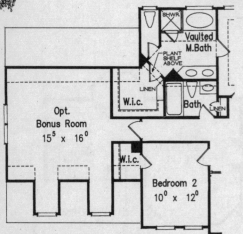

SECOND FLOOR W/ OPT. BONUS ROOM

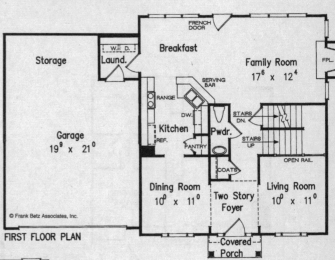

FIRST FLOOR PLAN

© Frank Betz Associates, Inc.

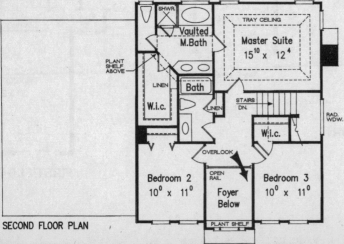

SECOND FLOOR PLAN

238

Units	Single
Price Code	E
Total Finished	2,340 sq. ft.
First Finished	1,132 sq. ft.
Second Finished	1,208 sq. ft.
Basement Unfinished	1,132 sq. ft.
Garage Unfinished	514 sq. ft.
Dimensions	56'4"x39'6"
Foundation	Basement
	Crawl space
	Slab
Bedrooms	4
Full Baths	2
Half Baths	1
First Ceiling	9'
Second Ceiling	8'
Primary Roof Pitch	12:12
Max Ridge Height	33'
Roof Framing	Stick
Exterior Walls	2x4

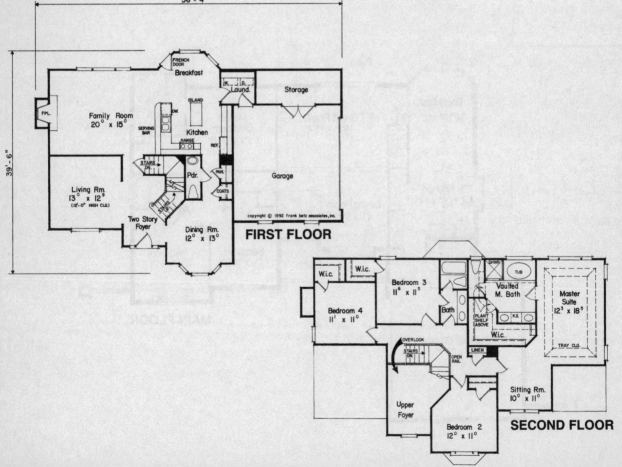

FIRST FLOOR

SECOND FLOOR

copyright © 1992 frank betz associates, inc.

Units	Single
Price Code	B
Total Finished	1,746 sq. ft.
Main Finished	1,746 sq. ft.
Basement Unfinished	1,560 sq. ft.
Garage Unfinished	455 sq. ft.
Dimensions	65'10''x56'
Foundation	Basement
Bedrooms	3
Full Baths	2
Primary Roof Pitch	9:12
Secondary Roof Pitch	10:12
Max Ridge Height	21'9''
Roof Framing	Truss
Exterior Walls	2x4

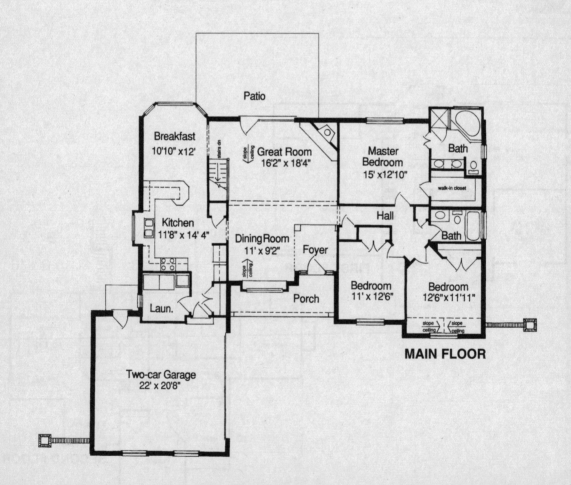

Patio

Breakfast
10'10" x 12'

Great Room
16'2" x 18'4"

Master Bedroom
15' x 12'10"

Bath

walk-in closet

Kitchen
11'8" x 14' 4"

Hall

Bath

Dining Room
11' x 9'2"

Foyer

Laun.

Porch

Bedroom
11' x 12'6'

Bedroom
12'6"x 11'11"

MAIN FLOOR

Two-car Garage
22' x 20'8"

Rear Elevation

Units	Single
Price Code	A
Total Finished	1,400 sq. ft.
First Finished	1,400 sq. ft.
Basement Unfinished	1,400 sq. ft.
Garage Unfinished	528 sq. ft.
Dimensions	50'x28'
Foundation	Basement
	Crawl space
	Slab
Bedrooms	3
Full Baths	2
First Ceiling	8'
Primary Roof Pitch	6:12
Max Ridge Height	17'
Roof Framing	Stick
Exterior Walls	2x4, 2x6

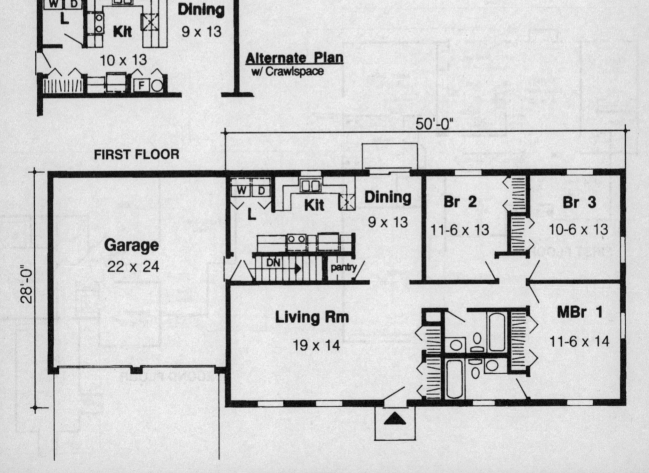

Alternate Plan
w/ Crawlspace

Dining 9 x 13
Kit 10 x 13
W D L
F

FIRST FLOOR

50'-0"

28'-0"

Garage 22 x 24

W D L
Kit
Dining 9 x 13
Br 2 11-6 x 13
Br 3 10-6 x 13
DN pantry
Living Rm 19 x 14
MBr 1 11-6 x 14

241

Units	Single
Price Code	F
Total Finished	2,601 sq. ft.
First Finished	2,003 sq. ft.
Second Finished	598 sq. ft.
Bonus Unfinished	321 sq. ft.
Basement Unfinished	2,003 sq. ft.
Garage Unfinished	546 sq. ft.
Dimensions	60'x61'
Foundation	Basement
	Crawl space
	Slab
Bedrooms	4
Full Baths	3
Primary Roof Pitch	12:12
Max Ridge Height	31'6"
Roof Framing	Stick
Exterior Walls	2x4

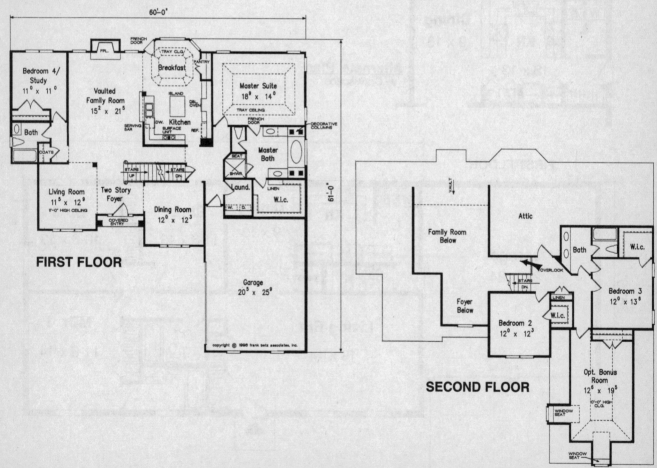

FIRST FLOOR

SECOND FLOOR

copyright © 1996 frank betz associates, inc.

242

Units	Single
Price Code	H
Total Finished	3,040 sq. ft.
First Finished	1,478 sq. ft.
Second Finished	1,562 sq. ft.
Basement Unfinished	1,478 sq. ft.
Garage Unfinished	545 sq. ft.
Porch Unfinished	100 sq. ft.
Dimensions	72'6''×35'
Foundation	Basement Slab
Bedrooms	4
Full Baths	3
Half Baths	I
First Ceiling	9'
Second Ceiling	8'
Vaulted Ceiling	10'
Tray Ceiling	9'4''
Primary Roof Pitch	12:12
Secondary Roof Pitch	6:12
Max Ridge Height	30'
Roof Framing	Stick
Exterior Walls	2x4

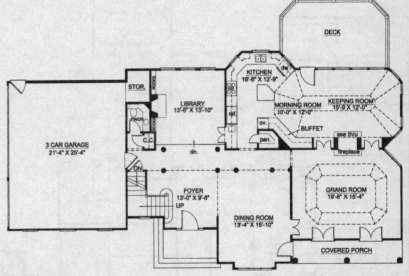

FIRST FLOOR

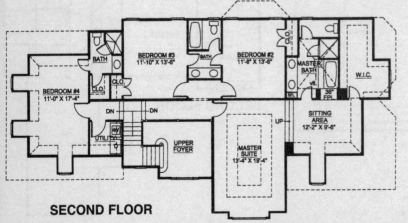

SECOND FLOOR

Units	Single
Price Code	H
Total Finished	3,083 sq. ft.
First Finished	2,429 sq. ft.
Second Finished	654 sq. ft.
Bonus Unfinished	420 sq. ft.
Basement Unfinished	2,429 sq. ft.
Garage Unfinished	641 sq. ft.
Dimensions	63'6"x71'4"
Foundation	Basement, Crawl space
Bedrooms	3
Full Baths	3
Half Baths	1
Primary Roof Pitch	12:12
Max Ridge Height	34'9"
Roof Framing	Stick
Exterior Walls	2x4

FIRST FLOOR

- RADIUS WINDOW
- K.S.
- Vaulted M.Bath
- Hers
- His
- MIRROR
- SHWR
- SEAT
- PLANT SHELF ABOVE
- LINEN
- FRENCH DOORS
- Pwdr.
- TRAY CLG.
- TRAY CEILING
- Master Suite 16⁰ x 19⁰
- STAIRS DN.
- OPEN RAIL
- BOOKSHELVES
- Sitting Room / Den 14⁰ x 14⁸
- TRAY CLG.
- FRENCH DOORS
- Two Story Foyer
- Dining Room 13⁰ x 16⁶
- ARCHED OPENING
- ARCHED OPENINGS
- Two Story Family Room 18⁸ x 18⁴
- FRENCH DOOR
- Vaulted Keeping Room 13⁵ x 14³
- RAD. WDW.
- FPL
- RAD. WDW.
- VAULT
- VAULT
- FRENCH DOOR
- DESK
- K.S.
- FPL.
- PANTRY
- COATS
- Breakfast
- ISLAND
- SURFACE UNIT
- DW.
- Kitchen
- DBL OVEN
- REF.
- Laund.
- SINK
- W.
- D.
- Terrace
- Three Car Garage 20⁶ x 30³
- © Frank Betz Associates, Inc.

SECOND FLOOR

- RADIUS WINDOW
- Family Room Below
- W.i.c.
- LINEN
- Bedroom 3 14⁰ x 12⁰
- OPEN RAIL
- OVERLOOK
- NICHE
- STAIRS DN.
- PLANT SHELF ABOVE
- W.i.c.
- K.S.
- Foyer Below
- Bedroom 2 13⁰ x 12⁹ 11'-0" HIGH CEILING
- Bath
- K.S.
- Bath
- W.i.c.
- PLANT SHELF
- Opt. Bonus Room 12⁵ x 22⁹

Photography by Donna & Ron Kolb, Exposures Unlimited

Units	Single
Price Code	C
Total Finished	1,782 sq. ft.
Main Finished	1,782 sq. ft.
Basement Unfinished	1,735 sq. ft.
Garage Unfinished	407 sq. ft.
Dimensions	67'2"x47'
Foundation	Basement
Bedrooms	3
Full Baths	2
Primary Roof Pitch	7:12
Secondary Roof Pitch	9:12
Max Ridge Height	20'
Roof Framing	Truss
Exterior Walls	2x4

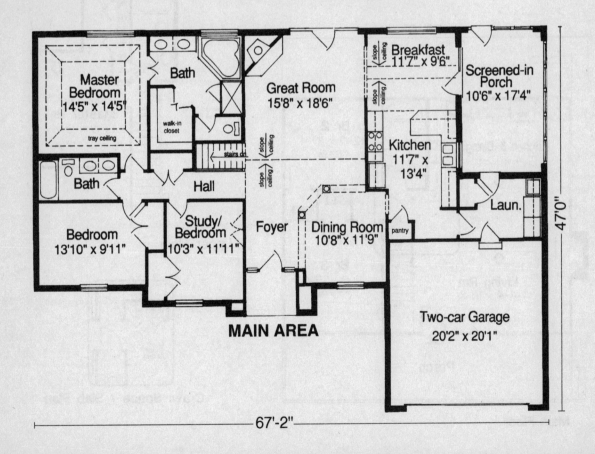

Master Bedroom 14'5" x 14'5" — tray ceiling

Bath

walk-in closet

Bath

Bedroom 13'10" x 9'11"

Study/ Bedroom 10'3" x 11'11"

Hall

stairs dn

slope ceiling

Foyer

Great Room 15'8" x 18'6"

Breakfast 11'7" x 9'6" — slope ceiling

Screened-in Porch 10'6" x 17'4"

Kitchen 11'7" x 13'4"

Laun.

Dining Room 10'8" x 11'9"

pantry

Two-car Garage 20'2" x 20'1"

MAIN AREA

47'0"

67'-2"

Photography supplied by Michele Evans Christy

Units	Single
Price Code	A
Total Finished	1,328 sq. ft.
Main Finished	1,013 sq. ft.
Upper Finished	315 sq. ft.
Basement Unfinished	1,013 sq. ft.
Dimensions	36'x36'
Foundation	Basement
	Crawl space
	Slab
Bedrooms	3
Full Baths	2
Main Ceiling	8'
Upper Ceiling	7'6"
Primary Roof Pitch	10:12
Max Ridge Height	23'6"
Roof Framing	Stick
Exterior Walls	2x4, 2x6

Rear Elevation

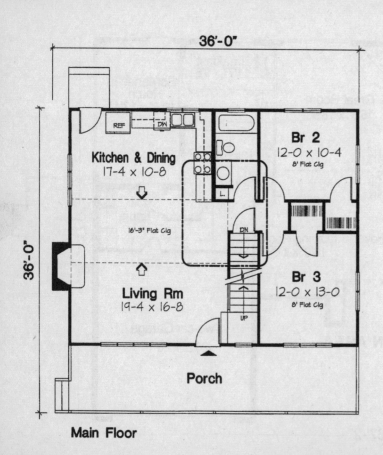

Main Floor

36'-0"

36'-0"

Kitchen & Dining
17-4 x 10-8

16'-3" Flat Clg

REF   DW

Br 2
12-0 x 10-4
8' Flat Clg

DN

Living Rm
19-4 x 16-8

Br 3
12-0 x 13-0
8' Flat Clg

UP

Porch

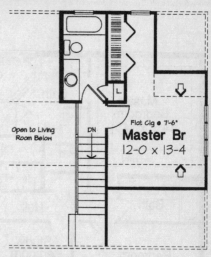

Upper Floor

Open to Living
Room Below

Flat Clg @ 7'-6"

DN

Master Br
12-0 x 13-4

Crawl Space / Slab Plan

FURN   WH

Crawl
Space
Access

Units	Single
Price Code	E
Total Finished	2,394 sq. ft.
First Finished	1,814 sq. ft.
Second Finished	580 sq. ft.
Bonus Unfinished	259 sq. ft.
Basement Unfinished	1,814 sq. ft.
Garage Unfinished	461 sq. ft.
Dimensions	55'4"x52'
Foundation	Basement Crawl space
Bedrooms	4
Full Baths	3
First Ceiling	9'
Second Ceiling	8'
Primary Roof Pitch	12:12
Max Ridge Height	30'6"
Roof Framing	Stick
Exterior Walls	2x4

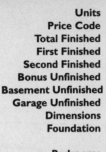

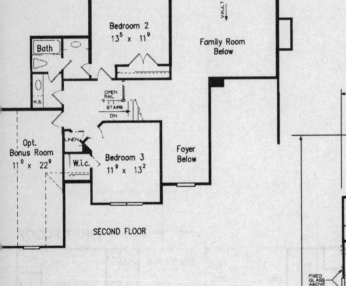

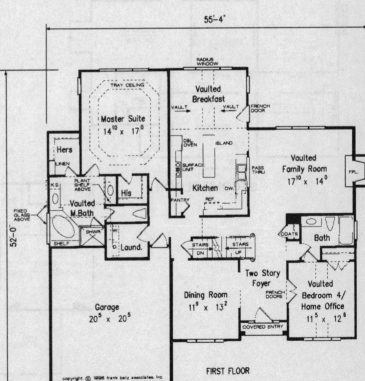

247

Units	Single
Price Code	G
Total Finished	2,832 sq. ft.
First Finished	1,920 sq. ft.
Second Finished	912 sq. ft.
Basement Unfinished	1,920 sq. ft.
Garage Unfinished	538 sq. ft.
Porch Unfinished	15 sq. ft.
Dimensions	70'x40'
Foundation	Basement
	Slab
Bedrooms	4
Full Baths	3
Half Baths	1
Primary Roof Pitch	12:12
Secondary Roof Pitch	10:12
Max Ridge Height	28'
Roof Framing	Stick
Exterior Walls	2x4

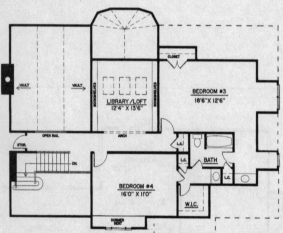

SECOND FLOOR

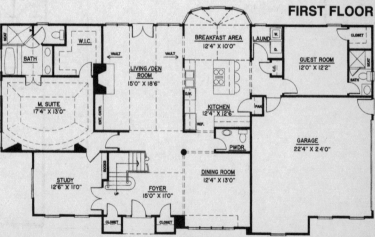

FIRST FLOOR

Garlinghouse Award Winning Designers

the best in the business... since 1907

2000 Platinum Designers

- Ahmann Design, Inc.
- Corley Plan Service
- Design Basic, Inc.
- Donald A. Gardner Architects, Inc.
- Fillmore Design Group
- Frank Betz Associates, Inc.
- Jannis Vann & Associates, Inc.
- Perfect Plan
- Rick Garner
- Studer Residential Design, Inc.

2000 Gold Designers

- Alan Mascord Design Associates
- Archival Designs
- Chatham Home Planning, Inc.
- Greg Marquis
- James Fahy Design
- L.M. Brunier & Associates, Inc.
- Landmark Designs
- Larry E. Belk
- Living Designs
- National Home Planning Service
- Patrick J. Morabito, AIA
- Sater Design Group
- Vaughn A. Lauban Designs
- W.D. Farmer F.A.I.B.D.
- Wesplan Building Design, Inc.

Plan # 98455

Design by Frank Betz Associates, Inc.

BL ML ZIP		See order pages & index for info
Units	Single	
Price Code	E	
Total Finished	2,349 sq. ft.	
First Finished	1,761 sq. ft.	
Second Finished	588 sq. ft.	
Bonus Unfinished	267 sq. ft.	
Basement Unfinished	1,761 sq. ft.	
Garage Unfinished	435 sq. ft.	
Dimensions	56'x47'6"	
Foundation	Basement, Crawl space	
Bedrooms	4	
Full Baths	3	
First Ceiling	9'	
Second Ceiling	8'	
Primary Roof Pitch	12:12	
Max Ridge Height	31'6"	
Roof Framing	Stick	
Exterior Walls	2x4	

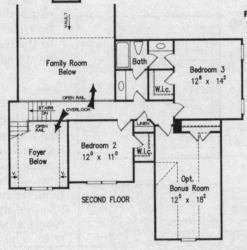

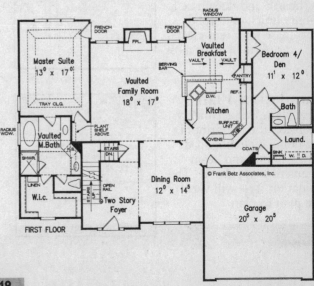

Exterior Elevations

Scaled drawings of the front, rear, sides of the home. Information pertaining to the exterior finish materials, roof pitches and exterior height dimensions.

Cabinet Plans

These plans, or in some cases elevations, will detail the layout of the kitchen and bathroom cabinets at a larger scale. Available for most plans.

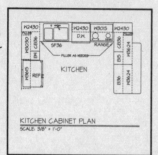

Typical Wall Section

This section will address insulation, roof components, and interior and exterior wall finishes. Your plans will be designed with either 2x4 or 2x6 exterior walls, but most professional contractors can easily adapt the plans to the wall thickness you require.

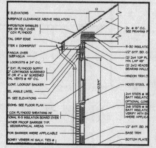

Fireplace Details

If the home you have chosen includes a fireplace, the fireplace detail will show typical methods to construct the firebox, hearth and flue chase for masonry units, or a wood frame chase for a zero-clearance unit. Available for most plans.

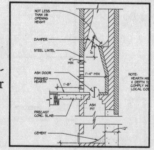

Foundation Plan

These plans will accurately dimension the footprint of your home including load bearing points and beam placement if applicable. The foundation style will vary from plan to plan.

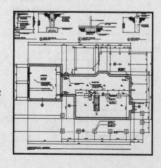

Roof Plan

The information necessary to construct the roof will be included with your home plans. Some plans will reference roof trusses, while many others contain schematic framing plans. These framing plans will indicate the lumber sizes necessary for the rafters and ridgeboards based on the designated roof loads.

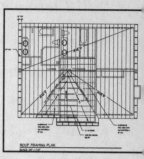

Typical Cross Section

A cut-away cross-section through the entire home shows your building contractor the exact correlation of construction components at all levels of the house. It will help to clarify the load bearing points from the roof all the way down to the basement. Available for most plans.

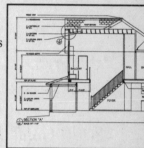

Detailed Floor Plans

The floor plans of your home accurately dimension the positioning of all walls, doors, windows, stairs and permanent fixtures. They will show you the relationship and dimensions of rooms, closets and traffic patterns. The schematic of the electrical layout may be included in the plan.

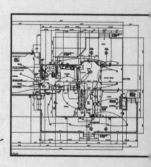

Stair Details

If stairs are an element of the design you have chosen, the plans will show the necessary information to build these, either through a stair cross section, or on the floor plans.

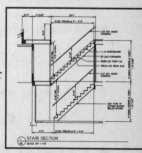

Reversed Plans Can Make Your Dream Home Just Right!

You could have exactly the home you want by flipping it end-for-end. Simply order your plans "reversed." We'll send you one full set of mirror-image plans (with the writing backwards) as a master guide for you and your builder.

The remaining sets of your order will come as shown in this book so the dimensions and specifications are easily read on the job site...but most plans in our collection come stamped "reversed" so there is no confusion.

As Shown   Reversed

We can only send reversed plans with multiple-set orders. There is a $50 charge for this service.

Some plans in our collection are available in Right Reading Reverse. Right Reading Reverse plans will show your home in reverse, with the writing on the plan being readable. This easy-to-read format will save you valuable time and money. Please contact our Customer Service Department to check for Right Reading Reverse availability. There is a $135 charge for Right Reading Reverse. **RRR**

Remember To Order Your Materials List

Available at a modest additional charge, the Materials List gives the quantity, dimensions, and specifications for the major materials needed to build your home. You will get faster, more accurate bids from your contractors and building suppliers — and avoid paying for unused materials and waste. Materials Lists are available for all home plans except as otherwise indicated, but can only be ordered with a set of home plans. Due to differences in regional requirements and homeowner or builder preferences... electrical, plumbing and heating/air conditioning equipment specifications are not designed specifically for each plan. **ML**

What Garlinghouse Offers

Home Plan Blueprint Package

By purchasing a multiple set package of blueprints or a vellum from Garlinghouse, you not only receive the physical blueprint documents necessary for construction, but you are also granted a license to build one, and only one, home. You can also make simple modifications, including minor non-structural changes and material substitutions, to our design, as long as these changes are made directly on the blueprints purchased from Garlinghouse and no additional copies are made.

Home Plan Vellums

By purchasing vellums for one of our home plans, you receive the same construction drawings found in the blueprints, but printed on vellum paper. Vellums can be erased and are perfect for making design changes. They are also semi-transparent making them easy to duplicate. But most importantly, the purchase of home plan vellums comes with a broader license that allows you to make changes to the design (ie, create a hand drawn or CAD derivative work), to make copies of the plan, and to build one home from the plan.

License To Build Additional Homes

With the purchase of a blueprint package or vellums you automatically receive a license to build one home and only one home, respectively. If you want to build more homes than you are licensed to build through your purchase of a plan, then additional licenses may be purchased at reasonable costs from Garlinghouse. Inquire for more information.

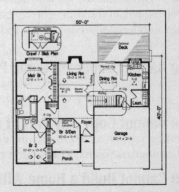

Modify Your Favorite Design, Made Easy

Questions?

Call our customer service department at 1.860.343.5977

#1 Modifying Your Garlinghouse Home Plan

Simple modifications to your dream home, including minor non-structural changes and material substitutions, can be made between you and your builder by marking the changes directly on your blueprints. However, if you are considering making significant changes to your chosen design, we recommend that you use the services of The Garlinghouse Design Staff. We will help take your ideas and turn them into a reality, just the way you want. Here's our procedure!

When you place your Vellum order, you may also request a free Garlinghouse Modification Kit. In this kit, you will receive a red marking pencil, furniture cut-out sheet, ruler, a self addressed mailing label and a form for specifying any additional notes or drawings that will help us understand your design ideas. Mark your desired changes directly on the Vellum drawings. NOTE: Please use only a **red pencil** to mark your desired changes on the Vellum. Then, return the redlined Vellum set in the original box to us.

Important: Please roll the Vellums for shipping, *do not fold*.

We also offer modification estimates. We will provide you with an estimate to draft your changes based on your specific modifications before you purchase the vellums, for a $50 fee. After you receive your estimate, if you decide to have us do the changes, the $50 estimate fee will be deducted from the cost of your modifications. If, however, you choose to use a different service, the $50 estimate fee is non-refundable. (Note: Personal checks cannot be accepted for the estimate.)

Within 5 days of receipt of your plans, you will be contacted by a member of the design staff with an estimate for the design services to draw those changes. A 50% deposit is required before we begin making the actual modifications to your plans.

Once the design changes have been completed to your vellum plan, a representative will call to inform you that your modified Vellum plan is complete and will be shipped as soon as the final payment has been made. For additional information call us at 1-860-343-5977. Please refer to the Modification Pricing Guide for estimated modification costs.

#2 Reproducible Vellums for Local Modification Ease

If you decide not to use Garlinghouse for your modifications, we recommend that you follow our same procedure of purchasing Vellums. You then have the option of using the services of the original designer of the plan, a local professional designer, or architect to make the modifications.

With a Vellum copy of our plans, a design professional can alter the drawings just the way you want, then you can print as many copies of the modified plans as you need to build your house. And, since you have already started with our complete detailed plans, the cost of those expensive professional services will be significantly less than starting from scratch. Refer to the price schedule for Vellum costs.

Important Return policy: Reproducible Vellum copies of our home plans are copyright protected and only sold under the terms of a license agreement that you will receive with your order. Should you not agree to the terms, then the Vellums may be returned, unopened, for a full refund less the shipping and handling charges, plus a 20% restocking fee. For any additional information, please call us at 1-860-343-5977.

Ignoring Copyright Laws Can Be A $1,000,000 Mistake

Budget
r dream home
P QUOTE
s the answer!

Why? Do you wish you could quickly find out the building cost for your new home without waiting for a contractor to compile hundreds of bids? Would you like to have a benchmark to compare your contractor(s) bids against? Well, Now You Can!!, h Zip-Quote Home Cost Calculator. Zip-Quote is ly available for zip code areas within the United tes.

w? Our Zip-Quote Home Cost Calculator will ble you to obtain the calculated building cost to nstruct your new home, based on labor rates and lding material costs within your zip code area, with- the normal delays or hassles usually associated with bidding process. Zip-Quote can be purchased in separate formats, an itemized or a bottom line for- t.

How does Zip-Quote actually work?" When you call order, you must choose from the options available, your specific home, in order for us to process your er. Once we receive your Zip-Quote order, we cess your specific home plan building materials list ough our Home Cost Calculator which contains up- date rates for all residential labor trades and building terial costs in your zip code area."The result?" A culated cost to build your dream home in your zip de area. This calculation will help you (as a con- ner or a builder) evaluate your building budget.

ll database information for our calculations is fur- hed by Marshall & Swift, L.P. For over 60 years, rshall & Swift L.P. has been a leading provider of t data to professionals in all aspects of the construc- n and remodeling industries.

tion 1 The **Itemized Zip-Quote** is a detailed lding material list. Each building material list line m will separately state the labor cost, material cost d equipment cost (if applicable) for the use of that lding material in the construction process. This lding materials list will be summarized by the indi- ual building categories and will have additional lumns where you can enter data from your contrac- 's estimates for a cost comparison between the differ- t suppliers and contractors who will actually quote u their products and services.

ption 2 The **Bottom Line Zip-Quote** is a one line mmarized total cost for the home plan of your choice. is cost calculation is also based on the labor cost, terial cost and equipment cost (if applicable) within ur local zip code area. Bottom Line Zip-Quote is ailable for most plans. Please call for availability. st The price of your Itemized Zip-Quote is based

upon the pricing schedule of the plan you have select- ed, in addition to the price of the materials list. Please refer to the pricing schedule on our order form. The price of your initial Bottom Line Zip-Quote is $29.95. Each additional Bottom Line Zip-Quote ordered in conjunction with the initial order is only $14.95. Bottom Line Zip-Quote may be purchased separately and does NOT have to be purchased in conjunction with a home plan order.

FYI An Itemized Zip-Quote Home Cost Calculation can ONLY be purchased in conjunction with a Home Plan order. The Itemized Zip-Quote can not be pur- chased separately. If you find within 60 days of your order date that you will be unable to build this home, then you may exchange the plans and the materials list towards the price of a new set of plans (see order info pages for plan exchange policy). The Itemized Zip- Quote and the Bottom Line Zip-Quote are NOT returnable. The price of the initial Bottom Line Zip- Quote order can be credited towards the purchase of an Itemized Zip-Quote order, only if available. Additional Bottom Line Zip-Quote orders, within the same order can not be credited. Please call our Customer Service Department for more information.

An Itemized Zip-Quote is available for plans where you see this symbol. `ZIP`

A Bottom-line Zip-Quote is available for all plans under 4,000 sq. ft. or where you see this symbol. `BL` Please call for current availability.

Some More Information The Itemized and Bottom Line Zip-Quotes give you approximated costs for con- structing the particular house in your area. These costs are not exact and are only intended to be used as a pre- liminary estimate to help determine the affordability of a new home and/or as a guide to evaluate the general competitiveness of actual price quotes obtained through local suppliers and contractors. However, Zip-Quote cost figures should never be relied upon as the only source of information in either case. **Land, landscaping, sewer systems, site work, contractor overhead and profit, and other expenses are not included in our building cost figures. Excluding land and landscaping, you may incur an additional 20% to 40% in costs from the original estimate.** Garlinghouse and Marshall & Swift L.P. can not guar- antee any level of data accuracy or correctness in a Zip- Quote and disclaim all liability for loss with respect to the same, in excess of the original purchase price of the Zip-Quote product. All Zip-Quote calculations are based upon the actual blueprints and do not reflect any differences or options that may be shown on the published house renderings, floor plans, or photographs.

the Garlinghouse company

Order Code No. HONH1

Order Form

Plan prices guaranteed until 8/8/01 — After this date call for updated pricing

_____ Foundation

____ set(s) of blueprints for plan #_____ $_____

____ Vellum & Modification kit for plan #_____ $_____

____ Additional set(s) @ $50 each for plan #_____ $_____

____ Mirror Image Reverse @ $50 each $_____

____ Right Reading Reverse @ $135 each $_____

____ Materials list for plan #_____ $_____

____ Detail Plans @ $19.95 each

     ❏ Construction   ❏ Plumbing   ❏ Electrical $_____

____ Bottom line ZIP Quote@$29.95 for plan #_____ $_____

____ Additional Bottom Line Zip Quote

     @ $14.95 for plan(s) #_____ $_____

Zip Code where building _____

____ Itemized ZIP Quote for plan(s) #_____ $_____

Shipping (see charts on opposite page) $_____

Subtotal $_____

Sales Tax (CT residents add 6% sales tax, KS residents add 6.15% sales tax) (Not required for other states) $_____

TOTAL AMOUNT ENCLOSED $_____

Send your check, money order or credit card information to:
(No C.O.D.'s Please)

Please submit all <u>United States</u> & <u>Other Nations</u> orders to:
Garlinghouse Company
P.O. Box 1717
Middletown, CT. 06457

Please Submit all <u>Canadian</u> plan orders to:
Garlinghouse Company
102 Ellis Street
Penticton, BC V2A 4L5

ADDRESS INFORMATION:

NAME: _____

STREET: _____

CITY: _____

STATE: _____ ZIP: _____

DAYTIME PHONE: _____

EMAIL ADDRESS: _____

Credit Card Information

Charge To: ❏ Visa   ❏ Mastercard

Card # ⌊_│_│_│_│_│_│_│_│_│_│_│_│_│_│_│_│⌋

Signature _____ Exp. ____/____

IMPORTANT INFORMATION TO RE BEFORE YOU PLACE YOUR ORDE

How Many Sets Of Plans Will You Need?

The Standard 8-Set Construction Package

Our experience shows that you'll speed every step of construction an avoid costly building errors by ordering enough sets to go around. Each tradesperson wants a set — the general contractor and all subcontractors foundation, electrical, plumbing, heating/air conditioning and framers. Don get your lending institution, building department and, of course, a set for y self. * Recommended For Construction *

The Minimum 4-Set Construction Package

If you're comfortable with arduous follow-up, this package can save y few dollars by giving you the option of passing down plan sets as work progresses. You might have enough copies to go around if work goes exac scheduled and no plans are lost or damaged by subcontrators. But for only more, the 8-set package eliminates these worries.
* Recommended For Bidding *

The Single Study Set

We offer this set so you can study the blueprints to plan your dream h detail. They are stamped "study set only-not for construction", and you car build a home from them. In pursuant to copyright laws, it is <u>illegal</u> to repro any blueprint.

Our Reorder and Exchange Policies:

If you find after your initial purchase that you require additional sets of plans yo purchase them from us at special reorder prices (please call for pricing details) vided that you reorder within 6 months of your original order date. There is a $. reorder processing fee that is charged on all reorders. For more information on reordering plans please contact our Customer Service Department.

Your plans are custom printed especially for you once you place your order. I that reason we cannot accept any returns.

If for some reason you find that the plan you have purchased from us does n meet your needs, then you may exchange that plan for any other plan in our co tion. We allow you sixty days from your original invoice date to make an exchan the time of the exchange you will be charged a processing fee of 20% of the to amount of your original
order plus the difference in price between the plans (if applicable) plus the cost ship the new plans to you. Call our Customer Service Department for more inf tion. Please Note: Reproducible vellums can only be exchanged if they are unop

Important Shipping Information

Please refer to the shipping charts on the order form for service availabl your specific plan number. Our delivery service must have a street address o Route Box number — never a post office box. (PLEASE NOTE: Supplying a P. number <u>only</u> will delay the shipping of your order.) Use a work address if no home during the day.

Orders being shipped to APO or FPO must go via First Class Mail. Please include the proper postage.

For our International Customers, only Certified bank checks and money c are accepted and must be payable in U.S. currency. For speed, we ship inter al orders Air Parcel Post. Please refer to the chart for the correct shipping co

Important Canadian Shipping Information

To our friends in Canada, we have a plan design affiliate in Penticton, BC relationship will help you avoid the delays and charges associated with shipr from the United States. Moreover, our affiliate is familiar with the building re ments in your community and country. We prefer payments in U.S. Currency. you, however, are sending Canadian funds please add 45% to the prices of t plans and shipping fees.

An Important Note About Building Code Requirements:

All plans are drawn to conform to one or more of the industry's major na building standards. However, due to the variety of local building regulations, y plan may need to be modified to comply with local requirements — snow loa energy loads, seismic zones, etc. Do check them fully and consult your local building officials.

A few states require that all building plans used be drawn by an architec registered in that state. While having your plans reviewed and stamped by su architect may be prudent, laws requiring non-conforming plans like ours to b completely redrawn forces you to unnecessarily pay very large fees. If your s has such a law, we strongly recommend you contact your state representativ protest.

The rendering, floor plans, and technical information contained within th publication are not guaranteed to be totally accurate. Consequently, no infor from this publication should be used either as a guide to constructing a hom for estimating the cost of building a home. Complete blueprints must be purc for such purposes.

For Our USA Customers:
Order Toll Free — 1-800-235-5700
Monday-Friday 8:00 a.m. to 8:00 p.m. Eastern Time
or FAX your Credit Card order to 1-860-343-5984
All foreign residents call 1-800-343-5977

For Our Canadian Customers:
Order Toll Free — 1-800-361-7526
Monday-Friday 8:00 a.m. to 5:00 p.m. Pacific Time
or FAX your Credit Card order to 1-250-493-7526
Customer Service: 1-250-493-0942

Please have ready: 1. Your credit card number 2. The plan number 3. The order code number ➡ **HONH1**

arlinghouse 2000 Blueprint Price Code Schedule

1 Set	4 Sets	8 Sets	Vellums	ML	Itemized ZIP Quote
$350	$395	$455	$550	$60	$50
$390	$435	$495	$600	$60	$50
$430	$475	$535	$650	$60	$50
$470	$515	$575	$700	$60	$50
$510	$555	$615	$750	$70	$60
$555	$600	$660	$800	$70	$60
$600	$645	$705	$850	$70	$60
$645	$690	$750	$900	$70	$60
$690	$735	$795	$950	$80	$70
$740	$785	$845	$1000	$80	$70
$790	$835	$895	$1050	$80	$70
$840	$885	$945	$1100	$80	$70

Additional sets with original order $50

Shipping — (Plans 1-59999)

	1-3 Sets	4-6 Sets	7+ & Vellums
Standard Delivery (UPS 2-Day)	$25.00	$30.00	$35.00
Overnight Delivery	$35.00	$40.00	$45.00

Shipping — (Plans 60000-99999)

	1-3 Sets	4-6 Sets	7+ & Vellums
Ground Delivery (7-10 Days)	$15.00	$20.00	$25.00
Express Delivery (3-5 Days)	$20.00	$25.00	$30.00

International Shipping & Handling

	1-3 Sets	4-6 Sets	7+ & Vellums
Regular Delivery Canada (7-10 Days)	$25.00	$30.00	$35.00
Express Delivery Canada (5-6 Days)	$40.00	$45.00	$50.00
Overseas Delivery Airmail (2-3 Weeks)	$50.00	$60.00	$65.00

Design by Studer Residential Design, Inc. | **Plan # 97727** | **BL** See order pages & index for info

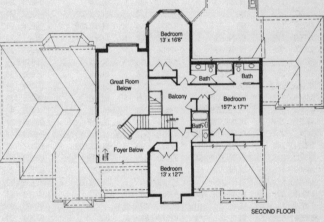

SECOND FLOOR

Units	Single
Price Code	L
Total Finished	4,562 sq. ft.
First Finished	3,364 sq. ft.
Second Finished	1,198 sq. ft.
Dimensions	98'6"x61'5"
Foundation	Basement
Bedrooms	4
Full Baths	3
Half Baths	1
Primary Roof Pitch	8:12
econdary Roof Pitch	12:12
Max Ridge Height	31'
Roof Framing	Truss
Exterior Walls	2x4

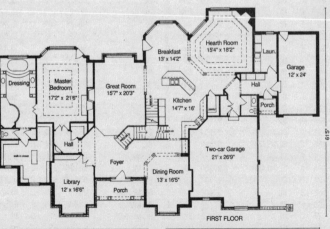

FIRST FLOOR

Order Today! 1-800-235-5700 or order online at
www.familyhomeplans.com

Index

Option Key

BL Bottom-line Zip Quote	**ML** Materials List Available	**ZIP** Itemized Zip Quote	**RRR** Right Reading Reverse